The Economist in Parliament:
1780–1868

The Economist in Parliament: 1780–1868

Frank Whitson Fetter

Duke University Press   Durham, North Carolina   1980

To the memory of my parents
Frank Albert Fetter *1863–1949*
Martha Whitson Fetter *1868–1954*

Contents

Preface

This book is the outgrowth of an earlier study of the British monetary and banking controversy between 1797 and 1875, which I published in book form in 1965 as *The Development of British Monetary Orthodoxy* (Harvard University Press, Cambridge). The purpose of that book was not limited to analyzing the theory underlying the policies adopted, but also aimed to set the decisions reached in the political and economic philosophy of the time and to consider the influence of politics and personality on the policy decisions that were reached.

In the course of the study I was impressed by the role that economists, as members of Parliament, had played not only in the discussions of monetary and banking questions, but also of a wide range of economic and political issues. In addition to such great figures in the history of economics as Henry Thornton, David Ricardo, Robert Torrens, and John Stuart Mill, many other members of Parliament with substantial credentials as economists played an important role in parliamentary debates and legislative policy making. From this observation came the decision to do intensive research on their parliamentary roles and to write this book.

I have not attempted to judge the influence of the writings and nonparliamentary activities of these economists, nor have I attempted to estimate the legislative influence of economists not in Parliament—men such as Thomas Robert Malthus, John Ramsay McCulloch, Nassau Senior, and Thomas Tooke—who were advisers to government, members of royal commissions, or witnesses before parliamentary committees. The book is limited to the activity and influence of economists as members of Parliament.

The hard core of the research was in the parliamentary records of debates and voting, and of parliamentary committees. An important source for the electoral campaigns of the economists, revealing how they were elected and what policies they supported in their campaigns, were contemporary newspapers. I consulted all available private papers of parliamentary economists for information bearing on their parliamentary elections and on their parliamentary careers.

A large part of the research, outside of printed parliamentary records, was done in 1970 and 1971 while I was a visitor at the Institute of Historical Research of London University. I am grateful to Mr. Taylor Milne, then secretary of the Institute, and to its staff for their many courtesies and for the help they gave in arranging for interlibrary loans, putting me in touch with manuscript collections, and answering my innumerable questions about parliamentary politics. Mr. E. L. C. Mullins, in charge of the History of Parliament Trust that is associated with the Institute, gave generously of his time and his wide knowledge of members of Parliament and their campaigns.

Helpful in providing background information on the parliamentary careers of these economists was manuscript material in the British Museum, the National Library of Scotland, the National Library of Ireland, the National Library of Wales, the National Register of Archives, the Scottish Record Office, the Public Record Office of Northern Ireland, the Ipswich Public Record Office, the Bodleian Library at Oxford, the Libraries of the University of Birmingham, the University of Cambridge, the University of Durham, the University of Hull, the London School of Economics, the University of London, the University of Nottingham, University College (London); the Public Libraries of Birmingham, Bolton, Derby, and Shrewsbury; the Lambeth Castle Library (London), the John Rylands Library (Manchester), and the Church Missionary Society (London). I am grateful for the many courtesies and the assistance I received from the directors and staffs of these organizations.

Lord Congleton made available to me the papers of Sir Henry Parnell, later 1st Lord Congleton, at his home at Ebbisbourne Wake (Wilks), and his gracious hospitality and that of Lady Congleton left me with most pleasant memories of my research at their home. Mr. D. W. H. Neilson, the owner of the Wilmot Horton papers on deposit at the Derby Public Library, graciously permitted me to examine them and to quote from them. Material at the Kress Library of the Harvard Graduate School of Business Administration and at the Goldsmiths' Library of the University of London filled in many details about the writings and careers of parliamentary economists. To the staffs of these libraries I am grateful. I appreciate the many courtesies of the staff of the Baker Library at Dartmouth College and the provision of the study in which I did much of my research in printed parliamentary records and wrote most of this book. I am indebted to the Royal Economic Society and to Mr. Piero Sraffa for permission to quote from *The Works and Correspondence of David Ricardo* (Cambridge, 1951–73), and to Mr. Sraffa for good counsel.

A research grant from Dartmouth College, when I was visiting professor in 1967–68, facilitated the preliminary research for this book. A grant from the National Endowment for the Humanities in 1970–71 made possible eight months of research in England, and also covered the expenses of research assistants while in Hanover.

The late Professor Arthur Cole, librarian of the Baker Library of the Harvard School of Business Administration, gave me, over the years, much good advice on the subject of this book. Professor R. S. Sayers and Lord Robbins, both formerly of the London School of Economics, and Mr. J. Keith Horsefield, formerly of the International Monetary Fund, have been helpful and wise in their counsels and patient in listening to and responding to my many questions. I benefited from these discussions, even though I did not always follow their advice. Professor Maurice O'Connell of Fordham University generously shared with me information on economists in Parliament that he had collected in connection with his editing of the correspondence of Daniel O'Connell, and I profited from our discussions about parliamentary actions affecting Ireland. Many interchanges of ideas in 1970 and 1971 with Mr. Paul Sturges, who for several years was collecting material for the *Economists' Papers: 1750–1950*, published by the Royal Economic Society, clarified a number of points. Professor William Grampp, of the University of Illinois at Chicago, shared with me his wide knowledge of British economic controversies in the first half of the nineteenth century. Professor Sydney Checkland of the University of Glasgow gave me good counsel on a number of points and made available to me correspondence between John Gladstone and Kirkman Finlay. Professor A. W. Coats of the University of Nottingham was a helpful adviser, and put me on the trail of material that I would otherwise have missed. Mr. Horsefield, and Professor David Roberts of Dartmouth College, read an earlier version of this book; Professor Sayers read chapters 6 and 7, and Professor R. D. C. Black of Queen's University, Belfast, read chapters 9 and 10. I benefited from their searching and constructive criticism. Many students, both in London and in Hanover, have by their research assistance lightened my work. Mrs. Dorothy Clarke, an experienced London researcher who for over two decades has helped me in running down British records, was again invaluable in handling difficult research tasks. Mrs. Alice Weymouth has for over six years typed this manuscript in its changing versions, and her keen eye and good editorial judgment frequently saved me from duplication of ideas and mistakes in phrasing and in citations.

Some of the conclusions of my early research were given in a talk before the History of Economic Thought Conference in Manchester, in September 1971, and a brief summary of this talk is in *History of Economic Thought Newsletter* (number 7, 1971). A number of ideas and phrases in the book, particularly in the last chapter, draw heavily on a paper given at the meetings of the International Economic History Association in Copenhagen in August 1974 and published in revised form in an article in the *Journal of Political Economy* in October 1975, "The Influence of Economists in Parliament on British Legislation from David Ricardo to John Stuart Mill."

Frank Whitson Fetter

Hanover, New Hampshire
March 1978

References to Parliamentary Debates
and to Voting

P.H. – Cobbett's *Parliamentary History*, for Years 1780–1803.

1 H – Hansard's *Parliamentary Debates*. First Series, 1803–1820.

2 H – Hansard's *Parliamentary Debates*. New Series, 1820–1830.

3 H – Hansard's *Parliamentary Debates*. Third Series, 1830–1868.

Up to the middle 1830s *Hansard*, when giving names in voting, usually lists only the minority; from then on more frequently, but not always, it gives the names of both majority and minority. When, in the text or footnote, I give the names on only one side of a question, it is because names on the other side of the question are not in *Hansard*.

In all statements about total votes, I have used the figures reported in *Hansard*. This total figure does not include the tellers, or the pairs in the few cases where pairs are listed. However, when I give the names of those voting with the majority or with the minority I also include anyone paired or a teller.

The Economist in Parliament:
1780–1868

Chapter 1

The Economists Who Sat in Parliament

No economist today believes that economics was invented by Adam Smith and reached its pinnacle of perfection in John Stuart Mill. Yet there is a significance in the development of British economics from Smith to Mill much greater than is sometimes recognized by those who have read too deeply in the *General Theory* and accepted too uncritically the Keynesian picture of the great issue of classical controversy as that between Ricardo and Malthus over the significance of demand. In a broad sense man has always been concerned with economic issues, in deciding what material things to produce, in finding out how best to produce them, and in determining how the fruits of production are to be shared. Primitive man, even before the development of writing or even of speech, had to make decisions, without sophisticated rationalization, that suggest the type of decision making discussed in advanced seminars in the Cambridges of England and of the United States. Biblical times had their economic problems. There is an economic literature of Greece and Rome, in particular dealing with taxation and with the consequences of changes in the money supply; and more than one economist has found in classical experience a warning of the "lessons of history" against policies as far removed in time as the repeal of the Corn Laws or the New Deal legislation of Franklin D. Roosevelt.

Nature of Early Economic Literature

But economic decisions in ancient times, and even in the Western world until after the breakup of the feudal system, touched only a small part of the life of man. Actions in the economic field were made largely on the basis of authority or of custom, originating in beliefs accepted without question from the experience of the past or from the dictates of church, feudal lords, or emerging national states. Men carried on economic practices largely because someone told them to, not because of any rational judgment that such action would result in a larger personal or national income or a more equitable distribution of income. The three-field system, payment of tithes, restrictions by local guilds—all represented economic policies not determined by economic analysis but part of a hierarchical organization of society.

In the two centuries before 1750 what economic analysis there was, either in England or on the Continent, related principally to problems of cities—and in particular seaports—that had managed to escape the grip of feudal control. Foreign trade, the balance of payments, causes of exchange-rate fluctuations, influence of the precious metals upon prices, details of coinage, the beginnings of banking—it was with such topics that a large part of the writings of the predecessors of Adam Smith had dealt. Up to the middle years of the eighteenth century Italy, with a wide-ranging foreign trade, and monetary and banking operations associated with that trade, produced an extensive economic literature. Most of it, however, dealt only with a limited segment of the economic life of the country. The sort of problems with which Adam Smith, Thomas Robert Malthus, David Ricardo, Robert Torrens, and John Stuart Mill were later concerned—how a whole economy operates—played little part in the prenineteenth-century Italian economic literature.[1]

It is no accident that, despite the early preeminence of Italy in the production of specialized economic tracts, analysis on the functioning of the economic system should have had its roots in England. In the last part of the eighteenth century Italy was not moving forward economically. In the same period the industrial revolution was gathering momentum in England and bringing to inland cities and countryside the new problems, hitherto largely confined to small groups in seaports, of explaining economic behavior when the voice of authority no longer provided the answers to what people should produce, how they should produce it, or what should be paid for labor or for products.

---

1. Much of this early Italian literature is reprinted in *Scrittori Classici Italiani di Economia Politica*, 50 vols. (Milan, 1803–16).

Development of Organized Economic Analysis

Economics as an organized and systematic analysis, as distinguished from episodic insights and individual comments about production or discussion of coinage and foreign exchange, came into flower only when two conditions existed, or at least were held out as desirable:

1. The opportunity for men to decide how they would allocate resources to maximize some material advantage, free from the constraint of a political system, a social order, or a religious belief that forbade new ways of doing things that would disturb the status quo.
2. The belief that an increase in the supply of goods and services available to a nation, and sometimes but not always, to the common man, was a desirable objective.

These changes did not come fully born within the economic system; they were part of a larger philosophical and political change that took on increasing strength in the late eighteenth century. In a broad sense the rise of political economy was part of the Enlightenment, of the revolt against authority, of the belief in the rationality of man. It is more than a coincidence that the Declaration of Independence was signed and the *Wealth of Nations* published in the same year.

Adam Smith had well stated the view that the market was the best place for the making of economic decisions, and that these decisions should be made by rational men seeking to further their own economic interests. But this was not the central theme of the revolution in thinking associated with classical economics. The central theme was the role of reason, rather than tradition or authority, in directing all aspects of organized society. For Smith and his followers the greatest misuse of tradition and authority was in the making of economic decisions. Laissez-faire has all too frequently been thought of as the heart of classical economics, whereas it was in fact the economic policy that in most cases the classical economists thought reasonable. Economists were not going back on their principles when they argued that in particular situations it was not rational to abjure authority and to leave decisions to an unregulated market. They were simply honoring the belief for which they were spokesmen in the economic field—the spirit of the Enlightenment. And by the same token, the efforts of many economists, from Smith through Mill, in favor of education, a wider diffusion of political power, and a removal of religious discrimination, should not be considered as an excursion by economists into foreign fields, but rather as evidence of the pervasive spirit of rationality that had inspired so many men to become economists.

Until well into the nineteenth century no one made his income from being an economist; rather one had to have some other source of income to make it possible to be an economist. It was in effect an avocation of a gentleman of inquiring mind. The possession of paper, pen and ink, some leisure, and intellectual curiosity about the economic problems of a changing world were the only entrance qualifications in the heyday of British classical economics. You became a political economist by publishing something relating to an economic problem, and perhaps announcing that you were a political economist.

Economists in Parliament

A high proportion of British economists from Adam Smith to John Stuart Mill wanted change—and in particular change that would increase economic wealth by breaking up monopolies and allowing labor and resources to be used more effectively. These changes in most cases called for political action—not only repeal of laws that maintained ancient privileges and hampered a better allocation of resources, but also a change in political power that would bring into Parliament men who believed in such change. That is the major explanation of a situation that has no parallel before or after in Britain, nor at any period in any other country: the large number of economists who became members of the national legislature. David Ricardo and John Stuart Mill head the list in fame, and there were others who are still names to conjure with, such as Thomas Attwood, Richard Cobden, Francis Horner, William Huskisson, Henry Parnell, George Poulett Scrope, Henry Thornton, Robert Torrens, Richard Whately, James Wilson, Samuel Jones Loyd (Lord Overstone), Lord King, and the Earl of Lauderdale. In addition, many others sat in Parliament who played a prominent role in the economic controversies of their time, and in some cases produced an impressive volume of literature, although their names today are overshadowed by the luster of more famous contemporaries.

Hence, to get the full picture of the role of British economists from Smith to Mill, it is important to consider not only what they wrote but what they did as members of Parliament. In the period of neoclassical economics from Mill to Keynes economists could make their influence felt in academic chairs, as civil servants, and in membership on and testimony before royal commissions. This was partly because the broad objectives for which the economists of the classical period had argued had in major degree been achieved— the breaking down of monopoly barriers and the abolition of the more extreme cases of diversion of public revenues for the benefit of favored groups. Furthermore, to an increasing degree neoclassical economists were discussing what private business, administrative bodies, or the Bank of England should do, and not what Parliament should do or stop doing, as was the case in the first half of the nineteenth century.

To evaluate the role of economists in Parliament over the ninety years from Smith to Mill, it is first necessary to decide who are to be considered economists. This presents a problem familiar to logicians and statisticians, of circular reasoning and biased samples. Any conclusions as to why economists wanted to get into Parliament, how they got into Parliament, and what they stood for and what their influence was in Parliament, depends in considerable degree on what persons are classed as economists. For example, if the brothers Attwood and Frederick Muntz are included in the fraternity, the views of parliamentary economists on monetary policy are very different from what they are if we accept the general attitude of John Stuart Mill and John Ramsay McCulloch that such heretics were not worthy of the name of economist.

Certainly not all, if any, economists will agree with my choice of the sixty-two members of Parliament considered to be economists.[2] The principal test applied was organized writing on an economic subject, but there were several men who left no such legacy and yet whose parliamentary careers give them a strong claim for inclusion

2. The sixty-two men, and biographical details, are given in Appendix I. The twenty-five members of the Political Economy Club who were in Parliament but are not covered are listed in Appendix II. Appendix VI gives brief information of the unsuccessful attempts of several economists to secure seats in Parliament.

as economists. In the period under survey a large proportion of the leading lights of classical economics were members of the Political Economy Club, founded in 1821 to debate the great economic issues of the day.[3] Before 1868, 109 men had been members of the club, 52 of whom had been, at some time until then, members of Parliament. However, about half of these club members in Parliament were passive economists, who had joined the club primarily for the claret, the venison pastry, the good companionship, and to hear the controversies. W. J. Blake never published a word on economics, never spoke in four years in Parliament, and in forty years of membership never participated in a discussion at the club. There were other cases hardly less extreme, and if one leaves them out, the Political Economy Club provided twenty-seven economists to Parliament.

In addition many contributors to economic analysis who sat in Parliament were not members of the club. Francis Baring, Horner, and Thornton died before its founding. Monetary heretics like the Attwoods, Frederick Muntz, Edward Cayley, E. D. Davenport, and Scrope would hardly have been welcomed. Joseph Hume was turned down, for membership, presumably because of his abrasive persistence in pressing his own ideas. In many cases the claim of those who were not members of the Political Economy Club to be called economists needs no argument; examples are Cobden, Horner, Thornton, and Wilson. John Sinclair, the brothers Attwood, Cayley, Davenport, Muntz, and Scrope were concerned with the same problems as were the more conventionally classical economists, and their views, emotionally oriented as they sometimes were, were an important force in the controversies of the time. Henry Brougham and Hume may not figure prominently in the history of economic theory—Schumpeter does not index them in his *History of Economic Analysis*—but both of them thought and argued in economic terms of how resources could be used most effectively to maximize output, and how output should be allocated. And they—and in particular Hume—were influential in Parliament in pressing for economic reforms.

3. A history of the club, by Henry Higgs, a list of all its members and of all topics discussed at meetings, and diary entries and letters about the meetings are in *Political Economy Club*, vol. 6 (London: Macmillan, 1921).

Background and Training of Parliamentary Economists

Almost every profession and station in life provided its parliamentary economists: Robert Torrens, the colonel of Marines who did his early economic writing as a relief from the boredom of garrison life, and Perronet Thompson, the army officer, who read Adam Smith in preparation for his duties as governor of the new colony of Sierra Leone; Joseph Hume, trained as a physician, who acquired a small fortune in the service of the East India Company before entering politics; David Ricardo, the stockbroker who, having first made money beyond the dreams of avarice, under prodding from James Mill found more satisfaction in trying to explain how nations got rich than in making himself still richer; his nephew John Lewis Ricardo, financier and business promoter; the Irish country gentlemen Henry Parnell and Thomas Spring Rice; the Scottish country gentleman and agricultural reformer Sinclair; the lawyers Brougham, Horner, George Pryme, and Isaac Butt; the bankers Thornton, Matthias and Thomas Attwood, Alexander and Francis Baring, George Grote, Samuel Jones Loyd, and George Goschen; the clergymen Edward Copleston and Richard Whately; John Stuart Mill, philosopher and civil servant; Scrope, geologist and philanthropically minded country gentleman; the journalists William Cobbett and James Wilson; the businessmen Kirkman Finlay, John Fielden, James Morrison, Muntz, and Richard Cobden; young members of the nobility such as Lord King, Lord Howick (later 3d Earl Grey), and Lord Henry Petty (later 3d Marquess of Lansdowne), influenced by the ideas of Adam Smith and the philosophy of the Enlightenment; the Scottish lawyer and country gentleman the Earl of Lauderdale, whom the *Dictionary of National Biography* describes as "a violent-tempered, shrewd, eccentric man, with a fluent tongue, a broad Scottish accent, and a taste for political economy," and whose wide-ranging activities included fighting a duel with Benedict Arnold. Four were directors of the Bank of England: Alexander Baring, Thomson Hankey, John Gellibrand Hubbard, and George Goschen. And all but five were included in the *Dictionary of National Biography*.

A word is in order about two men included, who should not, some might argue, be called economists, even by a liberal interpretation: Cobbett and Sir William Molesworth. These men thought primarily in political terms, yet their emotionally charged political statements constantly involved economic ideas. Cobbett, low as the rating he might receive in a graduate seminar in economic theory, in his diatribes against inflation,[4] monopoly, inequitable taxation, and the abuses of church revenues, had an impact on the economic thinking of others and on economic policy that makes it impossible to ignore him as a force in British economics. Molesworth never published anything on economics as such, but he was the friend of a number of members of the Political Economy Club and reflected the ideas of economists. His great concern was with stopping the transportation of convicts to Australia, its colonization by free settlers, and the development of colonial self government. He was the principal spokesman in Parliament for the economic ideas of Edward Gibbon Wakefield, who advocated that Australian land should be disposed of at a price that would prevent an uneconomic dispersal of population, and that the proceeds of land sales should be used to assist free immigration.

Among the sixty-two men are three whose activities outside Parliament give them substantial credentials as economists but who played virtually no role in Parliament. For this study their parliamentary careers are important only to show that not all economists were from the same mold, nor were they inspired by an ambition to translate economic ideas into political action. In 1800 Walter Boyd wrote an important brochure on the causes of exchange-rate fluctuations, and later two pamphlets on the sinking fund, and gave penetrating testimony in 1797 before the Commons and Lords Committees on the Bank of England. Yet in thirteen years in Parliament he only spoke twice, voted only three times in listed divisions, and never served on a committee. William Jacob's works on the corn trade and on the production and consumption of gold and silver are still important sources for the economic historian, but in seven years he spoke only fourteen times, served on only two minor committees, and voted only three times in listed divisions. Samson Ricardo, a brother of David Ricardo, was a member of the Political Economy Club, wrote two important pamphlets on banking prob-

4. A French doctoral thesis by Marie de Kergaradec deals with Cobbett's monetary views: *William Cobbett. L'inflation et la déflation* (Paris, 1935).

lems (one of which included a reprint of his brother's *Plan for the Establishment of a National Bank*), yet in his two years in Parliament never spoke and never served on a committee. Furthermore Samuel Jones Loyd, although as Lord Overstone from 1850 active in parliamentary affairs in the Lords, as a member of Commons from 1819 to 1826 never spoke, never was on a committee, and voted only eight times in listed divisions.

Over the years fellow economists have pointed out to me a dozen or more members of Parliament whose claim to be called economists they thought as good as, if not better than, some of those here included, in particular Edmund Burke, John Leslie Foster, and John Charles Herries. I can simply say that I carefully considered what these men wrote and what they said in Parliament, and the decision not to include them was deliberate. Burke's parliamentary activity on economic affairs was almost all before 1780, and even that was largely focused on political corruption and patronage rather than on economic cause and effect. Both Foster and Herries wrote brochures on foreign exchange familiar to students of the Bullion controversy of Napoleonic years, but aside from that contributed little to economic analysis either in or out of Parliament.

None of the sixty-two parliamentary economists had formal training in economics, but many had read the important economic literature of the time, and in particular the *Wealth of Nations*. There was no instruction in Political Economy at Cambridge until 1816, when Pryme started his lectures; none at Oxford until 1825, when Nassau Senior became the first holder of the Drummond professorship. There is no evidence, however, that any of the economists here considered were influenced in their economic ideas by the instruction at Oxford and Cambridge, or even that they attended the infrequent lectures. However, Brougham, Horner, Petty, and the Earl of Lauderdale attended the Edinburgh lectures of Dugald Stewart, the pupil of Adam Smith, and there are some indications that the thinking of all four was influenced by these lectures. When McCulloch gave his public lectures in London in 1825, Lord Landsowne was a regular attender, and Wilmot Horton, Huskisson, Parnell, Whitmore, and Lord King came occasionally.[5] Lord Howick, twenty-three

5. D. P. O'Brien, *J. R. McCulloch, A Study in Classical Economics* (London: George Allen & Unwin, 1970), pp. 50–53.

years old, ambitious for a political career and eager to learn of the
new science of political economy, in 1825 was a private pupil of
McCulloch's.[6] One can only speculate how many ideas in speeches
given by economists in Parliament were based on notes taken on the
words of Stewart or of McCulloch.

Types of Parliamentary Economists

The sixty-two parliamentary economists fall into three main
groups, although few, if any, conformed neatly to any one type. First
were those who correspond most closely to the academic economist:
the man with a philosophic and inquiring mind, trying to explain
the upheavals in economic relations, and also to guide policy in behalf of interests that went beyond his own personal gain. Outstanding examples are Brougham, Butt, Fawcett, Horner, Lord King,
John Stuart Mill, Parnell, Pryme, David Ricardo, Rice, Scrope,
Thompson, Thornton, Torrens, Whately, and Wilson. Some of these
men drew on business experience but their role was primarily that
of the observer; they all had a quality of mind that in a later era
would have made them strong candidates for a university professorship, and Butt, Fawcett, Pryme, and Whately held professorships.

A second group were bankers and businessmen, writing about a
particular problem closely associated with their day-to-day experience and using their experience in the world of affairs to strengthen
that analysis. David Ricardo—and particularly the early Ricardo of
the Bullion controversy—and Thornton fit this prototype and also
the first type of the more detached observer. The Attwoods, Alexander and Francis Baring, William Clay, John Fielden, George J.
Goschen, Thomson Hankey, John G. Hubbard (later Lord Addington), and Lord Overstone fall into this general group.

In a broader sense anyone who stands for political office is a politician, even though only as a by-product of his desire to make effective his ideas. In addition to the two types of economists just
mentioned several men in Parliament who participated in the great

6. In the Grey of Howick papers at the University of Durham is a file entitled "Papers
Written for McCulloch," and the entry in the catalog reads: "Essays on various aspects of
economics, evidently written for criticism by McCulloch in 1825, with some comments." Among
items in the file is the undated draft of a long letter from Howick, probably written in 1825
and intended for McCulloch, raising a number of acute questions on topics they had recently
"discussed at considerable length."

economic debates, and whose names are linked with historic economic legislation, were basically politicians whom the accidents of history forced to be economists. The outstanding case was Robert Peel. Peel's name is associated with the three most important economic measures in the first half of the nineteenth century—the Act of 1819 for resumption of cash payments, the Bank Charter Act of 1844, and the repeal of the Corn Laws in 1846. Yet Peel contributed virtually nothing to the economic analysis that lay back of these measures, and his basic reason for sponsoring them was to maintain a politically stable society. He was a master politician and a superb broker in the economic ideas of others. Less striking examples are Nicholas Vansittart (later Lord Bexley) and John Charles Spencer (Lord Althorp, and later 3rd Earl Spencer), who as parliamentary spokesmen and as chancellors of the Exchequer were influential in guiding financial and monetary policy but who contributed little to economic analysis. A few men among the sixty-two here considered would qualify both as economists who were in Parliament and as important political figures who wrote on economics. Parnell is an outstanding example: his name would figure in economics had he, untouched by political ambitions, simply written, and he would figure in political history had he made no contribution to the theory of foreign exchange. To a lesser degree this could be said of Charles Jenkinson (later Lord Hawkesbury, and 1st earl of Liverpool), George Rose, Huskisson, Rice, James Graham, and Robert Wilmot (later Robert Wilmot Horton).[7]

7. Appendix III lists the economist members of each Parliament from 1780 to 1868.

Chapter 2

From Economist to Legislator

A high percentage of the economists in Parliament were politically Whigs, Radicals, or Independents. Party affiliations were less strict than in twentieth-century politics, and many men owed their seats to family influence, local personal popularity, or the support of a patron; and in several cases it is difficult to say whether a man is to be classed as an Independent, a Radical, or as a Whig, particularly as Radicals and Independents generally voted with the Whigs on important issues. But even recognizing the difficulty in an exact classification of the sixty-two economists by political affiliation, the picture is clear and would not be changed by individual shifts that those who disagree with my listing might make: thirty eight Whigs or Liberals, eleven Tories or Conservatives, nine Radicals or Independents, and four who shifted their party sympathies (Alexander Baring, Isaac Butt, Graham, and the Earl of Lauderdale).[1]

The great majority of the economists in Parliament, particularly until 1850, wanted in some way to change the existing order, usually by stopping the government, the Bank of England, the Church of England, the Church of Ireland, or the Universities of Oxford and Cambridge from doing what they were then doing. They were well to the left of center by the standards of the age. They were liberals in the historic sense of being receptive to, even eager for, orderly changes to be defended in the light of reason. Many bits of evidence, both circumstantial and direct, suggest that a high percentage of parliamentary economists had a sense of mission, and that it was to advance their ideas, rather than to add to their personal political power or to their wealth, that they sought parliamentary seats.

Economists' Roads to Parliament

With the exception of the two clerical members (Edward Copleston, bishop of Llandaff; and Richard Whately, archbishop of Dub-

---

1. The political classification of individuals is given in Appendix I.

lin), and of Lord King, who never sat in the Commons before inheriting his title, these sixty-two economists in Parliament, no matter how much they may have differed in their professional background, their approach to economics, or their party affiliations, had one thing in common: they had to be elected. The economists in Parliament, both before and after the Reform Act of 1832, provided examples of literally every road to Westminster open in an age of venality, political corruption, and lavish election expenses.

British and Irish elections, even after the Reform Act of 1832, were a far call from the principle of "one man, one vote." The situation was so different from that of modern democracies that some description of the electoral system before the Reform Act, and of the changes that act brought about, is essential to an understanding of the process by which an economist could become a member of the Commons. The constituencies were a patchwork of historical accidents with the basis of electoral power varying greatly from one to another.[2] Before the Union with Ireland in 1800 there were 558 seats in the Commons, of which 45 were for Scotland, and 513 for England and Wales. The Union added one hundred seats for Irish constituencies.

Electoral Franchise in England and Wales

Constituencies in England and Wales were of three main types: counties, cities, and boroughs. The franchise in counties was based on a property test (the forty-shilling freehold franchise) that limited the voters to a small fraction—sometimes less than 2 percent—of the residents.[3] Most of the counties were dominated by landed gentry, who, under the electoral system that ended only in 1872 with the introduction of the secret ballot, frequently put pressure on tenants, retainers, and tradesmen to vote for a particular candidate.

The franchise in boroughs and cities varied widely, but for present purposes it is enough to say that in the great majority of cases it was narrowly restricted, with its roots deep in history. The largest electorate in such a constituency was about 17,000 in the City of

2. A large part of this discussion of constituencies is based on Edward Porritt, *The Unreformed House of Commons, Parliamentary Representation before 1832*, 2 vols. (Cambridge: Cambridge University Press, 1903).
3. Details of the county franchise are given in Porritt, 1, Chap. 2, "The County Franchise."

Westminster; the smallest electorate was in the borough of Gatton, with six houses and one voter. Old Sarum, which, thanks to the crusading of journalist Cobbett became the most famous of the "rotten boroughs"—as boroughs of limited franchise were often called—had no residents and seven electors but sent two members to Parliament. In addition to boroughs owned or dominated by individuals, sometimes referred to as pocket boroughs or nomination boroughs, there were so-called Treasury boroughs where the government, by control of the votes of government employees and of tradesmen dependent on government patronage, could control or greatly influence an election.

There were twenty-seven corporation boroughs, which, regardless of what they may have been in origin, by 1832 had become, according to Porritt, primarily "organizations for returning members to the House of Commons, and for defending and maintaining the exclusive right to make such elections." Voters in corporation boroughs were few—according to Porritt, in no case over sixty—and voting had nothing to do with residency. Corporations were almost always controlled by a single person or closely knit faction that could handpick its candidates. In Porritt's words: "In the last century of the unreformed Parliament nearly one half of the members had no constituents to whom they had any responsibilities."[4]

The English Reform Act of 1832 made a comprehensive change in the allocation of parliamentary seats, as between individual boroughs, cities, and counties, but did not change the total numbers. It gave representation to twenty-one towns and cities—officially described as boroughs—heretofore represented only by county members for whom their residents voted, increased county members by sixty-five, and provided for uniform franchise requirements in both counties and boroughs. The net effect was to make it easier for economists to secure seats for the newly enfranchised towns and cities, and for other constituencies where the franchise was broadened.

Electoral Franchise in Ireland and Scotland

The electoral situation in Ireland[5] before 1832 was essentially the same as in England: county, city, and borough constituencies with a

4. 1:309.
5. Porritt, 2, chap. 107, describes the Irish electoral situation between the Union and 1832.

limited franchise; the domination of the county elections by the big landowners, and many boroughs where the government or a single man could return whom they pleased. The Irish Reform Act of 1832 made less change in Irish electoral arrangements than in England, although it did increase the number of Irish seats from 100 to 105.

In Scotland[6] parliamentary representation before the Reform Act was even less democratic than in England and Ireland, and probably also less venal. The Scottish counties elected thirty members; sixty-four royal burghs were divided into fourteen groups, each group electing a member; and Edinburgh elected a member. The tight control exercised in both counties and burghs by a small oligarchy made bribery, at least of the cruder sort, unnecessary. The situation is indicated by the remark of Sir Walter Scott, who, when visited in 1826 by the Russian Prince Davidoff and his tutor, took them to an election "to see our quiet way of managing the choice of a national representative."[7] Election for the Scottish burghs, other than Edinburgh, was by a system comparable to the election of an American president by the Electoral College: in each group of four or five burghs, one representative from each burgh had a vote. Hence, at a maximum, the members of the Commons from the burghs were chosen by the votes of five men. These electors in turn were chosen by a very small electorate; according to Porritt a burgh seldom had more than fifty electors, and in 1831 "only one thousand and three hundred and three persons had any direct and legal part in the election of the fifteen members from the Scottish burghs."[8] Brougham's statement in the Lords debate in 1832 on the Reform bill for Scotland was substantially correct:

From the Tweed to John o' Groats, throughout the whole length of the country, there is not within the memory of man, the knowledge of anything like a popular election. As far back as the records of authentic history go there never has been anything deserving the name, or even approaching to a popular election, anything like an election for borough or city, anything which would convey to the mind of an Englishman, or a Welshman, or an Irishman, a notion of what an election is.[9]

6. Ibid., 2, chaps. 33 and 39, describes the Scottish electoral situation before 1832.
7. *The Journal of Sir Walter Scott* (New York, 1890), 1:220.
8. Porritt, 2:128.
9. Ibid., 2:142, quoting from the *Mirror of Parliament* (London: Longman, Brown, Green, and Longmans, 1828–41), 60 vols.

The Scottish Reform Act of 1832 greatly widened the electorate. Burgh members were increased from fifteen to twenty-three, county members were reduced from thirty to twenty-two, and the franchise was given to all £10 householders.

The Economists' Paths to Westminister

There were in all nearly 330 elections that gave seats to the fifty-nine economists who stood for Parliament—Copleston, Whately, and King never faced an electorate—and they embraced literally every path by which an economist who wanted to make his voice heard in politics, or the aspiring young politician who became in spite of himself a framer and defender of economic policy, could travel to Westminster. At one extreme were situations in which a borough owner, the government, or a powerful landowner—particularly but not only before the Reform Acts of 1832—could regard a seat as private property, and approval of a candidate as tantamount to election. An Irish rotten borough, Cashel, provided Peel's first seat in 1809, which his father gave him as a present a few weeks after his twenty-first birthday. Henry Parnell was elected in 1802 for the pocket borough of Portarlington, in Ireland, nominated by his father-in-law, the Earl of Portarlington. Vansittart entered Parliament in 1796 for the Treasury borough of Harwich; in 1802, 1807, and 1808 he was elected for Old Sarum.

Hume, in his election for Weymouth and Melcombe Regis in 1812, and David Ricardo, in his two elections for Portarlington (seventeen electors, all controlled by the Earl of Portarlington), in clear violation of the law secured their seats by outright purchase.[10] Before his second election for Portarlington, after the death of George III in 1820, there were reports that Ricardo might contest the County of Gloucester, where he had a country estate. His remarks in a letter to his friend Hutches Trower are a commentary on the electoral situation both in a county and a pocket borough: "My late constituents at Portarlington appear to be a very good tempered set of gentlemen, and will I am assured elect me without hesitation to the next Parliament. The report of my being a candidate for the county

---

10. A detailed account of Ricardo's purchase of his seat is given in Piero Sraffa, ed., *Works and Correspondence of David Ricardo* (Cambridge: Cambridge University Press, 1952–62), 5:xiii–xix. Hereafter cited as Ricardo, *Works.*

of Gloucester never had the least foundation. . . . I do not soar so high, and am the most unfit of all men to engage in an undertaking so difficult and so expensive as that of contesting a county with an old and powerful family."[11]

But such phrases as "pocket borough" or "domination of a county," common in political literature of the period, sometimes over-simplified a complex situation. Often the terms could be taken literally as meaning that pointing a finger or an approving nod would insure a man's election, but sometimes they meant only that the owner or patron would throw his influence, and perhaps his money, in favor of a candidate. This, however, did not always assure election if the candidate or his sponsor was personally unpopular.

Francis Horner, chairman of the Bullion Committee of 1810, was elected in three pocket boroughs—St. Ives, Wendover, and St. Mawes—with the support of Whig noblemen. Horner's account of his first campaign in St. Ives, a fishing village in Cornwall, sounds more like a rough-and-tumble campaign today than electoral pro-cedure in an unreformed pocket borough: "I never made so many vows, or shook so many by the hand, in the whole course of my life. They were nearly thirty fishermen of pilchards, every one of them styled captain . . . I shook every individual voter by the hand, stink-ing with brine and pilchard juice, repeated the same smiles and ca-joleries to every one of them, and kissed some women who were very pretty."[12] Yet even with the support of Horner by the dominant interest in the borough his two opponents polled 93 and 86 votes as against his 128.

At the other extreme from rotten and nomination boroughs were constituencies where the electorate ran into several hundreds or even the thousands, and no individual or family exercised a pre-dominant influence. Among elections in such constituencies before 1832 were Thornton's eight victories—only two uncontested—in Southwark, with the largest electorate except Westminster; Rice's one defeat and four victories (two uncontested) in Limerick City; Parnell's nine victories in Queen's County—six uncontested but three hard-fought contests; Poulett Thomson's narrow victories in

11. Ibid., 7:162–63. In 1816 Ricardo had earlier declined the suggestion that he stand for the borough of Worcester (7:110); and in 1822 rejected the idea that he stand for Liverpool (9:182).

12. Leonard Horner, ed., *Memoirs and Correspondence of Francis Horner, M.P.* (London, 1843), 1:380–81.

Dover in 1826 and 1830; and Western's six victories (three uncontested) and one defeat in Essex. Between the two extremes of nomination and pocket boroughs and large electorates were all gradations of personal or governmental influence, tradition, or venality.

Expenses of Economists' Elections

The expenses of economists' elections presented as diverse a pattern as did the type of constituencies that they represented. As already mentioned, David Ricardo, and Hume in his first election, purchased their seats outright, and Howick and Western had heavy expenditures in hard-fought contests. Howick, although his father, the second Earl Grey, was a large landowner in Northumberland, in 1831 spent over £17,000—roughly equivalent in purchasing power to $500,000 today;[13] Western, in Essex, where he was an important landowner, spent over £4,000 in the 1830 election, over £3,000 in 1831, and over £1,700 in 1820.[14] Graham's election for Hull in 1818 cost him at least £6,000;[15] Wilmot's election for Newcastle-under-Lyme in 1818, in which he polled 299 votes, cost him £8,000.[16] However, from a variety of circumstantial evidence—the financial means of candidates, specific statements, or the lack of charges of bribery—it appears that, considering the political practices of the day, large money outlays by economists seeking parliamentary seats were the exception.

In the case of Horner, sponsored for his three constituencies by Whig patrons, election expenses appear to have been minimal. In other situations, particularly where a group of leading citizens invited a man to stand, it was with little or no expense to him. This seems to have been true of Thomas Attwood in Birmingham, John Stuart Mill in Westminster, Perronet Thompson in Bradford, Torrens in Ashburton and Bolton, and Hume in Kilkenny. And there is the case of Thornton, of awesome personal integrity, who, when offered in 1780 a virtually sure seat in Hull by the Wilberforces, refused to stand when he learned that it was the local custom for a

13. Election records in Grey of Howick Papers, University of Durham.
14. Election records in Essex County Record Office.
15. J. T. Ward, *Sir James Graham* (New York: St. Martin's Press, 1967), p. 34, speaks of Graham as having to borrow £6,000 to cover election expenses.
16. H. J. M. Johnson, *British Emigration Policy, 1815–1830* (Oxford: Clarendon Press, 1972), p. 147.

candidate to pay two guineas to each voter. He then stood for and was elected eight times in his native Southwark, a community of prosperous tradesmen who did not need to look to election bribery as a source of income, and to whom as taxpayers there was a pocketbook appeal in Thornton's campaign ditty:

> Nor place nor pension e'er got he,
> For self or for connexion,
> We shall not tax the Treasury
> By Thornton's re-election.

That Thornton was not the ordinary politician, and Southwark not an ordinary constituency, is indicated by *The Times'* report of his speech to the electors after his victory in 1796: "He then spoke of the mischief that arose from dealing out continual flattery to the lower classes; for his own part, he said, that as he had not gained their votes by intoxicating them with liquor, so neither had he gained them by intoxicating them with extravagant and absurd praise."[17]

Economists' Electoral Promises before Reform Act

The arguments of economists in support of their candidacies covered a wide spectrum. In the some 185 uncontested elections—much more common in the unreformed Parliament—rarely if ever was anything said publicly by the candidate as to the policies he stood for. In only 20 of the 83 successful candidacies of economists from 1780 until the election of 1818 was there a contest. And even in most of the contested elections, until the general election of 1818, a public statement on issues, economic or of any other nature, does not appear to have played any part in the candidacy of an economist elected to a parliamentary seat. The closest approach reported in the press, to a stand on economic issues in an election campaign, was the cautious remark of Thornton in the 1796 campaign: "The reform in the representation for which he would vote, would neither lower immediately the price of bread, nor give coats to those who were without them."[18] Insofar as there were contests, they usually involved a small electorate. Only two economist members of Parlia-

17. 3 May 1796, p. 4.
18. *The Times*, 30 May 1796.

ment up to 1818—Thornton in Southwark, and Lord Althorp in Northamptonshire—polled over 1800 votes; and in only three other cases did a successful candidate have over 300 votes. Francis Baring was elected in Chipping Wycombe in 1794 with 29 votes; Huskisson in Liskead in 1804 with 21 votes; Charles Jenkinson (later earl of Liverpool) in Saltash in 1784 with 11 votes; Rose in Christchurch in 1801 with 30 votes; Western in Maldon in 1807 with 29 votes.

The war with France, beginning in 1793, had pretty well inhibited any debate, even in contested elections, over political issues. Views on the war undoubtedly influenced some voting, but I find no record of any election in which an economist was involved when the war was debated. Much the same can be said of parliamentary reform. Sentiment for such reform, which had been gaining strength in the 1780s, was virtually driven underground after the outbreak of the Revolution in France. It was not only that some reformers, reacting against the excesses of the Revolution, turned against all reform as tainted with Jacobinism; but many who still favored reform felt it useless or politically unwise to urge publicly a movement that many upper-class English then felt was akin to treason.

The permanent settlement of Napoleon on St. Helena released the pent-up sentiment for change—particularly for parliamentary reform, the removal of Catholic disabilities, and for dealing with the problems of taxation, money and banking, and the Corn Laws in an atmosphere freed from the overriding considerations of war policy. Economists were on the move politically. They came increasingly to compete in the more open constituencies and to make specific statements on the hustings on the policies they would oppose or support if elected. Hume was elected in 1818 for Aberdeen burghs, in a defeat for entrenched interests; in the same year Torrens put up a stiff contest in a by-election in Rochester before going down to defeat, in 1820 stood for Gloucester county but withdrew before the polling, and in 1826 was elected for Ipswich, only to be unseated on petition after serving a few weeks; Pryme was defeated in Cambridge in 1820 and 1826; Cobbett stood unsuccessfully for Coventry in 1820—the first of three attempts that finally brought him in for Oldham in 1832; Rice was defeated for Limerick City in 1818 but was returned for that constituency in 1820; in 1818 Graham was returned for Hull, as was Wilmot for Newcastle-under-Tyne; Loyd for Hythe in 1819; William Wolryche Whitmore for Bridgnorth in 1820; and Brougham, although already in a safe seat in Winchelsea, in 1818 made the first of his three unsuccessful campaigns to break the political power of the Lowther family in Westmorland County.

For Ricardo, standing for an Irish pocket borough in which he never set foot, the money paid to the Earl of Portarlington was an effective substitute for a political platform. But in the case of many other economists in the immediate post-Napoleonic years, their campaigns brought out that they stood for reform, both political and economic. The emphasis, however, was political reform—in particular reform of Parliament and removal of Catholic disabilities. There appears to have been a widespread assumption that until there was a reform that would bring into Parliament members more representative of public opinion and more concerned with removing economic injustice, there would be little chance of changing or abolishing the Corn Laws, reforming Church tithes, reducing wasteful expenditures, or eliminating pensions or sinecures for favorites of government; and until Catholic disabilities were removed peace in Ireland would never be achieved, no matter what economic reforms might be introduced.

Of Brougham's 1818 campaign in Westmorland *The Times* (7 July 1818) reported: "Mr. Brougham's friends . . . see in him the champion of their independence, the asserter of their rights, and the deliverance from their thraldom of an aristocratic domination, and which has long deprived them of all exercise of their electoral franchises."

In the speech opening his campaign in Hull in 1818 Graham said: "Ministerial extravagance and undue influence are objects of my entire abhorrence, and all my efforts have been used in resisting them, whether in the shape of places, sinecures or pensions. . . . I love peace rather than war. . . . I am a friend to religious as well as civil liberty, and see no reason why men should be put into danger or difficulty on account of their religious opinions. . . . I am a friend to reform in Parliament. . . ."[19]

In the same election Hume, who had left his home in Scotland twenty-three years before to make a fortune in India, accepted the invitation of a group of reformers to stand for the Aberdeen burghs,

19. Quoted in Ward, p. 30.

and won in a campaign in which he stressed parliamentary reform, reduced expenditures, and a smaller army. His postelection speech was no idle boast, that he was *"the independent, unshackled representative of the only free and independent borough in Scotland."*[20] Pryme, in his 1826 campaign, supported free trade and the removal of Catholic disabilities.[21] Poulett Thomson, in a speech after his victory in Dover in 1826, said "he could not but congratulate the freemen of having rescued their town from the disgrace of being a Government Borough."[22] Howick's program, in his unsuccessful campaign in Northumberland in 1826, was:

1. Rigid economy in public expenditure.
2. Lightening of taxation.
3. Catholic emancipation.
4. Parliamentary reform on moderate scale.
5. Abolition of slavery provided only that due regard be paid to the sacred rights of property.[23]

Whitmore, an ardent free trader who had represented Bridgnorth since 1820, said in an election speech in 1830: "To monopoly in the common sense of the word, I am and ever have been a decided enemy," and spoke of the evils of "an enormous debt—overwhelming taxation," and was critical of the East India Company monopoly.[24] Huskisson, in a letter to the freemen of Liverpool at the 1830 election, barely a month before his death, said:

. . . it is essential to lighten the pressure upon the springs of our productive industry. This can only be attained—

1st. By a positive diminution of taxation. Already an important and valuable remission of taxes has been effected.

2dly. By such a modification of the remaining burdens (as far as they may be necessary) as, by a more equitable distribution, may especially relieve the industrious classes.

3dly. By getting rid, as speedily as possible, of all monopolies affecting commerce & the free agency of the community in their capital & labour, for monopoly is not only a tax upon these two great sources of wealth, but

20. *Report of . . . Montrose* (Montrose, 1854), p. 34. A full account of Scottish electoral practices in 1818, and of Hume's election that year, is given in this brochure.

21. *Cambridge Chronicle and Journal,* 16 June 1826.

22. *Kent Herald,* 26 June 1826.

23. As given in an unpublished thesis by R. Job, "The Political Career of Henry Third Lord Grey," submitted for the degree of M. Litt. at University of Durham, 1959.

24. *The Shrewsbury Chronicle and North Wales Advertiser,* 6 August 1830.

a tax of the worst sort. The boon which it affords to the privileged party is very far from being the measure of the injury which it inflicts upon all the rest of the community.

4thly. By giving to the utmost every facility, not incompatible with the rights of property, to the expansion & development of those internal improvements which the progress of knowledge & the discoveries of science are daily pointing out, for the purpose of rectifying errors, of correcting abuses, & of increasing the civilization of mankind.[25]

In several of the elections up to 1832 it was reported in the press that clergy of the Established Church opposed economist candidates. During Torrens's campaign in Ipswich in 1826 the *Suffolk Chronicle* (24 June 1826) said of the opposition to Torrens: "The Admiralty has sent forth its commands, and a host of the clergy have done all in their power to overthrow the independent interest in the Borough."

Economists' Electoral Promises after Reform Act

Increasingly, beginning in 1832, economists in their campaigns stressed the economic policies they supported. Undoubtedly one reason for this development was the enlargement of the franchise and the creation of new urban constituencies, not controlled by a patron or by an arm of government. Also, as a result of Catholic emancipation in 1829 and parliamentary reform in 1832, political issues played relatively a lesser role in campaign appeals, and with the rising tide of free trade sentiment the public was more concerned with economic issues. Thomas Attwood, whose activities in the Birmingham Political Union had been an important force in the passage of the Reform Act, since 1816 had favored an expansionary monetary policy, and probably the main reason for his support of parliamentary reform was the belief that a legislature more responsive to public opinion would lead to a larger money supply.[26] Attwood was elected in 1832 for newly enfranchised Birmingham, and served seven years. Attwood and also Muntz, who succeeded to his seat, were vigorous critics of the gold standard. Outside Birmingham, I can find no evidence that the monetary question was ever a cam-

25. From a memorandum in the Horton papers at Derby.
26. In my Introduction to *Selected Economic Writings of Thomas Attwood* (London: London School of Economics and Political Science, 1964), pp. xx–xxii, I discuss briefly the relation between Attwood's monetary views and his activity for parliamentary reform.

paign issue, either before or after 1832, although at least six other economists—Matthias Attwood, Alexander Baring, Cayley, Davenport, Graham, and Torrens—in other settings were critical of the gold standard.

The Reform Act did not, however, stop the economists from campaigning on political issues. This was partly because, particularly in the 1830s and 1840s when so many economist politicians were in varying degrees under the influence of Utilitarianism and Philosophical Radicalism, the same people who wanted economic change also wanted political change for its own sake. After 1832 the franchise was by democratic standards, still narrowly restricted with about 14 percent of adult males eligible to vote, and the system of open voting continued, to be ended only by the adoption of the secret ballot in 1872. Hence the pre–1832 campaign argument that political reform was essential continued to have force and voter appeal. This was particularly true after the repeal of the Corn Laws, the repeal or reduction of many other duties, the virtual elimination of colonial preference, and the repeal of the Navigation Acts had removed from the arena of campaign controversy the major economic issues of the two decades following the Reform Act. So again in the 1850s and 1860s political issues became more frequent in the election campaigns of economists. At first glance this situation might seem to be a return to that previous to 1832, where for economists political issues overshadowed economic issues. Yet there was a basic difference in the role of the political issues before 1832 and after the early 1850s. Before 1832, even though most economists favored economic change, they stressed political issues because they felt they were a prerequisite to economic reforms. After the early 1850s the stress was on political and civil rights issues for their own sake. The great economic objectives had been won, and the full achievement of political, religious, and civil rights changes were thought of, not as a prerequisite to economic change, but as the logical release of the public from the grip of monopoly in the broadest sense, through extension of the franchise, abolition of university tests, disestablishment of the Church of Ireland, abolition of church rates, and removal of Jewish disabilities.

The three issues raised most often by economists in campaigns after the Reform Act were free trade and the repeal of the Navigation Acts; electoral reform and the ballot; and elimination or re-form of tithes together with reduction or elimination of the privileges of the Church of England and of the Church of Ireland. Of these the most frequently mentioned issue was free trade or tariff reduc-tion. At least eight economist candidates—Lord Howick, Cobden, Gisborne, Hume, Sir George Cornewall, Lewis, J. L. Ricardo, and Samson Ricardo—in electoral campaigns between 1841 and 1852 spoke in favor of free trade. Three economists—Hume, J. L. Ri-cardo, and Wilson—urged repeal of the Navigation Acts. Five econo-mists urged further extension of the franchise, and only one—Graham in 1837—expressed outright opposition. Fawcett, Perronet Thompson, and Torrens spoke in favor of the ballot, and two econo-mists, Graham and Hubbard, opposed it, although Hubbard's op-position was lukewarm and indicated that he then (in 1859) thought that it was just a matter of time before the ballot was enacted. Gis-borne, J. L. Ricardo, and Wilson all favored an extension of civil and religious liberty—a broad phrase that in differing contexts could cover anything from abolishing oaths which prevented non-adherents of the Church of England from receiving degrees at Cam-bridge and Oxford, to permitting Jews to sit in Parliament without taking the Christian oath. Frequently criticized by economists when on the hustings were tithes and the privileged position of the Church of England.

Rarely did a candidate present a complete program in specific terms, but the voting record and speeches in Parliament suggest that the platform of Perronet Thompson in the Hull election of 1835 represents the views of a high proportion of economist candi-dates of the 1830s and 1840s:

Free Trade
Extension of the Suffrage
Shortening of the duration of Parliaments
Ballot
End of corporal punishment in the Army
End of Slavery and Slave Trade
Church Establishment: "I follow the Master who said: 'Whatsoever you would that Men should do unto you, do ye also unto them.' "[27, 28]

27. *The Hull Advertiser*, 19 June 1835.
28. In the context of Thompson's known attitude, this cryptic remark was probably criticism of the Church of England and the Church of Ireland.

In his Bolton campaign of 1832 Torrens supported Reform, and spoke favorably of "household suffrage, triennial parliaments, and vote by ballot"; was the uncompromising advocate of reduction of taxation "in every Department of State"; favored "total abolition of the Corn Laws"; was for "the total abolition of tithes—for the repeal of the duty on salt, hops, soap, and in short for the repeal of every tax which pressed on the industry of the people."[29] In a new political setting, John Stuart Mill, when a candidate for Westminster in 1865, in response to questions, stated his position on specific issues:[30]

a. Further parliamentary reform, but opposition to the ballot.
b. No religious disabilities.
c. Death duties on land.
d. Flogging abolished, both in the army and outside, except for crimes of violence.
e. Government to interfere as little as possible in strikes and lockouts.

Such presentations of a political platform were, however, rare, and in most cases the views of candidates came out only in isolated remarks, statements by supporters as to why they would vote for a man, or even criticism by opponents of a man's views.

The Religious Issue in Economists' Elections

In the 1840s and 1850s religious feelings were fanned by the issue of "Papal aggrandizement," i.e., the assumption by Catholic bishops of territorial titles like those held by bishops of the Church of England; the debate over the parliamentary grant to the Catholic Seminary at Maynooth, Ireland; and the question of Church of England control over public education. A number of comments in the press suggest that for several years many voters were more concerned over these issues than over the Navigation Acts or tax policy. That politics can make strange bedfellows is suggested by the comment in *The Bradford Observer* (18 July 1852) that Thompson's defeat was due to "an unprincipled coalition of Methodists, Orangemen, and Roman Catholics," the charge being that the Catholics voted against him because of his support of the bill to forbid the assumption of territorial titles by Catholic clergy, and the Methodists and

29. *The Bolton Chronicle*, 15 Dec. 1832.
30. Michael St. John Packe, *The Life of John Stuart Mill* (London: Secker and Warburg, 1954), p. 440.

Orangemen voted against him because of his support of the grant to the Catholic seminary at Maynooth.

Daniel O'Connell and Economists' Campaigns

Probably the greatest personal abuse of any economists came to Gisborne and Hume, who, when defeated in English constituencies, were, with the support of Daniel O'Connell, elected for Kilkenny county in 1837 and Carlow Borough in 1839, respectively. *The Carlow Sentinel* denounced Gisborne as an "adventurer," as an "imported candidate" brought in by "the Government, the demagogues, and the Carlow priesthood" acting conjointly.[31] There was no economist upon whom more vituperation of the conservative press was heaped than upon Hume. When he lost his Middlesex seat in 1837 *The Times* gloated:

The county is no longer disgraced by a man whose knowledge of its interests is precisely equal to his acquaintance with the wants and interests of the nation at large—a man entirely devoid of all fixed and definite views of statesmanship, that is, of the science of legislation and civil government—a man who has no faculty of perception as to the merits of any political measure beyond its mere arithmetical bearings—a man profuse of vulgar speech, but of all else niggard—a man who set up in business as a demagogue, with no capital but that of an uneducated, reckless and malignant partisan of change—a man who understood the English character so little as to pay court to it by virtually denying the superintendent providence of the Almighty. . . .[32]

To such abuse Hume's supporters answered:

The *Morning Post* advances one serious charge against Mr. Hume, which we must on his behalf plead guilty to. Mr. Hume, it appears, is neither a gambler nor a frequenter of clubs. His time has not been spent in the pest houses in the neighborhood of St. James's, where some of the opulent and honourable representatives of English Toryism spend their midnight hours in the practice of elegant debauchery and mutual peculations. What taste he must have!—how vulgar must be his propensities!—how intolerably honest he must be! For him the black eyes of purchased passion have no charms; and there exist for him no attractive quality to the roulette table nor the marked card.[33]

31. 9 Feb. 1839; 13 July 1839.
32. 5 Aug. 1837.
33. Quoted in the *Kilkenny Journal*, 12 Aug. 1837, from the *Morning Freeman*.

In contrast to the experience of Gisborne and Hume was that of Parnell and Rice. They had long represented Irish constituencies; both had been supporters of Catholic emancipation and in many other ways had championed the cause of Ireland. They stopped short, however, of favoring repeal of the Union, and in 1832 O'Connell vowed vengeance on all who opposed repeal. Parnell withdrew as a candidate for his old seat for Queen's County because he felt that he had no chance of winning. In a by-election the following year he was returned unopposed for Dundee. Rice got the message of O'Connell's wrath early in the campaign, for there is no record that he ever was a candidate for his old seat in Limerick City in 1832. He stood for the borough of Cambridge and was elected along with Pryme, the professor of economics at Cambridge.[34]

Charges of Corruption in Economists' Campaigns

It would be professionally flattering to think that the campaigns of economists were on a higher ethical level than the run-of-the-mill campaigns. That was undoubtedly true in the case of Thornton and John Stuart Mill, but, particularly if we can believe the claims of their defeated rivals, was not always true in other elections. As an example, after Scrope's reelection in Stroud in 1841, the opposition press reported that in his campaign "influence and intimidation in every shape was brought to bear upon the more dependent voters."[35] And when Pryme, first holder of the Chair of Political Economy later occupied by Marshall and Pigou, was victorious in 1837, the *Cambridge Chronicle* said his victory was obtained by "cash in hand to afford the Elector [opposed to Pryme] a jaunt out of town on the day of Election," and spoke of "obstinate ones made incapable of voting by drink—of others locked up during the whole time of polling—of some gorged with beer to the critical point at which the vote could be secured by the continued attentions of a hired conductor for those candidates whose names were incessantly dinged in their ears," and concluded that "the victory of the Radicals at Cambridge

34. In the Rice papers in the National Library of Ireland in Dublin is a wealth of material on the candidacies of Rice and Pryme in 1832. As in so many campaigns of economists the emphasis was not so much on specific economic issues as on breaking the power of the Establishment.

35. *Gloucestershire Chronicle*, 3 July 1841.

is nothing more than the victory of a corrupt faction steeped in hypocrisy and double dealing."[36]

The Great Issues in Parliament, 1780–1868

To appraise the role of economists who were in Parliament between 1780 and 1868 it is important to set in perspective the great issues with which Parliament grappled in those years. In 1780, four years after the publication of the *Wealth of Nations*, Britain was still in the early stages of the Industrial Revolution. The country was primarily agricultural. The Bank of England was over eighty years old, but in no sense was it a central bank with public responsibilities. It was a private monopoly that served as a fiscal arm of government. Other banking services were in large part supplied by small unincorporated unit banks catering to local needs. Monopoly, in manifold forms, permeated the whole fabric of life, economic, political, and religious. The country was honeycombed with regulations, some governmental, some of private organizations, that by restricting the activities of a large part of the population gave a monopoly of power to favored and selected groups. The East India Company had a monopoly of trade with the Orient; British shipowners had a monopoly of the carrying trade; British agriculture had a virtual monopoly of the home market; many guilds had a monopoly of business. To a large extent goods were produced and sold, not on the basis of the decisions of producers or the wishes of buyers, but on the basis of some authoritarian restraint.

Much of the *Wealth of Nations* was an attack on the unreasonableness of these restraints, and on the philosophy that inspired them. Smith had articulated a feeling against monopoly and restraint that was to become increasingly vocal over the next three-quarters of a century. In that period a large part of the people who called themselves political economists were trying to explain both why an economic system would be more productive if these restraints were lessened or removed and how a system would function if the forces of the market were substituted for such restraints.

Adam Smith's criticism of the deadening hand of the past and the dampening effect of monopoly was aimed largely toward direct

36. 20 July 1837.

economic effects. Yet many passages in the *Wealth of Nations* showed that Smith's concern about "the wretched spirit of monopoly" also touched on problems, not economic in a narrow sense, that reflected both his particular beliefs and the general philosophy of the Enlightenment. Among these were education of the people; inadequacy of English university education; evils of government by an exclusive company; the "oppressive aristocracy" of Ireland, "an aristocracy founded in the most odious of all distinctions, those of religious and political prejudice";[37] a critical attitude toward tithes and even toward state support of religion.

For more than a decade after 1780 the handful of economists in Parliament that included the earl of Liverpool, the earl of Lauderdale, Sir Francis Baring, Sir John Sinclair, Rose, and Thornton, several of whom were to play an important parliamentary role in later years, had only a limited impact on debate and legislation. Much of what they had to say dealt with details of politics and of the affairs of the East India Company, and with the ending of the American Revolution. On two important economic measures debated in the 1780s, the commercial treaty with France and proposals to loosen restrictions on Irish trade, the economists had little to say, and there is no record as to how they voted on these measures.

But the French Revolution, and in particular the war with France beginning in February 1793, opened a whole range of economic and political issues in which the increasing number of economists in Parliament were to play an important role. These issues were ones with which a generation that had read Adam Smith, or at least had been influenced by his ideas, felt that they had a particular competence to advise: What economic policy best contributes to increase the wealth of a nation? How can the wretched spirit of monopoly be removed from the whole fabric of national life? For nearly three quarters of a century these questions were under almost continuous Parliamentary debate and economists were active in those debates.

Appendix: *A Note on Parliamentary Procedure*

A bill, before being passed by the Commons, had to be approved four times, by (1) permission to introduce the bill, which was usually

---

37. Cannan edition, 2:430 (London: Methuen, 1904).

a formality; (2) first reading and approval, also in most cases a formality in that a vote in favor did not necessarily mean that the member approved but simply that he favored further discussion; (3) second reading, which in most cases was the most important vote, as usually a bill approved on second reading was given final approval on third reading although sometimes with amendments; (4) third reading. Hansard frequently has no record of approval on third reading after a bill was passed on second reading, or at least no record of the votes of individual members.

Until 1836 recording of the votes of individual members was quite irregular. In previous years in many cases there is simply the statement that the bill was approved or disapproved, and when individual votes were given it was usually only for the minority. Occasionally bills were killed by voting that they be considered in six months.

Procedure in the Lords was much the same, except that as few bills originated there, the first step of giving permission to introduce a bill was rare. In the earlier years, and occasionally nearly to the end of the period covered, frequently there is no mention of one or more stages in the legislative history of a bill; and there are cases where the Lords consider a bill referred to as already approved by the Commons, but of which there is no mention of it in the proceedings of the Commons.

Chapter 3

The Economists and International
Trade

Central to the doctrines of Smith and the classical economists
were the gains from the division of labor, as determined by decisions in the market. This analysis covered the whole range of economic life, but the most historic controversy over division of labor
was in international trade. For the first twenty years of the period
there were no head-on parliamentary clashes over foreign trade,
and the few remarks on the subject were largely incidental. Lord
Hawkesbury's (later earl of Liverpool) comment in a discussion of
trade with Portugal, on the "benefit" of a reciprocal exchange of
commodities[1] was about the limit of parliamentary contribution to
the theory of international trade.

Early Debate on Corn Laws

Several committees on the corn trade between 1793 and 1802
dealt largely with factual details, but over four decades of almost
continuous debate on the Corn Laws began in 1804, with the appointment of the Select Committee on Petitions Relating to the Importation and Exportation of Corn.[2] Western, an indefatigable
spokesman for agriculture, was the only economist on the committee. Its report recommended a series of measures, the net effect of
which was to restrict the import of corn, and Western sponsored
legislation[3] incorporating the recommendations.[4] In the course of the
debate, in which Western was the only economist to make any substantive remarks, he advanced an economic argument that was made

1. P. H., vol. 26, 527, 21 Feb. 1787.
2. P.P., 1803–4 (96), 5:699 [33].
3. 45 Geo. III, c. 109.
4. William Smart, *Economic Annals of the Nineteenth Century*, 2 vols. (London: Macmillan,
1910–17), 1, chap. 6, "The New Corn Law," discusses the committee report and the subsequent legislation.

repeatedly in the next forty years by agricultural spokesmen, that restrictions on corn imports would in the long run make for lower prices. Without saying it in so many words, the Western position, contrary to the later view of David Ricardo and Torrens, was that corn production was in the long run subject to decreasing costs, and that therefore a larger domestic production would mean a downward sloping cost curve. As Western put it, "It was a measure to prevent the recurrence of that scarcity, which had been felt in so dreadful a manner some years ago; and, ultimately, make the price of corn moderate and cheap. . . . It was as much for the interest of the consumer, as it was for the grower of corn, that such a regulation as was contained in that bill should take place."[5]

For the following decade there was virtually no discussion of the Corn Laws, but in 1813 a Select Committee on the Corn Trade was appointed and on it were eight economists: Parnell (chairman), Alexander Baring, Giddy, Huskisson, Peel, Thornton, Vansittart, and Western. The committee report was a curious mixture of arguments, including Western's claim of a decade earlier that in some not clearly defined way restrictions on imports would lead to reduced production costs. If not written by Parnell or Western, the report certainly reflects their thinking at the time, and it is strange that Alexander Baring, Giddy, or Thornton should have agreed to a report so out of line with their views stated elsewhere, although no one filed a minority report. Parnell, in submitting the committee's report, bolstered his case with the argument that dependence on foreign grain involved "sending our money to improve other countries."[6]

Nothing came of the committee's report at the time. The following year Parnell again raised the question and a new committee was appointed, with the same economist members as the previous year, plus Finlay. In debate Alexander Baring and Finlay opposed new restrictions on corn imports, on what were essentially freedom of trade arguments, and Horner in a forceful speech said such measures would "permanently increase the price of corn,"[7] but Huskisson, Giddy, and Vansittart supported Parnell's position, mixing together the idea of decreasing costs with the political danger of

5. 1 H, 5:1087, 20 July 1804.
6. 1 H, 26:645, 15 June 1813. An analysis of the report and of Parnell's speech is given by Smart, *Economic Annals*, 1, chap. 20, "The Coming of the Corn Laws."
7. 1 H, 27:877, 13 May 1814.

depending on foreign food. In the Lords, Lauderdale, following the Parnell analysis, said of the proposed bill that "in its effect he had no hesitation in saying it would lower the price."[8] The net result of the long legislative wrangle was practically nil—the bounties on the export of grain were dropped but import duties were left unchanged. Outside Parliament the Corn Law controversy produced the pamphlets of Malthus, Torrens, Robert Wilson, and Sir Edward West, and Ricardo's first economic writing outside the field of money and banking.

Corn Law of 1815

In 1815 a new corn law was passed, increasing sharply the restriction on imported corn. This event was preceded by the most extended debate to that time on any economic topic other than the bullion debate of 1811. The arguments of Alexander Baring, Horner, and Lord King showed a good understanding of the economic concept of international division of labor and of costs at the margin, and drew on the authority of Adam Smith. Baring, taking a view suggestive of that taken by the Anti-Corn Law League a quarter of a century later, said that "the whole mass of the country ought not to be compelled to pay a high price for bread, that the experiment of cultivating barren lands might be tried,"[9] and that he believed the bill "was substantially a measure having no other effect but that of raising a considerable revenue from the consumer of bread for the purpose of raising the rents of land."[10] And then, anticipating the view that agitation for parliamentary reform was furthered by the economic views of an unreformed Parliament, he said: "The measure, if carried, would be more efficacious toward producing a reform in that House, than any speech that hon. baronet [Sir Francis Burdett, then a strong supporter of parliamentary reform] had made or could make." In the Commons, Baring, Finlay, and Horner were in the minority when the bill was approved 245–77,[11] and King was one of the seventeen Lords to oppose a bill that 144 favored.[12]

8. 1 H, 27:1068, 6 June 1814.
9. 1 H, 29:830, 17 Feb. 1815.
10. 1 H, 30:9–10, 6 March 1815.
11. 1 H, 30:124–25, 10 March 1815.
12. 1 H, 30:205, 15 March 1815.

Corn Law Debates to 1844

For the next five years, with the monetary question, repressive action by the Liverpool government on civil rights, and the trial of Queen Caroline for adultery holding the center of the political stage, there was little parliamentary discussion of the specifics of the Corn Law, and no new legislation. In 1821, in opposing a government proposal for changing the method of figuring the average price of corn for purposes of determining the duty, David Ricardo gave a forecast of a view that was soon to gain increasing strength: "Much had been said as to a remedy for the distress of the agriculturalist: he was of opinion, that the only remedy for that distress was the total repeal of the corn laws and, sooner or later, a measure of that sort would be adopted."[13]

The Corn Law of 1815 forbade all importation of foreign wheat and wheat products when the price was below 80s. the quarter, and other grains at varying prices; and all importation of Canadian wheat when the price was below 67s. the quarter. Above those figures grain could be imported free of duty. Such provisions created a serious administrative problem in determining the price of grain; and the prohibition on foreign imports at a price below 80s. made possible wide fluctuations below that figure. The early 1820s produced much argument by economists, but no specific results. Western wanted more protection than had been given in the 1815 law, and again showed his lack of understanding of increasing costs at the margin: "The British farmer had not sufficient security and encouragement, or he would fertilize every acre in the kingdom."[14] On the same day, in a long speech opposing the appointment of a committee to inquire into the agricultural distress, Ricardo explained lucidly the idea of varying costs of wheat production on different soils: "You might thus have fifty remunerating prices according as your capital was employed on productive or unproductive lands."[15] Alexander Baring restated his opposition to the existing corn laws; and Wilmot, the great advocate of emigration, who had been elected in 1818, "agreed with the remarks that had been made by the hon. member for Portarlington [Ricardo], but yet he thought they were

13. 2 H, 4:944–45, 26 Feb. 1821. In Ricardo, *Works*, 4:79.
14. 2 H, 1:651, 30 May 1820.
15. 2 H, 1:671–76, 30 May 1820. In Ricardo, *Works*, 5:49–56.

rather theoretical than practical."[16] Similarly the unpredictable Brougham contributed nothing to theory, but in the course of his remarks made an aside about "the subtleties of the hon. member for Portarlington or the ingenuity of the hon. member for Taunton [Alexander Baring]."[17] A new economist voice against the Corn Laws came from Whitmore, elected in 1820 and soon to be a member of the Political Economy Club, who said that "it was no longer politic to force the cultivation of corn in bad land."[18] Several members made reference to "political economy," and Huskisson said: "Whatever ridicule might be attempted to be thrown on political economy, it could not be discredited."[19]

On 29 April 1822 Ricardo, at the close of a speech on agricultural distress, proposed amending the Corn Laws so that when wheat went above 70s. it could be imported freely at a duty of 20s., with a gradual reduction to 10s., and that a drawback or bounty be allowed on the export of wheat.[20] Huskisson moved a series of counterresolutions that pointed in the same direction, but were less sweeping, thus marking a further step in a move from his extreme Corn Law position of 1814 and 1815 to his virtual free trade position of 1827. Ricardo's amendment was defeated 217–25, but in the minority were the economists Althorp, Brougham, Hume, Ricardo, and Whitmore.[21]

In 1823 Whitmore moved to bring in a bill to lower the importation price on foreign corn to 60s., stressing that the existing exclusion figure of 80s. had been a cause of large price fluctuations.[22] In the debate Ricardo, while objecting to any fixed price at which imports would be barred, supported Whitmore's motion as a move in the right direction.[23] The motion was lost 78–25, with Hume, Ricardo, Rice, and Whitmore in the minority.[24]

With Ricardo's death in 1823 the economists in Parliament lost their most articulate critic of the Corn Laws; but Whitmore, Hume,

16. 2 H, 1:720, 31 May 1820.
17. 2 H, 1:683–92, 30 May 1820.
18. 2 H, 4:1150, 7 March 1821.
19. 2 H, 7:445, 8 May 1822.
20. 2 H, 7:199–202, 29 Apr. 1822. In Ricardo, *Works*, 5:155–59.
21. 2 H, 7:470, 9 May 1822.
22. 2 H, 7:264–69, 26 Feb. 1823.
23. 2 H, 8:280–82, 26 Feb. 1823. In Ricardo, *Works*, 5:251–58.
24. 2 H, 8:288, 26 Feb. 1823.

and soon two young members elected in 1826—E. P. Thomson, a London merchant, later to be governor general of Canada; and Lord Howick, fresh from studying political economy with Mc-Culloch—kept pressing their economic arguments. Hume said: "But if the trade in corn were thrown open, it would afford a vent for those manufactures; and every knife or stocking that went abroad would produce a profit, that would enable the manufacturer to pay his portion of the interest of the national debt."[25] Howick, showing that he had profited from McCulloch's teaching, was sarcastic about the idea that British agriculture should have protection because of poor soil or climate: "If such a principle were admitted, the country might as well give up agriculture at once, and build hot-houses and grow sugar canes."[26] And Parnell stated that he had changed his position since 1815, cited Ricardo approvingly, stressed the relation between exports and imports, and recognized the existence of increasing costs with the extension of production to poorer lands.[27] The free trade view was still held by only a small minority of Parliament, but the economists kept up the attack and provided votes in favor of lower duties far out of proportion to their numbers.[28] In the Lords Lansdowne, and even more, King, both of whom had attended McCulloch's London lectures, attacked the Corn Laws, with a good understanding of increasing costs of production on poorer land. King repeatedly referred to the Corn Laws as a "job of jobs," and a comment by him anticipating Keynes's use of the word "propensity" is indicative both of his own stand and of the views of those Lords who wanted no alteration in existing law:

Some had requested him to desist, hinting that his speeches were like sermons in Lent, and repeated as often. Others were of opinion that he had a vicious propensity to make corn cheap; and as they thought that a vicious propensity in him, he must suppose that they considered a disposition to make corn dear a virtuous propensity.[29]

25. 2 H, 17:99–100, 27 March 1827.
26. 2 H, 19:221, 29 Apr. 1828.
27. 2 H, 16:1101–8, 9 March 1827; 17:102–4, 27 March 1827.
28. On 28 April 1825 Whitmore's motion for a committee on the Corn Laws was defeated 187–47 with five economists in the minority (2 H, 13:298); in April 1826 Whitmore's motion on the state of the Corn Laws was defeated 250–81, with five economists in the minority (2 H, 15:370–71); on 27 March 1827 an amendment by Hume for a reduction on the corn duty was defeated 140–16, with Howick, Hume, and Thomson in the minority (2 H, 17:105–9); and on several other votes there was a similar pattern.

King's unceasing attack on the Corn Laws inspired these lines from
the poet Thomas Moore:

> How can you, my Lord, thus delight to torment all
>   The Peers of the realm about cheapening their corn?
> When you know, if one hasn't a very high rental,
>   'Tis hardly worth while being very high born.
>
> So cease, my dear Baron of Ockham, your prose,
>   As I shall my poetry—neither convinces;
> And all we have spoken, and written but shows,
>   When you tread on a nobleman's corn how he winces.[30]

In 1827 a government-backed measure, due largely to Huskisson's influence, reduced the sliding scale duties. Parnell, completing a shift in his views that had taken place during several years, was now an out-and-out critic of the Corn Laws. Huskisson died in 1830, but the new voices of Torrens, Morrison, Clay, Pryme, Thomas Attwood, and Scrope were added in the early 1830s to the attacks on existing law, and in the 1830s and early 1840s the legislative history of the Corn Laws could be summarized as unsuccessful attempts, largely spearheaded by the economist members, to repeal the Corn Laws, or at least to substitute a low fixed duty for the sliding-scale duty.

In 1833 a motion to bring in a bill to amend the Corn Laws was defeated 74–47, with economists providing seven of the minority.[31] Peel, reflecting a view he took on so many questions that the most important test to be applied to a measure was its effect on the class structure, said: "He would not consent to a Repeal of the Corn laws, because it would make a great and sudden revolution in the relations of the different classes of society,"[32] and later referred to the "constitutional" importance of maintaining the "landed interest."[33] Torrens contributed an oratorical outburst: "Those who were endeavouring to keep up the system of restriction and monopoly were contending against an irresistible power—they were contending

29. 2 H, 15:36, 21 March 1826.
30. Quoted in Smart, 2:381.
31. 3 H, 18:976, 18 June 1833.
32. 3 H, 21:693, 21 Feb. 1834.
33. 3 H, 22:443, 19 March 1834. See also 45:678–88, 19 Feb. 1839.

against the power of knowledge, and struggling with the omnipotence of truth," adding that "there was no possible limit to the prosperity of England, if the ports were only thrown open to foreign corn."[34] Hume's motion for a committee on the Corn Laws was overwhelmingly defeated, 312–155, but economist thinking is indicated by thirteen economist votes in the minority as against seven in the majority.[35]

The debate continued, with little result. Molesworth pictured England with too much labor and capital and not enough land, and said the repeal of the Corn Laws would be equivalent to increasing the supply of land.[36] Increasingly the economists opposed to the Corn Laws were stressing economic analysis, whereas Matthias Attwood, Cayley, Graham, Peel, and Lord Ashburton (formerly Alexander Baring), supporting the Corn Laws, resorted less and less to economic analysis, and laid more emphasis on protecting landlords' interests and maintaining the "constitution." Howick, in a speech that must have pleased his early teacher, McCulloch, gave a sweeping defense of free trade: "Sir, I am persuaded that such will ever be the result of our interfering, by means of complicated and artificial regulations, with the natural order of things, and with that beautiful mechanism of society, which seems to me to bear so clearly the impress of unerring wisdom and divine benevolence."[37] In 1838, by a vote of 361–172, and in 1839 by a vote of 220 to 150, critics of the Corn Laws were defeated,[38] with two-thirds or more of the economists in the minority.

In 1841 the parliamentary economist critics of the Corn Laws had two new articulate voices in Cobden and John Lewis Ricardo, the nephew of David Ricardo. Cobden, in his criticism of the Tory party, neatly summarized the idea that economists' opposition to monopoly covered the whole range of life: "It consisted of monopolists of every kind; monopolists of religion, monopolists of the franchise, monopolists of sugar, monopolists of corn, monopolists of timber, monopolists of coffee."[39] Cobden also repudiated the idea that the

34. H, 21:1220, 1222, 5 March 1834.
35. 3 H, 21:1345, 7 March 1834.
36. 3 H, 37:596–601, 16 March 1837.
37. 3 H, xxxxvi, 550, 13 March 1839.
38. 3 H, 45:691, 19 Feb. 1839; 32:1042, 9 May 1838.
39. 3 H, 60:1054, 24 Feb. 1842.

price of food regulated wages and made clear that he expected the repeal of the Corn Laws to raise real wages: "It is not from the wretched that great things can emanate; it is not a potatoe-fed population that ever led the world in arts or arms, in manufacturing or commerce."[40] In 1842 a motion of Villiers, later a member of the Political Economy Club, for repeal of all corn duties, was defeated 393–90, with Cobden, Fielden, Muntz, and J. L. Ricardo in the minority and Cayley, Graham, and Peel in the majority.[41] In the Lords Brougham, Lansdowne, and Monteagle (formerly Rice) led the attack on the Corn Laws, and Monteagle, in a shift from his earlier lukewarm attitude toward change in the Corn Laws, sounded like an echo of Cobden: "There can be no permanent rest, no quiet, no safety with reference to this subject, until the trade in corn shall be as free as air, as far as protection is concerned."[42]

There were a number of straws in the wind in the early 1840s suggesting that the storm of total repeal might soon break. Western expressed concern that Peel had repudiated his earlier views on protection.[43] Peel, ever the pragmatist, said in regard to a small amendment of the Corn Laws just passed: "If they do not prove calculated to increase the prosperity of the country, if they should prove inadequate to meet the distress of the country, in that case I shall be the first to admit that no adherence to former opinions ought to prevent their full and careful revision."[44] And the following year Gisborne, who described himself as a "practical farmer," said that Peel had adopted free-trade principles, and then taunted the Tories: "Every hon. member on the opposite benches knew that the Corn-laws were at that moment doomed; he had said so elsewhere, and he repeated it here."[45] In 1844 Villiers's motion that the House go into a committee to consider resolutions for the repeal of the Corn Laws was badly defeated, but with nine economists in the minority of 124, and Graham the only economist other than Peel in the majority of 328.[46]

40. Ibid., 1046.
41. 3 H, 60:1082, 24 Feb. 1842.
42. 3 H, 62:775, 19 Apr. 1842.
43. 3 H, 62:612–15, 18 Apr. 1842.
44. 3 H, 64:1345–46, 11 July 1842.
45. 3 H, 69:152, 10 May 1843.
46. 3 H, 75:1549–52, 26 June 1844.

Repeal of Corn Laws in 1846

In 1846 Peel proposed that the Corn Laws be repealed or greatly reduced and that other duties be reduced,[47] and ensuing debates added little to what had already been said on either side by the economists. However, it provided an opportunity for the supporters of free trade to indulge in self-congratulation and to put in a good word for political economy. Clay poked fun at the idea that the Peel program was an abandonment of protection, which—in line with the comments that Western and Gisborne had made earlier—he said had already been abandoned on many points.[48] Scrope, in criticism of a speech supporting the Corn Laws, said:

The hon. Member does not seem to be aware that the principle he declaims against as a cold dogma of a stern political economy is the one sole vivifying principle of all commerce—the stimulus to all improvement—the mainspring of civilization—the principle, namely, of obtaining the largest and the best result at the least cost—in other words, to get the most you can of what you want for your money or your labour. . . . I call on you then no longer to interfere between the people and their spontaneous supplies of food—no longer by unwise and unjust laws to prevent the industrious classes of this country from availing themselves of the ample means which God and nature have placed at their disposal for obtaining, by the exercise of their unrivalled skill and energy, an abundant supply of the first necessaries of life.[49]

Cobden was lyrical about political economy: "I know there are many heads which cannot comprehend and master a proposition in political economy. I believe that study is the highest exercise of the human mind, and that the exact sciences require by no means so hard an effort."[50]

Peel's bill was approved on second reading 302–214, with eleven economists in the majority, and Matthias Attwood and Cayley the only economists in the minority.[51] In the Lords, in the most important vote on Peel's bill, it was approved 211–184, with Lansdowne, Brougham, Monteagle, Bexley, and Grey (the former Lord Howick) in the majority, and only the former free trader, Ashburton, and

47. 3 H, 83:239–85, 27 Jan. 1846.
48. 3 H, 83:985–86, 16 Feb. 1846.
49. 3 H, 83:1279, 1283, 20 Feb. 1846.
50. 3 H, 84:290–91, 27 Feb. 1846.
51. 3 H, 85:265–69, 27 March 1846.

the bishop of Llandaff (Edward Copleston) standing by the Corn Laws.[52] For all practical purposes this vote ended the parliamentary debate, by economists or anyone else, on the Corn Laws, although there appears to have been considerable discussion among agricultural spokesmen outside of Parliament about reopening the issue. A vote in 1850 made clear that restoration of the Corn Laws was, for that generation, a lost cause: a resolution to go into a committee on the Corn Laws was defeated 298–184, with eleven economists in the majority and Cayley the only economist in the minority.[53]

Debate on Other Trade Restrictions

The Corn Laws provided the most dramatic chapter in the first sixty years of the century in the parliamentary foreign economic policy debate. Yet possibly of even greater interest from the point of view of the relation of economic theory to economic policy are the debates on tariffs other than Corn Laws, and on commercial treaties and the Navigation Acts. They involved more subtleties of analysis and less emotional appeals than the Corn Law controversy.

In 1780 Great Britain had a complicated system of restrictions on shipping that in many ways had the same effect as restrictions on the import of goods, and preferential treatment to colonial trade. Most of what economists in Parliament said, and proposed in the way of change, drew on the argument that was back of the attack on the Corn Laws—the gains from the international division of labor. But there were two important differences in the settings of the controversies: the attack on the Corn Laws involved an attack of the monopolistic position of the landed gentry; much of the international economic debate other than on the Corn Laws raised questions of imperial policy in which economic analysis played but a minor role.

The earl of Liverpool (formerly Jenkinson) took a rigid mercantilist view of giving British shipping as complete a monopoly position as possible;[54] Rose on several occasions talked as if he were supporting an eternal verity not subject to debate that there should be special privileges for the colonies, and that the proper policy was

52. 3 H, 86:1405–6, 28 May 1846.
53. 3 H, 111:97, 14 May 1850.
54. P.H., 31:136–41, 2 Apr. 1794.

"never to permit a foreign ship to go where a British ship could be employed."[55] Likewise he objected to opening trade between the United States and the British West Indies. Little economic analysis went into Rose's argument; it was rather a simplistic, emotional view that there was a national gain when business was given to the British rather than to foreigners. Alexander Baring and Horner with their free-trade leanings were critical of the regulation of trade by license, but the thrust of their argument was pointed not so much to the trade theory involved as to abuses in the granting of licenses.[56]

After Waterloo, with the growing interest of manufacturers in foreign trade, concern over the network of regulations that crippled or blocked foreign trade became increasingly vocal. In 1814 and 1815 there were forewarnings of the developments of the 1820s: Huskisson moved for a committee to review ancient legislation preventing the export of wool;[57] Alexander Baring and Finlay, the Glasgow manufacturer with some pretensions as an economist, criticized the cotton duty,[58] primarily on the ground that a duty on a raw material weakened the country's international competitive power in manufacturing—an argument to be brought forward many more times in the following decades. Western, who viewed all economic issues from the narrow interests of agriculture, pictured any import of wool as a national injury,[59] but otherwise there was little opposition from economists to the free-trade trend. On 8 May 1820 Alexander Baring presented to the Commons the petition of merchants of London, drafted in large part by the merchant economist, Thomas Tooke, in favor of free trade.[60] Finlay, always a voice for manufacturing, in supporting similar petitions from the Glasgow Chamber of Commerce, said: "If the great man, Adam Smith, whose sentiments the petition contained, had but lived to see his doctrines thus expounded, it must have afforded him inconceivable pleasure."[61] In the Lords Lansdowne secured the appointment of a committee on foreign trade, of which he was chairman, and King and Lauderdale also members.[62] The following year, in moving for the reappointment

---

55. 1 H, 9:100–101, 12 March 1807; 9:684, 30 June 1807; 17:165, 22 May 1810.
56. 1 H, 14:259–60, 27 Apr. 1809.
57. 1 H, 27:991, 20 May 1814.
58. 1 H, 28:614–15, 6 July 1814; 30:173, 14 March 1815.
59. 1 H, 40, 1221–22, 18 June 1819; 2 H, 1:617–18, 26 May 1820.
60. 2 H, 1:166–82, 8 May 1820.
61. 2 H, 1:429, 16 May 1820.
62. 22 H, 1:546–65, 26 May 1820.

of the committee, Lansdowne said that relief to the country could only be obtained by removing foreign-trade restrictions and reducing taxes.[63]

Under the leadership of Huskisson, who became president of the Board of Trade in 1823, the severity of the Navigation Acts and of trade restrictions, particularly on trade with the colonies, was greatly eased. He sponsored the resolution, passed without recorded vote,[64] authorizing the king to extend to all countries that gave reciprocal treatment to British goods equality of duties and drawbacks on goods imported on ships of those countries. This was a breach in the Navigation Acts, and although its immediate practical consequences were not great, it was a harbinger of what was to follow. Other economists were urging Huskisson to move faster, but he opposed Whitmore's motion for a committee to investigate the differential sugar duties, which was defeated 161–34, with Hume, Ricardo, and Whitmore in the minority.[65]

The Budget of 1825, in the framing of which Huskisson is believed to have had an important hand, materially lowered duties on a wide range of products. In the debates on individual rates Brougham, Hume, Huskisson, and Parnell all had good words to say for free trade, and Brougham twitted the Tory government for adopting policies he had supported for years: "they had even enacted measures to legalize the damnable heresies of Adam Smith and the Scotch economists."[66] The debates are notable as being the turning point in the views of Alexander Baring, the ardent free trader of 1820, who, beginning on a small scale in 1824, and increasingly from then on, was a protectionist spokesman basing his argument more on domestic and international political considerations than on economic analysis.

On 21 March 1825, in an extended speech that was continued four days later,[67] Huskisson urged loosening the restriction on colonial trade, revision of many duties, and changes in the Navigation Acts. Parnell, now an out-and-out free trader, congratulated Huskisson; he was "greatly indebted to the right hon. gentleman for

63. 2 H, 4:824–28, 21 Feb. 1821.
64. 2 H, 9:795–99, 6 June 1823.
65. 2 H, 9:444–51, 22 May 1823.
66. 2 H, 12:54, 3 Feb. 1825.
67. 2 H, 12:1097–1116, 11 March 1825; 1196–1222, 26 March 1825. These speeches were also published separately.

having so clearly and manfully stated and illustrated the principles of economical science which ought to govern all legislation upon our commerce and industry," but hoped that Huskisson's proposals would not be considered final.[68] After a number of minor amendments the bill was passed without recorded vote.

Alexander Baring's split with his former free-trade associates was increasing, but he contributed virtually nothing to analysis, and in a self-serving way stressed how practical were his views as compared with those of theoretical economists. In 1826, in a discussion of the silk duties, he said that he had not abandoned free trade, "except as to the silk trade." He criticized the government opposition to raising the silk tariff: "No relief was to be granted, because it was contrary to the doctrines of the political economists and to right principles. The experience of practical men was as nothing in the scale"; and "He could not help referring to some of the extravagancies and absurdities of the writers, who were, on all hands, admitted to be amongst the ablest professors of the science of political economy. His late friend, Mr. Ricardo, had some of the most fanciful theories that could possibly be imagined."[69]

Debate continued in the late 1820s and 1830s, focused on three proposals: the desire of protectionists to restore silk duties; the desire of free traders to lower the duties on East Indian sugar and to drop the restrictions on trade with India and China. The familiar lineup among the economists continued, with Hume, Huskisson, Parnell, Poulett Thomson, and Whitmore leading the economists' espousal of freer trade. Thomson put his philosophy in capsule form: "In one single word lies the soul of industry—competition";[70] and Parnell said: "The country was loaded with protecting duties on protecting duties, and monopolies on monopolies, and distressed, by the millions of money taken out of the pockets of the people. . . ."[71] Matthias Attwood and Western continued in their restrictionist views, with Alexander Baring in the role of mixing support of the theory of free trade with alternating support and opposition to particular moves for liberalizing trade.

For nearly two decades the issues of tariff reduction, colonial

68. 2 H, 13:1222–42, 17 June 1825.
69. 2 H, 14:813–17, 24 Feb. 1826.
70. 2 H, 21:843, 14 Apr. 1827.
71. 3 H, 1:475–77, 12 Nov. 1830.

preference, the Navigation Acts, and the budget were so inter-twined that at times it is difficult to say just what economists thought on any one of these four issues, or just what issues they were sup-porting or voting for. The legislative setting for general tariff re-duction was much more propitious when the budget was in surplus; and weakening of opposition to an income tax, by making politically feasible a new source of revenue to offset the loss of import reve-nues, created a setting where tariff reduction had better chance of success.[72]

In the 1830s Lord Althorp, Gisborne, Hume, Morrison, Parnell, Rice, Poulett Thomson, Torrens, Whitmore, and after 1832 Thomas Attwood, Clay, Grote, Molesworth, Scrope, and Perronet Thomp-son, in varying degrees were urging the loosening of trade and ship-ping restrictions. In 1841 the powerful voices of Cobden and J. L. Ricardo were also raised in support of free trade.

Thomson succinctly stated the view, acquiring increasing but not yet universal acceptance among economists, that it was in the coun-try's interest to reduce if not eliminate colonial preference; to make unilateral tariff reductions; and to get rid of the privileges of British shipping. The increasing vigor of free-trade spokesmen and their proud appeal to the principles of political economy to support their views is shown in speeches by Thomson and Hume in 1835. In urg-ing unilateral reduction of tariffs Thomson said:

. . . it would be very inexpedient for this country to purchase its commodi-ties at a dearer market, because the country in which they could be ob-tained cheaper would not adopt our more liberal principles of commerce; such a course as that must have the effect of weakening the resources of our own industry, and depriving us of the means of competing with other countries in the markets for manufactured articles.[73]

And Hume, shortly thereafter, said in answer to a member who opposed a reduction in the timber duties:

. . . if the hon. Member claimed the right of going to the cheapest butcher and baker, why should he deny the privilege of going to the cheapest tim-ber merchant. . . . The hon. Member warned the House against the vision-ary theories of political economists, such as himself. He would warn the House against the hon. Member as not being a political economist, or, at

---

72. This point is discussed in Lucy Brown, *The Board of Trade and the Free Trade Movement* (Oxford: Clarendon Press, 1958), chaps. 9 and 13.

73. 3 H, 30:613, 17 Aug. 1835.

least, of being altogether ignorant of the subject. The hon. Member's arguments were as contrary to all rules of true political economy as they were to common sense . . . he had no hestitation in charging the hon. Member with being a theorist, and entirely ignorant of the true principles of political economy.[74]

After the repeal of the Corn Laws free traders with increasing assurance emphasized the benefits from division of labor, and from allocating capital to its most productive use. Perronet Thompson put the free-trade case neatly when, in opposing duties on copper and lead, he asked whether it was right to create distress in Bradford—where textiles were produced for export—in order to relieve distress in Cornwall—which faced foreign competition in copper and lead.[75] The protectionists, with the conversion of Peel to free trade, in effect abandoned any economic arguments to support their case, and were left with little more than emotional appeals for maintaining a trading monopoly within the British empire. Alexander Baring, now Lord Ashburton, said, in defending colonial preference, that the only reason to have colonies, except for naval stations, was "for the advantage of having a privileged trade with them."[76]

Debate over Sugar Duties

In the Lords, Lansdowne supported moves for tariff reduction and equalization of duties as between the East and West Indies.[77] Lord Ashburton continued to attack with increasing vigor his free-trade views of earlier years. Much of the debate and voting was on issues peripheral to the simple issue of tariff reduction, and this was particularly true in connection with the sugar duties, where complicating problems were the relation between the duty on East Indian and West Indian sugar, and the relation between the duty on West Indian and non-British sugar. Those who favored preferential duties on West Indian sugar made much of the idea that with the abolition of slavery in the West Indies sugar from there was at a disadvantage as compared with slave-grown sugar.

In 1841 the issue came to a head. Clay, Grote, Howick, Hume, Muntz, and Parnell were in favor of reducing the duty on non-Brit-

74. 3 H, 30:1320–21, 3 Sept. 1835.
75. 3 H, 101:608, 28 Aug. 1848.
76. 3 H, 88:520, 10 Aug. 1846.
77. 3 H, 57:516–17, 521–22, 23 Mar. 1841; 75:761–69, 13 June 1844.

ish sugar. There was increasing self-assurance in their statements, a confidence that they were the spokesmen both for economic truth and for national righteousness. As Clay put it, "The country began to apprehend the real nature of the contest between the two great parties in the state—the one party taking for its object the widening and freedom of trade, and the other advocating vested interests and the old system of monopoly and restrictions."[78] A key vote came on 18 May 1841, when a motion favorable to eliminating the preferential rate on West Indian sugar was defeated 317–281, with twelve economists in the minority, and only four—Matthias Attwood, Cayley, Graham, and Peel—with the majority.[79]

In 1846 the Commons, by a vote of 265 to 135, acted to end the discriminatory duties on slave-grown sugar. Eleven economists, including Peel, were in the majority, and Matthias Attwood was the only economist in the minority.[80] In the Lords Lansdowne,[81] Grey,[82] and Monteagle[83] favored the admission of slave-grown sugar; and Ashburton used the slavery argument to fortify his continuing opposition to practically any form of tariff reduction. Brougham, apparently torn between his long-standing support of free trade and his crusade of nearly a half-century against slavery and the slave trade, opted against letting in slave-grown sugar: "He did earnestly hope that their Lordships would not now treat the question as if it was merely one of commercial policy—they should bear in mind that there were involved in it considerations of religion, justice, humanity, and above all, considerations of the national character and credit."[84]

In the final analysis the so-called "moral" approach to the sugar duties played only a minor role in the positions taken by the economists. With the exception of Brougham and Perronet Thompson, like Brougham a lifelong crusader against slavery, economist members of Parliament lined up on the sugar duties as they might have been expected to had there been no complication of slavery. When in the Commons in 1850 an effort was again made to restrict the

78. 3 H, 58:369, 13 May 1841.
79. 3 H, 58:667–73, 18 May 1841.
80. 3 H, 88:180–84, 28 July 1846.
81. 3 H, 88:22–27, 27 July 1846; ibid., 515–19, 10 Aug. 1846.
82. 3 H, 88:536–42, 10 Aug. 1846; 59:229–38, 19 Feb. 1847.
83. 3 H, 79:477–81, 11 Apr. 1845; 88:523–27, 10 Aug. 1846.
84. 3 H, 88:22, 27 July 1846.

import of slave-grown sugar, the motion "that it is unjust and impolitic to expose the free-grown Sugar of the British Colonies and
Possessions abroad, to unrestricted competition with the Sugar of
Foreign Slave-trading countries" was defeated 275–234.[85] Eleven
economists, including Peel, were in the majority. With Matthias Attwood no longer in Parliament, the only economist to support the
motion was Perronet Thompson, who said that he had spoken on
free trade "from cart, and cask, and bench, and hustings, and trib-
une, and pulpit," but that free traders "never extended their doctrine to questions where the creation or maintenance of immorality
was concerned."[86]

Unilateral versus Bilateral Tariff Reduction

Had Torrens still been a member of the Commons, doubtless he
would have brought to bear on the tariff question some of the analytical acuteness he was contributing in his writings—specifically,
that unilateral tariff reduction might shift the terms of trade against
Britain, and foster price deflation.[87] But I find hardly a trace of this
theoretically important point among the comments of parliamentary economists in the quarter century after Torrens had first raised
it in the early 1830s. Most of the free traders were so concerned
with the broad issue of division of labor and the national advantages
that would flow from it that they were not interested in considering
a theoretical possibility that there might be even greater advantages
if the move toward tariff reduction were made by the slower process
of bilateral negotiation. And on the other hand, from 1830 on the
few protectionist-oriented economists thought more in terms of
maintaining the unity of the empire, or the social and political leadership of the landed gentry, than in developing the subtleties of
Torrens's analysis.

The issue of unilateral versus bilateral tariff reduction did play
some part in parliamentary tariff controversies from 1840 until
after the Cobden-Chevalier treaty of 1860, but never a major role.
Insofar as there was a theoretical difference of opinion it was largely
between economists who were agreed on the end result—an expan-

85. 3 H, 111:537, 593–96, 31 May 1850.
86. 3 H, 111:544, 31 May 1850.
87. See discussion on this point in Lionel Robbins, *Robert Torrens and the Evolution of Classical Economics* (London: Macmillan, 1958), pp. 182–231.

sion of foreign trade. The theoretical niceties of unilateral versus bilateral tariff reduction were simply engulfed in the rising tide of free-trade sentiment. Committed free traders might oppose the principle of making British tariff reduction dependent upon tariff reductions abroad, but if tariff reduction was accomplished that way they were not likely to object to the results because of a blemish on its theoretical purity. Out of this there arose the paradoxical situation that Peel, who before he openly admitted in 1846 his conversion to free trade had argued that tariff reductions should be made by bilateral negotiations,[88] nevertheless by repeal of the Corn Laws gave a great impetus to unilateral tariff reductions. On the other hand, Cobden had opposed bilateral negotiations on the ground that they were simply an effort by Peel to delay free trade: "Nothing could be more true than that the imports would regulate the exports, and all the much-talked of negotiations for commercial treaties were only intended to throw dust in the eyes of the people, and to maintain all the evils of the existing system."[89] And yet it was Cobden's negotiation of the commercial treaty of 1860 with France that gave England virtually complete free trade.

In addition to Cobden's opposition in the 1840s to making tariff reductions contingent upon tariff reductions abroad, other free-trade economists took the same view that increased imports would mean increased exports, and ignoring or waving aside the subtleties of Torrensian theory, held that it was in the country's interest to lower or eliminate duties regardless of the actions of other countries. J. L. Ricardo said that "the system of retaliation is more injurious to ourselves than to those towards whom we have adopted it," and moved that "no contemplated remission of duties be postponed, with a review to making such remission a basis of commercial negotiations with foreign countries."[90] The motion was beaten 135–61, with Cobden, Howick, and Ricardo in the minority, and Graham and Peel in the majority.[91] In the Lords the following year both Lans-

88. 3 H, 68:959–70, 25 Apr. 1843. In this speech Peel cited Torrens in support of the idea that tariffs should be reduced only by bilateral negotiations. He had made much the same argument in the debate the previous year (3 H, 63:1504, 13 June 1842).

89. 3 H, 68:970, 25 Apr. 1843.

90. 3 H, 68:902–13, 970–73, 25 Apr. 1843.

91. 3 H, 68:971–73, 25 Apr. 1843.

downe and Monteagle expressed a similar opposition to bargaining duties.[92]

In the 1860s, following the Cobden–Chevalier treaty, there was an aftermath of the controversy of the 1840s over unilateral versus bilateral tariff reductions that had no practical consequence at the time but shows how strongly free trade was entrenched among economists. Three economists—Lord Grey,[93] Lord Overstone,[94] and Northcote[95]—while approving of the substantive result of British tariff reduction regretted the means by which the reduction was achieved. As Northcote put it, "there were matters in connection with the Treaty which took off the keen edge of free-trade principles . . ."; and Overstone said: "I entertain grave doubts as to the expediency of having entered into any Commercial Treaty whatever." Thus England cemented its free-trade policy by an action of which several long-time free traders disapproved.

Theoretical Analysis of Preferential Duties

The parliamentary debate in the 1840s and early 1850s on preferential duties on colonial products, and in particular sugar, produced some high-class theoretical analysis that in large part anticipated that of a half century later in England in the setting of proposals for imperial preference, and in the United States in connection with the free admission of Hawaiian sugar after 1876 and with the Cuban reciprocity treaty of 1902. This was the effect of preferential treatment upon the Treasury, the home consumers, and colonial producers. Howick, in a debate in 1842 on the coffee duty, pointed out that "the difference between the duty levied on British and foreign coffee was a bounty levied on the British consumer for the advantage of the colonial grower."[96] In a debate three years later Cobden,[97] Clay,[98] and J. L. Ricardo[99] made essentially the

92. 3 H, 75:761–69, 679–732, 770–72, 13 June 1844.
93. 3 H, 156:1116–21, 16 Feb. 1860; 157:565–79, 15 March 1860.
94. 3 H, 157:596–608, 15 March 1860.
95. 3 H, 156:1525–37, 21 Feb. 1860; 157:188–94, 8 March 1860.
96. 3 H, 63:1499–1503, 13 June 1842.
97. 3 H, 78:440, 7 March 1845.
98. Ibid., 453–54, 497–505.
99. Ibid., 473.

same point, and Ricardo in particular sharpened up the point that preferential sugar duties took money away from consumers not for the benefit of the Treasury, but for the benefit of the West India planters.

Repeal of Navigation Acts

The economists who were in the forefront of the move for lower duties also led the fight for easing, and later for repealing, the Navigation Acts. This was part of a common pattern of economic analysis. If one believed that the forces of the market should determine the allocation of resources in the production of commodities, and that the buyers of commodities should have a choice as to where they would buy, then by the same token shipping services should have the same freedom. Any move to reduce restrictions on imports almost inevitably involved a criticism of the Navigation Acts. The price of wheat in the West Indies was raised because of import duties, and also because more expensive shipping had to be used. Much the same situation applied to timber in England: lower duties on Baltic timber and easing of the Navigation Acts would both make for lower timber prices. In the 1820s Huskisson's move for expanding foreign trade had dealt both with tariff rates and the Navigation Acts. There were a few minor modifications of the Navigation Acts in the 1830s and early 1840s, but in the late 1840s, with the Corn Laws repealed, and the free-trade movement in the ascendancy, the economists in both the Commons and the Lords began an all-out attack on the Navigation Acts. In this endeavor J. L. Ricardo played a leading role. His motion of 1847 for a committee on the Navigation Acts was adopted 155–61, with four economists, including Peel, in the majority, and no economist in opposition.[100] In addition to Ricardo, Hume and Peel were members of the committee. The next year in arguing for repeal Ricardo used the standard free-trade argument that repeal of the Navigation Acts would open trade opportunities and give work to the unemployed.[101] Wilson, Hume, Cobden, Perronet Thompson, and two recent converts to free trade, Graham and Peel, echoed the idea, and Cayley was the only economist to say a good word for the Navigation Acts. Cobden pointed

100. 3 H, 89:1007–20, 1058–59, 9 Feb. 1847.
101. 3 H, 98:1040–46, 15 May 1848.

out the waste of resources and the raising of costs to the British consumer that resulted from the Navigation Acts,[102] and Thompson, in line with his gift for putting the case for free trade in simple terms with popular appeal, pointed out that protection meant taking something away from better or more efficient workers.[103] And Graham, with the traditional zeal of a recent convert to a faith, in criticizing the Navigation Acts took issue with the idea of reciprocity and retaliation: "For what is retaliation? It is this—because some foreign nation does that which is more injurious to herself than it is to you, in the spirit of blind, vindictive passion you proceed to do that which is more injurious to yourself than it is to your rival."[104]

An effort to block complete repeal of the Navigation Acts, except as they applied for coastwise shipping, was defeated 275–214, with eleven economists, including Peel, in the majority, and Cayley the only economist to support the acts.[105] In the Lords, Grey, Lansdowne, and Monteagle were in the forefront of the move for repeal; and the sole economist to speak in defense of the Navigation Acts was the unpredictable Brougham, who, protesting his devotion to free-trade principles, bolstered his political support of the Navigation Acts by citing the authority of Adam Smith.[106] The critical vote in the Lords was 173–163 in favor of repeal, with Brougham and the bishop of Llandaff (Edward Copleston) the only economists opposing repeal.[107]

An attempt two years later to modify the action on the Navigation Acts received scant support. Wilson, with a parade of statistics, claimed that British shipping was more flourishing than before repeal of the Navigation Acts.[108] And Perronet Thompson, opposing any policy of retaliation, gave a pure distillation of free-trade doctrine. He said that a reduction of British restrictions helped the country, but that the benefits would be even greater if foreigners would reduce theirs, and concluded: "And the proposal put forward under the phrases of retaliation, reciprocity, and protection to the public, is, that in revenge for not having both, we should voluntarily cut off

102. 3 H, 99:613–30, 9 June 1848.
103. 3 H, 102:720–23, 14 Feb. 1849.
104. 3 H, 104:662–63, 23 Apr. 1849.
105. 3 H, 104:702–5, 23 Apr. 1849.
106. 3 H, 104:1344–55, 7 May 1849.
107. 3 H, 105:117–20, 8 May 1849.
108. 3 H, 118:1445–56, 24 July 1851.

the first."[109] A motion critical of the repeal of the Navigation Acts was defeated 158–50, with no economist voting for the motion and seven—Cobden, Graham, Lewis, J. L. Ricardo, Scrope, Perronet Thompson, and Wilson—opposing it.[110]

109. 3 H, 118:1462, 24 July 1851.
110. 3 H, 118:1465–66, 24 July 1851.

Chapter 4

Government Economic Activity and Regulation of Working Conditions

The legislative decision to repeal the Corn Laws and the Navigation Acts, and then to adopt international free trade across the board was the outstanding example of the victory of classical economics. But the question of the relation of government to economic life came up in other forms, and notably four: (1) government-sponsored monopolies; (2) direct government participation in economic production; (3) government-financed support of private industry; and (4) government regulation of economic activity, working conditions, in particular.

Government-Sponsored Monopolies

The two principal cases of government-sponsored monopolies were the Bank of England and the East India Company. As the controversy over the monopoly of the Bank of England was one part of the debate over monetary and banking policy, discussion of the attitude toward the bank's monopoly will be taken up in chapter 6. The monopoly position of the East India Company raised less complicated issues that everyone could understand, or at least about which one could have strong emotions. To oversimplify a complex situation, the company, as the result of a series of historical accidents, by the 1780s had a monopoly of all trade between Britain and China, of all trade between India and all parts of the world, and of all import of tea into Britain. These monopolies were in defiance of free-trade principles of allowing consumers to buy where they wished, and of allowing producers to decide where and how they would invest their capital and exercise their entrepreneural skills, and where they would sell their products. With British control of the seas after Trafalgar opening up larger vistas to the British interested in overseas trade and the increasing importance of tea in the

British diet, the East India Company's monopoly became a greater restriction on the free market at the same time that the principle of free trade was gathering strength.

The charter of the East India Company came up for renewal in 1812. Although the parliamentary debates centered more on political details and the terms of financial arrangements than on broad economic issues, there were on the legislative horizons clouds of free-trade sentiment that indicated the gathering storms of opposition to the company's monopoly. Lauderdale, still an ardent Whig, repeatedly criticized the company and urged a free trade with India.[1] With criticism of the company coming from many quarters, the real political argument was not whether the trading monopoly should remain untouched, but on the exact terms on which private trade would be allowed, and in particular the British ports which could participate in the trade. Brougham[2] and Horner[3] were in the forefront of the criticism of the monopoly position of the Company; Finlay urged the claims of private traders to trade with India;[4] and Thomas Attwood, not yet in Parliament, lobbied in Westminster against the renewal of the company's charter. Other than Vansittart, the only economist to defend the East India Company was Alexander Baring, whose devotion in principle to free trade, even at that time, sometimes took strange turns when specific problems arose. The new charter reduced somewhat the company's monopoly position, but still left it with the exclusive right to trade with China and to import tea, and allowed noncompany trade with India only from a few designated British ports.[5] In 1814 a motion for papers on the affairs of the East India Company—in the context showing a critical attitude toward the company—was defeated 62–23, but four economists—Grenfell, Horner, Parnell, and Western—were in the minority.[6]

The company's new charter was subject, upon three years' notice, to parliamentary review after 10 April 1831, and even before that date the economists in Parliament were mounting criticism against

1. 1 H, 22:108, 23 March 1812; 246–47, 9 Apr. 1812; 1080, 28 Apr. 1812; 26:710, 18 June 1813; 789–92, 21 June 1813; 1100–1101, 5 July 1813.
2. 1 H, 21:679–80, 6 Feb. 1812.
3. 1 H, 26:627–28, 14 June 1813.
4. 1 H, 26:683–84, 16 June 1813; 1013, 1 July 1813.
5. 53 Geo. III, c. 155.
6. 1 H, 27:928, 17 May 1814.

the monopolistic privileges of the company. Peel believed that a committee of inquiry would be in order,[7] and Huskisson,[8] Thomson,[9] Whitmore,[10] and Lansdowne[11] all were critical of the company's monopoly. As Huskisson put it, "He would not scruple to affirm, that more industry would have been called into employment if monopoly had never been in existence." The charter of the East India Company was renewed in 1833, but the company was stripped of its exclusive trade privileges: henceforth anyone could trade with India or China, and tea could be imported by anyone from anywhere in the world.

Government Participation in and Support of Business

The question of government interference in the market, or participation in business, came up in various forms, and revealed surprising differences of opinion among economists on specific issues. In 1822 when the potato crop failed in southern Ireland the government furnished direct relief, and also authorized the advance of money for undertaking or completing public works. Lansdowne reluctantly approved this deviation from laissez-faire purity: "That it was mischievous to interfere with the regular course of supply and demand in the market was a principle no less generally recognized; but, so singular was the situation of Ireland, that this great principle of political economy must be violated."[12] From Peel came much the same idea: "The Irish government were endeavouring to give relief in every possible way; not with strict regard to the principles of political economy, for unhappily the case was one that compelled them to set all ordinary rules at defiance."[13] And Rice urged prompt action on public employment: "He trusted that measures for employing the poor would be resorted to, and speedily; for while the legislature deliberated, the people perished."[14] The idea that government should itself carry on business was raised only in rare in-

7. 2 H, 22:271–76, 278, 282–83, 9 Feb. 1830.
8. 2 H, 23:179–80, 11 March 1830.
9. 2 H, 23:177–80, 11 March 1830.
10. 2 H, 22:532–33, 16 Feb. 1830.
11. 2 H, 22:253–55, 9 Feb. 1830; 1245–46, 4 March 1830; 3 H, 3:1737–38, 21 Apr. 1831.
12. 2 H, 7:1046–47, 14 June 1822. He said much the same thing on 10 May 1822, 7:472–73; and on 17 May 1822, 7:672–73.
13. 2 H, 7:1125, 17 June 1822.
14. Ibid.

stances. I find no suggestion that the government should provide assistance to railroad construction in Britain. But touches of the idea of government support of the economic infrastructure were raised passingly in the 1820s in connection with the debate on the Caledonian Canal, and decades later in connection with financial assistance to Irish railroads and government aid for workers' housing. In each case the topic was treated so briefly and involved so many political considerations that the economists' debates, although they have tantalizing comments suggesting an insight into ideas basic to developmental economics after World War II, gave no connected or organized theory. The Caledonian Canal across Scotland, approved in 1807 to be built at government expense, would have been an ideal case over which theoreticians of developmental economics a century and a half later could have had a field day of controversy. It produced no incisive analysis, however, probably because there was no clear-cut picture of what the canal was supposed to do: help the Royal Navy, assist shipping, give jobs to unemployed Scots, raise land values along its route, lower the cost of goods to consumers, or raise prices to producers. The only contribution of economists to the problem came in brief comments from Hume and Parnell in 1823 on an appropriation of £25,000 to complete the canal. Hume was in character when he opposed such an expenditure of public money "for the benefit of certain Highland gentlemen,"[15] whereas Parnell defended it on grounds of general public benefits.[16] The opportunity even for such limited discussion of a theory of infrastructure expenditures rarely arose—proposals of this type were outside the orbit of parliamentary contemplation. When, in 1829, the government sold the City canal to the West India Dock Company, a private party, Hume rejoiced: "He was not sorry that the canal had been disposed of, for, like other governmental undertakings, from the Caledonian to the Ridout canal, it had turned out an expensive failure."[17] But in 1839, when there was general agreement among men of all persuasions that something should be done about Ireland, but much dispute as to what that something should be, even Hume gave restrained support to government aid for Irish railroad construc-

15. 2 H, 7:1129, 18 Apr. 1823.
16. Ibid., 1130.
17. 2 H, 21:888, 16 Apr. 1829.

tion,[18] and for improving navigation on the Shannon. Rice gave a statement of allowable exceptions to private enterprise that would not sound out of place in a modern class on economic development.[19]

The strongest opposition to such departures from free-trade purity came from Peel, who, much as he at that time opposed free-trade doctrine in the foreign field, on aid to Irish railroads took a view more doctrinaire than might have come from Adam Smith or David Ricardo: "If these railroads were likely to turn out profitable speculations, why not leave them to the spontaneous exertions of the landowners and capitalists of Ireland? If they were likely to turn out unprofitable speculations, let them consider the unfairness of what they were about to do."[20] Pryme, the Cambridge professor of economics, in words with the ring of Adam Smith, expressed skepticism about using public monies on Shannon navigation: " . . . he had never understood that liberality in politics consisted in giving away the public money. It consisted in giving the people free and good Government, and franchises which they had never enjoyed before."[21] However, a motion to advance Exchequer bills for railroad construction in Ireland was carried 144–100, with Cayley, Howick, Hume, Parnell, Pryme, and Rice in the majority and no economist in the minority.[22]

A few months later five economists—Thomas Attwood, Gisborne, Howick, Hume, and Rice—were among the sixty-four who voted to go into committee on a bill to appropriate funds for improving navigation on the Shannon, and Pryme was the only economist in the minority of twenty-five.[23] During the famine years proposals for government economic activity in Ireland again came forward on a broader front. Peel, as on so many subjects, bent to political winds, and in 1846 said the government would consider, in individual cases, advances to Irish railroads.[24] Clay was willing to have the government advance part of the costs of Irish railroads: "He did not think much of the validity of the objections which had been

18. 3 H, 45:1107–11, 1 March 1839; 48:1017, 28 June 1839.
19. 3 H, 45:1090–97, 1 March 1839.
20. Ibid., 1089.
21. 3 H, 49:429, 17 July 1839.
22. 3 H, 45:1122, 1 March 1839.
23. 3 H, 49:433, 17 July 1839.
24. 3 H, 86:7–9, 4 May 1846.

made to the measure. It was said to be opposed to the principles of political economy. He could not admit that much weight should be attached to that objection."[25] Muntz said: "Though it might not be in strict accord with the doctrines of political economy that money should be advanced by the Government . . . it would be better, in his opinion, to deviate from the principles of political economy in order to feed the people."[26] And Monteagle felt that the idea that funds for Irish development should come from Ireland applied "to ordinary times and ordinary circumstances," but in the present situation the state "must interfere."[27] Scrope not only wanted the government to aid railroad construction, but also urged that waste lands be acquired by eminent domain and improved.[28] Other economists, including Brougham,[29] Graham,[30] Grey,[31] Hume,[32] and Molesworth,[33] felt that the government should stay out of such matters, although in some cases apparently it was more the belief that anything the government touched in Ireland involved patronage and corruption than economic analysis that determined their views. As Hume put it, "He objected to taking money from the pockets of the people of England and Scotland, not to benefit the Irish people, but for the advantage of a few speculators."[34] A resolution to make advances for railroads in Ireland was carried 208–75 on 30 April 1847, with Cayley, Clay, Muntz, and Scrope in the majority, and Gisborne, Graham, Hume, and Peel in the minority.[35] In 1851 Grey, in supporting the idea of local authorities in Ireland guaranteeing railroad loans, reiterated an old fear: "He thought that, especially when they were legislating for Ireland, they ought to be careful there was not some job intended."[36] Scrope stressed the idea of bringing wastelands into cultivation by government expenditure, and although the theory was not spelled out in detail, his proposals are

25. 3 H, 89:1402, 15 Feb. 1847.
26. 3 H, 79:836, 4 Feb. 1847.
27. 3 H, 90:672–73, 2 March 1847.
28. 3 H, 85:1198–1206, 28 Apr. 1846.
29. 3 H, 89:850, 852–53, 5 Feb. 1847.
30. 3 H, 93:1019–27, 28 June 1847.
31. 3 H, 90:670–72, 2 March 1847.
32. 3 H, 89:460–70, 25 Jan. 1847.
33. 3 H, 93:975–81, 28 June 1847.
34. 3 H, 93:1042, 28 June 1847.
35. 3 H, 92:297, 30 Apr. 1847.
36. 3 H, 116:126, 14 Apr. 1851.

familiar to readers of Adam Smith or to present-day theorists of economic development—that government aid sometimes makes possible improvements in production that no individual is prepared to undertake.[37]

But there was no continuous or organized discussion of either government economic activity or government financial support of private industry. Particular situations, like economic distress in Ireland, might force economists in Parliament to cast a vote or to say a few words, but one gets the feeling that the very consideration of such proposals, whether in approval or criticism, was intellectually distasteful, and that most economists were relieved when debate got back to a theme like free trade, university test oaths, the ballot, or the Church of Ireland, where they could think and speak with more assurance. Time moved on, however, and a sign that the high tide of laissez faire was passing among economists was the speech of Hubbard, a political conservative, in 1867 in support of a bill for a government subsidy for workers' housing: "Political economy in its true sense, and properly understood, could not discourage any object from being carried out concerning the welfare of the people."[38] Probably the best statement of economic-development theory came from John Stuart Mill only a month before the close of his short parliamentary career in support of loans to Irish fishermen even if similar loans were not extended to Scottish fishermen:

His answer was that Ireland was a more backward country than either Scotland or England. Government might very properly undertake to do things for a country which was industrially backward, which no one would expect from them in the case of a country which was in a more advanced and prosperous condition. . . . It was therefore incumbent on us, now that we were wiser and able to look upon our past conduct with shame, to legislate in an opposite direction, and even to risk if necessary the loss of small sums of money to advance that industry which we had formerly endeavoured to retard.[39]

Far more important in the economists' parliamentary activities than the question of direct government participation in economic life, or of government aid to private industry, was the regulation of working conditions and business practices.

37. 3 H, 94:164–66, 10 July 1847.
38. 3 H, 186:694, 27 March 1867.
39. 3 H, 192:2021–22, 24 June 1868.

Apprenticeship and Combination Acts

Apprenticeship laws, dating back to Elizabethan times, not only prescribed the number of apprentices but in other ways regulated entrance to a trade. As early as 1811 Giddy felt that "too minute legislation had gone abroad lately,"[40] and three years later expressed this view more forcibly when he defended "the general right of the inhabitants of this country, to employ the energies of their mind and body in the way they themselves pleased," and said that apprenticeship laws had checked "the progress of our arts and manufactures."[41] Not until 1823 did economists have anything further to say about apprenticeships. Huskisson, primarily on the ground that it was important for national defense, sponsored legislation to require all operators of merchant vessels to have a number of apprentices in proportion to tonnage. David Ricardo's criticism of the bill reads like a lecture on political economy:

He thought it was a maxim, that no person ought to be controlled in his own arrangements, unless such control was rendered necessary by paramount political circumstances. Now, no such necessity could be shown in support of this bill. In his opinion, it would not be more unjust to enact a law, that every surgeon should take a certain number of apprentices, to encourage the progress of surgical science, than it would be to pass this bill, rendering it imperative on the masters of merchant vessels to take a given number of apprentices, in order to encourage the increase of efficient seamen. He denied that this bill would cause an addition of one seaman to the number now in the service. So long as there was employment for seamen, there would be encouragement enough for them; and when there was not, those who were now here, would resort to foreign countries for employ. The only effect of the bill would be, to reduce the wages of seamen; and that alone would render it objectionable.[42]

Ricardo's motion to eliminate the compulsory provisions was defeated 85–6, with Grenfell, Hume, Ricardo, and Whitmore in the minority.[43]

The following year, after Ricardo's death, the economists achieved their first major victory in loosening the restraints on the freedom of labor. The Elizabethan laws against combination of workers had

40. 1 H, 20:518, 7 June 1811. He subsequently expressed the same idea, 25:1130, 3 May 1813.
41. 1 H, 27:880, 13 May 1814.
42. 2 H, 8:663, 24 March 1823; Ricardo, *Works*, 5:276–77.
43. 2 H, 8:666, 24 March 1823.

been made even more severe by the legislation of 1799 and 1800. In the early 1820s there was widespread criticism of these laws, both by economists as being contrary to the doctrines of their faith, and by labor spokesmen as an infringement on the rights of labor. Petitions against them came to Parliament in increasing numbers, Francis Place was quietly fanning the fires of opposition, and McCulloch's article critical of the combination acts in the January 1824 *Edinburgh Review* on "Combination Laws, Restraints on Emigration" had a powerful effect on public thinking. Hume's motion for a committee to investigate the matter was approved without opposition. In addition to Hume as chairman, the members included Gilbert, Huskisson, and Parnell. The committee recommended repeal of the combination acts, as well as of the acts forbidding the emigration of artisans and the export of machinery.[44] Repeal legislation[45] was approved with little debate and no recorded vote.

Repeal of the combination acts had an unusual aftermath. It was followed by an outbreak of strikes, and numerous petitions to Parliament to restore, at least in part, the combination acts. Huskisson[46] and Peel[47] referred to abuses since the repeal. As Huskisson put it: "The object of the bill [to restore the combination acts] was, to protect the weak against the strong—to afford to the man who chose to give his labour for a certain value, that protection against the combination of large bodies to which every man was entitled."[48] Alexander Baring said that "in his view of the subject, the mere crude simple repeal of those laws was one of the most mischievous measures that the House ever agreed to."[49] Hume was the only economist to defend the legislation passed a year before, and even he was on the defensive. Lansdowne felt that new legislation was necessary to curb abuses and "to protect the workmen against themselves. He wished every facility to be given both to masters and workmen to consult about the rise or fall of wages; but it was obvious, that no manufacture could be carried on, if workmen could dictate to the masters who should be employed, and to prevent men from exercising their right of labouring on whatever terms they might please.

44. 2 H, 11:811–14, 21 May 1824.
45. 5 Geo. IV, c. 95.
46. 2 H, 12:1288–1301, 29 March 1825.
47. 2 H, 12:1305–10, 29 March 1825.
48. 2 H, 13:1406, 27 June 1825.
49. 2 H, 13:361, 3 May 1825.

This was what never could be tolerated in a free country."[50] A bill was passed in both houses without recorded vote[51] that repealed the act of 1824 and also repealed the harsher provisions of the old combination acts, so the net result of the legislation of 1824 and 1825 was to increase substantially the activities that trade unions could carry on legally.

Spitalfields Acts

Another restriction of long standing also came under attack: the Spitalfields acts, which authorized magistrates to fix wages of journeymen silk workers in the London area. The principle of this legislation offended the increasingly vocal economists in Parliament, and to their voices were added the complaints of many in the silk business, who argued that the result of such controls was to drive the silk trade to areas where there was no such control. In 1823 a bill to repeal the acts was introduced by Huskisson and supported by Brougham and Hume. Ricardo spoke in favor of repeal, putting his argument in the broader concept of political economy:

Mr. Ricardo could not help expressing his astonishment that, in the year 1823, those acts should be existing and in force. They were not merely an interference with the freedom of trade, but they cramped the freedom of labour itself. Such was their operation, that a man who was disposed to embark in the trade could not employ his capital in it in London; and, as it might be inconvenient, in many instances to carry that capital out of London, the trade was necessarily cramped and fettered.[52]

The bill passed the Commons, 53–40, without recorded vote,[53] but was so weakened by amendments in the Lords that Huskisson reported that "it would neither conduce to the public interest, nor be consistent with his duty, to proceed further with it at present."[54] Ricardo wrote to his friend Hutches Trower a few days later:

We shall I hope go from Session to Session getting rid of some of the absurd regulations which fetter commerce till all shackles are removed. Huskisson behaved very well after I left London in refusing to have any thing to do with the Lords' amended bill respecting the magistrates inter-

50. 2 H, 13:1479, 4 July 1825.
51. 6 Geo. IV, c. 129.
52. 2 H, 9:149, 9 May 1823. Also in Ricardo, *Works*, 5:292.
53. 2 H, 9:833, 11 June 1823.
54. 2 H, 9:1541, 18 July 1823.

ference with wages in Spitalfields—the bill was quite spoiled, there was nothing left in it worth retaining.[55]

The following year Lauderdale reintroduced essentially the same bill that had been passed by the Commons the previous year,[56] and with little debate in the Lords, and none in the Commons, it became law.[57]

Labor Legislation for Women and Children

The most drawn-out, and theoretically and historically most significant controversies about the relation of the state to economic life were not over the abandonment of old controls, but over the introduction of new controls. The opinion of economists was almost unanimous against the old controls, but there were great differences of opinion about new controls. Proposals for new controls took on many forms, of which the most important were: (1) regulation of hours and conditions of work of women and children; (2) regulation of conditions of work of adult males; (3) regulation of rates, service, and safety of railroads; (4) regulation of gas and water companies; and (5) regulation of a miscellaneous group of practices, including payment of wages in kind, sale of alcoholic drink, industrial smoke, and bull baiting.

The first legislation regarding the employment of children—the Health and Morals of Apprentices Act of 1802[58] —had been sponsored by the elder Sir Robert Peel, and produced no comments, pro or con, from parliamentary economists. Sir Robert's attempt, in June 1815, to forbid the employment of all children under ten in factories, died after the first reading, and was ignored by economists except for a remark by Horner that the proposed bill as well as existing legislation did not go far enough.[59] The reintroduction of the bill the following year provided only a sketchy debate, in which Finlay, the Glasgow manufacturer who constantly took on the role of self-appointed spokesman for what he conceived to be Scottish economic interests, combined an attack on Sir Robert with the self-

---

55. Ricardo, *Works*, 9:318. 24 July 1823.
56. 2 H, 11:433–34, 4 May 1824.
57. 5 Geo. IV, c. 66. The vote in the Lords was 61–55, with no record of individual votes (2 H, 11:792–93, 21 May 1824). *Hansard* makes no mention of a vote in the Commons.
58. 42 Geo. III, c. 73.
59. 1 H, 31:625–26, 6 June 1815.

serving claim that the cotton mills of Glasgow were "not only situated most advantageously for health but were conducted upon the most liberal plan."[60] The only result was the appointment of a select committee, of which Finlay, Giddy, Horner, and Vansittart were members. In 1818 Sir Robert[61] introduced a bill forbidding the employment of children under nine, and limiting the hours of daily work of children to eleven. Except for the younger Peel, whose speech was both a defense of his father against personal attacks and a support of the bill,[62] no economist spoke in favor of the bill, but Finlay restated his opposition, principally on the grounds that "he was convinced that the effects of the present bill would operate more to the injury than the benefit of those for whom it was intended,"[63] and "would have the effect of driving children from a state of comparative ease and happiness to one of severity and hardship."[64]

Evidently the bill passed the Commons, although the vote was not reported in *Hansard*, for soon the Lords were considering the same bill. The eccentric Lauderdale, a complex character who alternated between criticism of political economy and doctrinaire views that were in line with Thomas Carlyle's caricatures of political economy, was the only economist to speak on the bill: "Were their Lordships prepared to encroach upon that great principle of political economy, that labour ought to be left free, and without taking upon themselves the trouble of investigating the subject?"[65] Despite Lauderdale's continuing opposition, a bill, substantially the same as proposed earlier by Sir Robert Peel, became law in 1819.[66]

A bill to stop the cleaning of chimneys by small children was defeated the same year. No economist in the Commons had any role in supporting the legislation, and *Hansard* has no record of its passage in the Commons. It evidently did pass, and in the Lords Lauderdale led the opposition, principally on the ground that machines could not do the job as well as boys, and that the bill's supporters "took a partial view of the evil they wished to cure, and did not look at the relation in which it stood to the general state of society. Hence

60. 1 H, 33:884–87, 3 Apr. 1816.
61. 1 H, 37:559–60, 19 Feb. 1818.
62. 1 H, 37:564, 19 Feb. 1818.
63. 1 H, 37:1262, 10 Apr. 1818.
64. 1 H, 38:368, 27 Apr. 1818.
65. 1 H, 38:579, 8 May 1818. Similar remarks of Lauderdale are on 548, 578–82, 647–48, 792–95.
66. 59 Geo. III, c. 66.

they were not aware of the extent of the mischief their remedy would produce."[67] Lansdowne supported the bill, which was lost 32–12, with individual votes not recorded.[68]

For nearly a decade, while the country was split over Catholic emancipation and parliamentary reform, the question of government regulation of working conditions of children was quiescent. But beginning in 1831 and continuing until 1868 there was continuous debate over such legislation. In the 1830s the driving force in the Commons was first Michael Sadler, and after he lost his seat in 1832, Lord Ashley, neither here considered economists, but before the decade was over many of the parliamentary economists had voiced an opinion. Both the debates and the numerous votes frequently leave the reader in doubt as to just how individual economists stood on factory legislation, for it appears that in some cases a man opposed a particular provision because he wanted an even stronger regulation, and in other cases a man who in principle opposed legislation nevertheless voted for it because he feared that failure to pass it would lead to an even more restrictive law. Certainly the voting does not support any conventional stereotype of a phalanx of economists opposing factory legislation on the ground that it ran counter to the laws of political economy.

The younger Peel urged caution in lowering the hours of children's labor below eleven and a half, because of the risk of "injuring the poorer classes, by causing them to be thrown out of employment altogether."[69] Hume said that Sadler talked "as if no other person but himself had any regard to the interests of humanity," and although not opposing his bill felt that because of the complicated issues involved it should be referred to a committee.[70] Althorp,[71] Gisborne,[72] Rice,[73] and Poulett Thomson[74] took a similarly reserved position. Torrens, who did not allow a philosophical devotion to the free market to interfere with action to help those in distress, said: "It was impossible to argue that the principles of political economy were opposed to those of humanity." He "admitted the truth of the principle, that

---

67. 1 H, 39:983, 15 March 1819.
68. 1 H, 40, 669–70, 24 May 1819.
69. 3 H, 9:1095, 1 Feb. 1832.
70. 3 H, 10:193–94, 10 Feb. 1832.
71. 3 H, 19:219–24, 5 July 1833.
72. 3 H, 17:91–94, 3 Apr. 1833.
73. 3 H, 17:105–7, 3 Apr. 1833.
74. 3 H, 19:248–49, 5 July 1833.

adult labour should be left free, but he contended, that this, like all other general principles, was liable to exceptions."[75] Matthias Attwood and Cobbett, poles apart on most issues, were agreed in their support of regulation. As Attwood put it: "The question was not a mere question of the feelings of Englishmen, but a question of the feelings of humanity—a question of the grossest injustice—of utter destruction, inflicted upon the feeble and the unprotected. It was not a question of pounds, shillings, and pence—not a point to be settled on the grounds of mercantile advantage."[76] Cobbett, never one to restrain words, said the language of Thomson "amounted to this—mammon against mercy,"[77] and turned loose his sarcasm at the suggestion that the proposed legislation would weaken England's competitive position in foreign trade: " . . . now it was admitted, that our great stay and bulwark was to be found in three hundred thousand little girls, or rather in one-eighth of that number. Yes: for it was asserted, that if these little girls worked two hours less per day, our manufacturing superiority would depart from us."[78] An amendment to the 1833 bill that the ten-hour day apply to children under eighteen, rather than to those under sixteen, was defeated 238–93, but the minority included the two Attwoods, Cayley, Cobbett, Fielden, and Torrens.[79] The final bill, more restrictive than anything heretofore, and with provisions for enforcement, was passed without a recorded vote, and without any comment in the Lords by economists.[80]

Among the economists Fielden continued to press for more restrictive legislation, while Poulett Thomson led a counteroffensive to remove the restrictions on the labor of twelve- and thirteen-year-olds, and expressed fear that the law of 1833 hampered competition in foreign markets.[81] His bill to weaken the act of 1833 was approved on the second reading, 178–176, with nine economists, including Peel, supporting it, and Thomas Attwood, Cayley, Fielden, and Perronet Thompson in the minority.[82] The bill died, never having come to a third reading.

75. 3 H, 10:21, 7 Feb. 1832; 19:901, 18 July 1833.
76. 3 H, 19:247, 5 July 1833.
77. 3 H, 19:249, 5 July 1833.
78. 3 H, 19:912, 18 July 1833.
79. 3 H, 19:913–14, 18 July 1833.
80. 3 & 4 Will. 4, c. 103.
81. 3 H, 33:737–40, 9 May 1836.
82. 3 H, 33:788–90, 9 May 1836.

The report in 1842 of the Royal Commission on Children's Employment, of which Thomas Tooke was a member, revealed such shocking conditions in mining that even most of those who a few years ago had opposed legislation now supported Ashley's bill. The rising young politician, Benjamin Disraeli, who opposed the bill, wrote to Lord Londonderry: "To my surprise the political economists were also in its favour."[83] Hume said: "Hundreds of thousands of pounds had been expended in trying to alleviate distress abroad, and nothing done to put an end to such scenes of misery at home."[84] Yet Matthias Attwood, who said that he had previously supported all of Ashley's and Sadler's measures to protect the "labouring classes," now used against the new bill the argument previously used against Sadler's and Ashley's legislation, and felt that this colliery proposal went too far, and would "throw many of the boys themselves out of employment, and inflict hardships on the class intended to be benefitted."[85] In the Lords Brougham, in a long speech, supported the bill, but with a warning against going too far in the exercise of "cheap virtue," and an indication that only in the case of children would he support any legislation to regulate conditions of labor.[86] On the whole, however, the economists stayed on the sidelines; they did not oppose the bill, nor were they strong spokesmen for it. Most of them undoubtedly had in mind what they considered far bigger game in the forest of national abuses—repeal of the Corn Laws. There was no recording of votes in either House on the bill.[87]

Much of the same ground was fought over, and essentially the same arguments made, when in 1844 Graham introduced a government bill increasing slightly the regulation on the labor of women and children, and Lord Ashley proposed amendments of a more restrictive nature. This debate, probably more than any previous debate, sharpened up the issue of the economic consequences of reducing hours of work—an issue which had previously been talked about and around, but never faced head on. Graham feared that a reduction of hours to ten would undermine British industry.[88] Clay,

---

83. J. L. Hammond and Barbara Hammond, *Lord Shaftesbury* (London: Constable and Co., 1923), p. 83.
84. 3 H, 63:1356, 7 June 1842.
85. 3 H, 64:1004, 5 July 1842.
86. 3 H, 65:571–78, 25 July 1842.
87. 5 & 6 Vict., c. 99.
88. 3 H, 73:1101–10, 15 March 1844.

by no means an unbending opponent of factory legislation—"His opposition to the Motion, arose, not from any bigotted adherence on his part to any dogma of economical science"—felt that the reduction in the hours of work from twelve to ten would cause a proportionally greater reduction in wages. This conclusion was based on the argument that reduction in output would be exactly proportional to reduction in hours of labor, and that as employers were in a stronger bargaining position than labor, the decrease in profits would be less than in wages.[89] Graham, Hume, Morrison, and Peel expressed similar views, but failed to apply any searching analysis as to what the economic consequences of reduced hours would be. The economists supporting a ten-hour day never faced up to the problem, although there are subliminal traces of an idea that somehow or other production would not decline with a decrease in hours of work, whereas those opposing a ten-hour limitation seemed to have assumed, *sub silencio*, that worker efficiency and industry efficiency would be unchanged.

Cobden was the only economist who came to grips with the theoretical issues involved:

. . . the question was whether a ten hours Bill would not involve a reduction of wages in a degree corresponding with the reduced labour, and whether this would not be a far more serious injury to the working classes than the saving of two hours work would be an advantage. This was a question from which there had been exhibited a great disposition on this occasion to shrink, though it was in reality the main point.

Cobden spoke of two ways to reduce hours without decreasing wages: (1) by increasing the speed of machinery; and (2) by raising the price of textiles, assuming a virtually price inelastic foreign demand for British textiles. He rejected both of these possibilities, but went on to say that a repeal of the Corn Laws, and of import duties on other foodstuffs, might enable workers to have as large a real income with a ten-hour day as with a twelve-hour day: "Let the hon. Gentlemen who really wished the labourers to work only ten hours, and to get the same wages as for twelve, support the hon. Member for Wolverhampton [C. P. Villiers, later a member of the Political Economy Club] when he next brought forward his Motion for a

89. 3 H, 73:1387–96, 22 March 1844.

repeal of the Corn Laws, and their object would speedily be effected."[90]

Howick, an admirer of Adam Smith, and on most issues an opponent of government interference in the market, quoted the passage from Smith that starts: "The property which every man has in his own labour, as it is the original foundation of all other property, so it is the most sacred and inviolable."[91] He then went on to say, in words with a ring of the environmentalism of the 1970s:

... while I subscribe to the principle in the sense in which it was meant to be laid down by the distinguished author I have quoted, I utterly deny that it applies to the question now before us. . . . I contend that you altogether misapply the maxim of leaving industry to itself when you use it as an argument against regulations of which the object is, not to increase the productive power of the country, or to take the fruits of a man's labour from himself and give it to another, but, on the contrary, to guard the labourer himself and the community from evils against which the mere pursuit of wealth affords us no security. The welfare, both moral and physical of the great body of the people, I conceive to be the true concern of the Government: national wealth, no doubt, rightly used, greatly contributes to that welfare, but he must indeed have a low and mean idea of our nature, who thinks that mere wealth is all in all to a nation, and who does not see that in the too eager pursuit of wealth, a nation like an individual, may neglect what is of infinitely higher importance.[92]

Probably the best indication of the views of economists was on an amendment by Lord Ashley that would have called for a ten-hour day rather than a twelve-hour day for women and young people, which would have for all practical purposes, given the factory practices of the times, also meant a ten-hour day for men. The ten-hour day lost 186–183. Seven economists, Clay, Gisborne, Graham, Hume, Morrison, Peel, and J. L. Ricardo, favored the twelve-hour day; and four, Cayley, Fielden, Howick, and Muntz, preferred ten hours.[93] Finally, after the defeat of this and other amendments to strengthen the bill, it was passed in the Commons, 136–7, with no economist in opposition,[94] and in the Lords without recorded vote.

The observer, from the vantage point of over a century and a

90. 3 H, 74:330–33, 26 Apr. 1844.
91. Cannan edition, 2:123.
92. 3 H, 74:641–43, 3 May 1844.
93. 3 H, 73:1460–63, 22 March 1844.
94. 3 H, 74:1108, 13 May 1844.

quarter later, should be cautious about interpreting opinions and votes on child labor legislation as simply a conflict between those who believed that a free market was the proper arbiter of hours and working conditions, and those who felt that children were not free bargaining agents and deserved the protection of the state. There was a graduation of opinion among economists that frequently makes it artificial to speak of one economist favoring factory legislation or of another as opposing it. Furthermore, statements that taken alone may have appeared to be in opposition to all state interference may in fact have been more connected with the feeling that further regulatory action might better take some other form. And almost always in the background of debate over regulation of child labor was the control of education called for by a particular bill—and specifically how much voice the Church of England was to have in such education. In some cases opposition to a provision in a bill seemed, in its larger context, to be a criticism of the Church of England rather than criticism of child labor legislation.[95]

Working conditions in the mines were so shocking that legislation of 1842 to remedy them had faced virtually no opposition from economists, but their reaction to Ashley's bill of 1845 regulating the employment of children in calico works showed that, at least for the moment, they were loath to support further regulation. Graham said of Ashley's bill: "I cannot view that alternative without a serious apprehension that a fatal effect will be produced on the trade and manufactures of the country."[96] Hume regretted that the bill had been introduced: "He feared it was only raising hopes that could not be realized, and encouraging people to meddle in other people's affairs, with which they had nothing to do."[97] He used this as an opportunity to say a good word for repeal of the Corn Laws: " . . . he could not give much credit to those who felt so much for the sufferings of children from over-employment, whilst they kept the food of those children dear."[98] And he made the point, not without basis, that if Parliament were to legislate against child labor, "let them begin with the farming children." Cobden objected to further

---

95. There is a suggestion both of the coverage problem and of the religious control of education in Hume's speech of 6 Feb. 1844 (3 H, 72:261–62).

96. 3 H, 77:659, 18 Feb. 1845.

97. 3 H, 77:660, 18 Feb. 1845.

98. 3 H, 78:1382, 2 Apr. 1845.

legislation, and in line with Hume's suggestion said that children in calico print works were better off than children in agriculture.[99] The most extreme opposition came from Brougham, who had a hair-trigger conscience about Negro slavery but when child labor was concerned sometimes fitted Carlyle's and Ruskin's view of the heartless political economist. He ridiculed the "humanity mongers." He "doubted whether it was within the province of the Legislature to find protection for children. The true protection of the child was that which Nature and Divine Providence had furnished it in the care of the parent."[100] Ashley's bill, in greatly emasculated form, was adopted without a recorded vote in either House.

The same general situation continued into the early 1850s, with Clay, Cobden, Gisborne, Graham, Peel, and J. L. Ricardo resisting further regulation and Cayley, Fielden (until his death in 1847), and Muntz favoring it. The voices of Hume and Graham became more strident, and the appeal to the laws of political economy more insistent. As Hume put it in the debate on the factories bill of 1847: "Some hon. Gentlemen—he did not think it was much to their credit—cast reflections upon the principles of political economy, not considering that it was by those principles that the best interests of the community were regulated."[101] Graham outdid Hume in justifying his opposition in the name of political economy:

... the question is, shall you by indirect legislation restrain industrious men from working twelve hours a day for the purpose of earning their livelihood, though they are willing to undergo the fatigue? ... [the bill was] a departure—a flagrant departure—from the strict rules of political economy—a science which in some quarters of this House appears to be treated almost with contempt, but it is a science which I have always considered as tending towards the benefit and general happiness of the nation; and I doubt if any legislation will be found safe if you depart from the great rules of that important science.[102]

Scrope said nothing in the debate—his great concern then was with Irish problems—but his infrequent votes were favorable to more regulation. The economists in the Lords were more receptive to regulation than were their economist colleagues in the Commons. Howick, since 1845 in the Lords as Earl Grey, stated the case: "[he

99. 3 H, 77:662–63, 18 Feb. 1845.
100. 3 H, 80:1028–29, 30 May 1845.
101. 3 H, 89:1074, 10 Feb. 1847.
102. 3 H, 90:773, 3 March 1847.

had] strong objections to interfering between labourers and their employers. But there was something so peculiar in the case of persons employed in factories, that he had come to the conclusion that Parliament was justified in interfering to extend protection to persons who were not able to protect themselves."[103] A crippling amendment to the factories bill of 1851 was carried 52–39, with four economists—Grey, Lansdowne, Monteagle, and Overstone—in the minority, and no economist in the majority.[104]

Acceptance of Principle of Labor Legislation

Grey's speech and the vote of the four economist Lords may be considered a turning point in the parliamentary economists' attitude toward labor legislation. From then on not only was the view of economists more favorable toward such legislation, but two—Butt, formerly professor of political economy at Trinity College, Dublin; and Fawcett, later Marshall's predecessor as professor of political economy at Cambridge—were leaders in promoting such legislation. In 1854 Butt, then a Tory Irish nationalist, but later to be the parliamentary leader of the Irish home rule movement, was in charge of a bill regulating working conditions in bleaching works. The bill was withdrawn, but Butt continued his sponsorship of such legislation, and in 1860 a law was passed, without recorded vote, putting bleach and dye works under the Factory Acts.[105] Either new economic ideas on the regulatory role of the State, the revelation in parliamentary reports of the terrible working conditions in bleaching and dyeing works, or the mellowing influence of old age were having their effects. Brougham and Graham did an about-face. Brougham said:

He thought it monstrous that children of seven and eight years of age should be kept eighteen hours at work, sometimes for three or four days together. . . . The Factories Act of 1844 had done great good—He wished to ask his noble Friend, the President of the Council [Earl Granville], whether any steps would be taken to extend the benefits of the Factories Act to persons engaged in bleaching and dyeing works?[106]

103. 3 H, 112:1362, 15 July 1850.
104. 3 H, 112:1371, 15 July 1850.
105. 23 & 24 Vict., c. 78.
106. 3 H, 156:1823, 27 Feb. 1860.

And the Graham of 1860 sounded very different from the Graham of the 1840s and 1850s:

He had said he had a confession to make. Experience had shown to his satisfaction that many of the predictions formerly made against the Factory Bill had not been verified by the result, and that, on the whole, that measure had contributed to the comfort and well-being of the working classes, while it had not materially injured the masters.[107]

These debates of 1860, for all practical purposes, marked the end of the appeal to political economy as against legislation to regulate working conditions. Particular provisions might be questioned on grounds of practicality or necessity, but no longer did opponents of such legislation wrap themselves in the mantle of political economy. Except for an unsuccessful attempt in 1867 by Fawcett to forbid night work in factories by children under fourteen, and to enact legislation regulating the labor of women and children in agriculture, this debate in 1860 marked the end, in the years through 1868, of economists' participation in the controversy over labor legislation.[108]

107. 3 H, 158:984, 9 May 1860.
108. 3 H, 186:1011–14, 2 Apr. 1867; 187:559–61, 14 May 1867; 189:481–82, 30 July 1867.

Chapter 5

Government Regulation of Business Practices

Working conditions were the most important controversy over the government's regulation of economic life in which economists played a role. But in many other problems, some fundamental, some trivial in themselves but involving larger principles, the economists had something to say.

Usury Laws

The long-standing but widely violated usury laws gave offense to the free-trade views of economists. In 1817 Parnell, cosponsor of a bill to repeal these laws, said that they "belonged to the darkest periods of the most ignorant times."[1] The bill made no progress, but the following year a committee on the usury laws was appointed. Alexander Baring, Brougham, Finlay, Huskisson, and Vansittart were members, and David Ricardo, not yet in Parliament, was the first witness before the committee.[2] The committee recommended repeal, and in February 1819 there was a brief and inconclusive discussion of the recommendations. Hume used the occasion for a lecture on political economy and the benefits of free trade:

Although this country had flourished under restrictive acts, he hoped the time was come when the principles established by the many able books on political economy would be recognised, and when every restriction would be removed from manufactures and commerce—from the efforts of industry, and the enterprises of speculation.[3]

In a debate two years later Ricardo supported repeal:

---

1. 1 H, 36:1267, 30 June 1817.
2. His evidence is in Ricardo, *Works*, 5:337–47.
3. 1 H, 39:422, 11 Feb. 1819.

He had had great experience in the money market, and could state the usury laws to have always been felt as a dead weight on those wishing to raise money. With respect to those concerned in the money market itself, the laws had always been inoperative; and during the war indirect means had been found of obtaining seven, eight, ten and fifteen per cent interest. The laws therefore occasioned inconvenience, but did no good.[4]

Althorp and Alexander Baring also supported repeal,[5] but Parliament took no action. Again in 1823, in his next to last speech in Parliament, Ricardo spoke in favor of repeal.[6] Subsequent legislation whittled away at the usury laws, but they were not finally repealed until 1854 in a bill of which Wilson was cosponsor.[7] Three veterans of free trade were in at the death of this old, restrictive legislation: in the Lords Lansdowne managed the bill,[8] Brougham supported repeal,[9] and in the Commons Hume got in a final word in favor of a measure he had first supported nearly thirty-five years before.[10]

Truck System of Wage Payment

In 1830 a bill came before the Commons to forbid the truck system by which workers were paid in goods, and to require all wages to be paid in money. Hume,[11] in the name of free trade, strongly opposed the legislation, but got scant support from other economists. Davenport,[12] Alexander Baring,[13] Gilbert,[14] Poulett Thomson,[15] Whitmore,[16] Althorp,[17] and Peel (even though it might be "opposed to the rigid rules of political economy"),[18] favored the legislation. The position of Althorp and Poulett Thomson is noteworthy as showing that even among dedicated free traders there were grada-

---

4. 2 H, 5:179, 12 Apr. 1821; also in Ricardo, *Works*, 5:110.
5. 2 H, 5:177–79.
6. 2 H, 9:1015, 17 June 1823. Also in Ricardo, *Works*, 4:323.
7. A note in Ricardo, *Works*, 5:335–36, traces this gradual abandonment.
8. 3 H, 135:581–83, 24 July 1854.
9. 3 H, 135:583, 24 July 1854.
10. 3 H, 135:1344, 4 Aug. 1854.
11. 2 H, 23:387, 16 March 1830; 25:595–607, 23 June 1830.
12. 2 H, 25:611, 23 June 1830.
13. 2 H, 25:874–75, 1 July 1830.
14. 3 H, 1:1163–64, 14 Dec. 1830.
15. 3 H, 1:1174–75, 14 Dec. 1830.
16. 3 H, 3:1257, 12 Apr. 1831.
17. 3 H, 3:1259, 12 Apr. 1831.
18. 2 H, 25:611–12, 23 June 1830.

tions of opinion as to just when it was appropriate for the state to intervene between employer and employee. Althorp said that "those hon. Members who had opposed this Bill had argued upon a false foundation. They had assumed, that the labourers were always competent to make contracts, whereas they were in every case in debt to their masters . . . and they were obliged to take goods from them at any rate."[19] And Poulett Thomson, who soon was to appeal to political economy in his opposition to factory legislation, said:

> With regard to the principles of political economy, he advocated them because they served as a fixed line to guide him, but he had never asserted that they were to approach that line under all circumstances, and at all times . . . he gave his support to the measure, he felt that it was calculated to prevent fraud, and protect the poor and ignorant.[20]

Western was the only economist, other than Hume, to oppose the bill,[21] although Torrens gave it only half-hearted support, saying that "as the working classes desired the measure, although it was at variance with strict principles, he was disposed to endeavour to gratify them."[22] And, as was true with many economists when regulatory measures were advocated, he put in a word for repeal of the Corn Laws as a more important step to improve the condition of the worker: "To attempt to abolish the truck-system while the Corn Laws and high taxes existed, would do little to mitigate the evils." The law was passed, with no record of the vote in either House.[23]

Licensing of Sale of Beer

A curious controversy involving the regulatory power of the state over the sale of beer mingled together a variety of considerations, often in a way that makes it virtually impossible to be sure of the thrust of the argument: the comparative social consequences of beer and spirits, the relation between the tax on malt and the tax on beer, the basis of a happy English family, the monopoly power of big brewers, or the special favors granted by venal licensing officials.

19. 3 H, 3:1259, 12 Apr. 1831.
20. 3 H, 1:1174–75, 14 Dec. 1830.
21. 3 H, 3:1256, 12 Apr. 1831.
22. 3 H, 6:1361, 12 Sept. 1831.
23. 1 & 2 Will. 4, c. 37.

And constantly running through the argument of the economists was the idea that eliminating licensing regulations was in line with the broad principle of free trade.[24]

The first economist to get into this many-sided dispute was Rose, who in 1790 defended an additional tax on malt against the charge that this would make it more expensive for the poor to brew their beer than to buy it.[25] And in 1816 Finlay was confident that the lower taxation of distilleries was "the only way to put down smugglers, by enabling the legal distilleries to provide a palatable liquor for the people of Scotland."[26] These comments on British drinking practices were but curtain-raisers for a controversy that began in earnest in 1822 and continued unabated for some fifty years. Brougham attacked the malt taxes on the ground that they raised the price of home-brewed beer, and thus encouraged tea drinking. Of tea he said: "It was a thin and meagre liquid, which gave neither strength to the body nor comfort to the mind, and which the British people were now obliged to use instead of that refreshing, inspiring, and truly British beverage, which their fathers had used in the good old times of England."[27] He also urged a reform of the licensing system, which he said frequently limited licenses to houses connected with a brewery.[28] No legislative action followed, but in 1825, when W. L. Maberly, a member of the Political Economy Club, introduced a motion to repeal the taxes on beer, Brougham in seconding the motion also attacked the licensing requirements:

Another advantage attendant upon throwing the trade open, would be found in providing the poor man with a cheap and wholesome beverage, which he might procure without the inconvenience of sending his daughters or other females of his family to the public house. . . . Gin would be, in great measure dispensed with; and his notion was, that the more the beer-shops could be brought into competition with the gin-shops the better.[29]

---

24. A full discussion of the controversy over the licensing of the sale of beer is given by Sidney and Beatrice Webb, *The History of Liquor Licensing* (London, 1903), chap. 4, "Free Trade in Theory and Practice" and chap. 5, "Legislative Repentance"; and by Brian Harrison, *The Victorians and Drink* (Pittsburgh: University of Pittsburgh Press, 1971), chap. 3, "Free Trade and the Beer Act."

25. P.H. 28:1172, 20 Dec. 1790.

26. 1 H, 33:566–67, 25 March 1816.

27. 2 H, 6:402–3, 15 Feb. 1822.

28. 2 H, 6:1459–60, 17 Apr. 1822.

29. 2 H, 13:380, 5 May 1825.

The motion was lost 88–23, with Hume and Western in the minority.[30] The move for removing the licensing requirement, although due in part to political considerations, was swept up in the wave of free-trade sentiment, and when the economist Edward Davenport entered Parliament in 1826, the economist-clergyman Sydney Smith urged him: "Advocate free trade in ale and alehouses."[31]

The Tory budget of 1830 repealed all taxes on beer. This action was followed shortly by legislation that ended the license requirement, and in effect opened the retailing of beer to all. Brougham, Hume, Huskisson, and Western favored the removal of the licensing requirement, no economist opposed the bill, and it was passed in both houses without a recorded vote.[32]

When an attempt was made the next year to restrict the sale of beer, Hume fought it on grounds of freedom of trade and tax equity. He opposed an attempt to close the shops to the poor man for beer, when the rich could buy champagne at any hour: "It was an attempt to perpetuate that tyranny over the people from which they had just escaped . . . as sugar, tea, soap and other articles were sold without restriction, so ought the sale of beer to be equally open."[33] He was soon urging the abolition or substantial reduction of the tax on malt, "because it would improve the morals of the people, by putting a stop to the quantity of ardent spirits which they consumed."[34] Thomas Attwood, as part of his distrust of government, opposed the return to a licensing system, for bestowing magistrates with control over licenses "would have the effect of converting honest and brave Englishmen into miserable slaves within a short time."[35]

The question of licensing the sale of beer and of reducing the tax on malt to encourage home brewing kept coming up intermittently, and when economists had anything to say, with the exception of Alexander Baring,[36] they spoke mostly in favor of beer versus gin, of home brewing versus commercial breweries, and freedom to sell

30. 2 H, 13:386, 5 May 1825. As the vote was taken shortly after Brougham's speech, his absence from the minority is puzzling. It is not clear whether the list is in error, or whether Brougham had left the House before the vote was taken.

31. Quoted in the Webbs, *The History of Liquor Licensing*, p. 118.

32. 11 Geo. IV & 1 Will. IV, c. 64.

33. 3 H, 6:545–46, 24 Aug. 1831. He expressed much the same idea in 3 H, 6:1135, 5 Sept. 1831.

34. 3 H, 16:913–14, 21 March 1823.

35. 3 H, 17:204–5, 17 Apr. 1833.

36. 3 H, 17:273, 18 Apr. 1833; 23:1132–33, 16 May 1834.

beer without license. Cobbett, who often had praised beer as a foundation of solid virtues, although he himself was a teetotaler, in typical Cobbett speech opposed increasing licensing restrictions: "It would not affect him—it would lay no tax on him; indeed the noble Lord could not tax him in the way of drink, unless he chose to lay a tax on cows' udders."[37] Muntz's judgment was: "He had yet to learn why beer was not to be sold as other articles."[38] Almost to his last days in Parliament Hume held to the view that "plentiful use of beer would prevent the consumption of ardent spirits, which worked so much evil in these Kingdoms."[39] And Cobden, near the end of his life, favoring abolition of the malt duties if consistent with a balanced budget, cited Adam Smith in support of the idea that cheap fermented liquor made for sobriety.[40] Not until 1869 were beer shops again required to be licensed.

Control of Air Pollution

Economists were no different from their parliamentary colleagues in their lack of concern about what today would be called environmental economics. With the increasing use of steam power there were frequent complaints, in the post–Napoleonic years, as smoke became a common feature of the urban landscape. In 1820 Brougham, Gilbert, Hume, and Vansittart were appointed on a committee to consider how the smoke of steam engines affected "health and comfort"; and Finlay was a witness before the committee. The next year a bill, with very mild provisions, was after brief discussion in the Commons—the only economist to speak was Gilbert, who hoped the law would not go too far—[41] and none in the Lords, passed without rollcall.[42] For the next three decades economists had little of significance to say about smoke, and when they did say anything, their general view was that smoke, like the trade in corn, should not be regulated. As J. L. Ricardo put it: "There were two parties affected by this Bill. The one was the party who was annoyed by smoke; the other was the party who lived by smoke.

37. 3 H, 20:799, 20 Aug. 1833.
38. 3 H, 53:310, 31 March 1840.
39. 3 H, 120:22–23, 23 March 1852.
40. 3 H, 174:1021–28, 14 Apr. 1864.
41. 2 H, 5:441, 18 Apr. 1821; 5:537, 7 May 1821.
42. 1 & 2 Geo. IV, c. 41.

Now, he could only say, on the part of his constituents, that they would have to give up business altogether if they were not allowed to smoke."[43] Graham[44] and Hume[45] opposed legislative measures, on grounds that, in modern phrase, elimination of smoke would interfere with the growth of the gross national product. Even Muntz, usually in the forefront of support of protective legislation, opposed legislation, principally on administrative grounds.[46] Lansdowne was the first economist to speak out in favor of antismoke legislation, and his remarks throw light on the popular arguments that evidently were being used against such legislation—he denied that it was merely for the benefit of the rich to protect their works of art.[47] Fifteen years later Grey, in connection with a plea for more stringent regulation of railroads, spoke of the need for smoke control.[48] Considering the oceans of smoke and soot that industrial Britain had poured forth in the previous half century, parliamentary economists as a group cannot be given high grades as environmentalists.

Regulation of Gas and Water Companies

On the problems of gas and water companies and railroads, economists had much more to say, and many comments showed great perceptivity as to the limitations of competition in those fields. As indicated earlier, there was virtually no suggestion that those services should be provided by the state; yet at the same time there was a sensing, soon to be articulated by several economists, that more than a simplistic view of competition was required to furnish the public with a good product at minimal cost. The doubts took several forms, of which the most important were: (1) the wastefulness of competition; (2) the need to fix prices to protect the public; (3) the need to supervise the financing of companies, both to protect individual investors and to curb disturbances to the money market; and (4) regulation of service, in particular safety regulations.

As early as 1817 Lauderdale opposed incorporating gas companies, feeling that individuals or partnerships could do the business

43. 3 H, 78:1368, 2 Apr. 1845.
44. 3 H, 107:205–6, 11 July 1849.
45. 3 H, 112:1437–38, 17 July 1850.
46. 3 H, 105:1262–63, 6 June 1849; 112:1438, 17 July 1850.
47. 3 H, 129:1752–55, 16 Aug. 1853.
48. 3 H, 192:419, 18 May 1868.

better;[49] and the next year he opposed a water monopoly, urging that the consumer should have the opportunity to choose between two or more companies.[50] In 1824 he blocked a bill giving a gas service monopoly to a corporation: "The granting of a monopoly of this kind would take away all the check which arose from competition."[51] Peel agreed with Lauderdale in thinking that the laws of the marketplace applied to public utilities as much as to any other business. He denied that it was a responsibility of the government to do anything about public complaints in regard to the water supply: "Roads, bridges, and the supply of markets, all of which were of consequence to the public, were not directly interfered with by government;— and by a parity of reasoning he was convinced that it ought not to interpose in the present instance."[52] He felt that the way to insure good service was to have competition from new companies.[53]

The great majority of economists, however, who had anything to say on the subject recognized that competition was not the proper policy in supplying water and gas. Even Hume's usually puristic view of competition gave way to economic realities when he supported a bill to give a monopoly to a London water company: "but as great risk would attend the experiment in the first instance, they asked for exclusive privileges for a certain period, in order to secure them against loss, and to insure them a reasonable profit on their capital so sunk."[54] Clay said that "everybody knew that the principle of competition could not be advantageously applied to a supply of water."[55] And over the years there were a number of other comments from economists to the same effect.

Regulation of Railroads

The same issue was debated in more detail in the railroad field. All railroads required parliamentary authorization, but in the beginning almost anyone could get a charter virtually free of restrictions. Shortly, however, questions arose as to adequacy of service,

49. 1 H, 36:559–61, 14 May 1817.
50. 1 H, 37:1184, 3 Apr. 1818; 1210–12, 8 Apr. 1818.
51. 2 H, 11:790, 21 May 1824.
52. 2 H, 19:1594–96, 1 July 1828.
53. 2 H, 21:1113–14, 7 May 1829.
54. 3 H, 28:537, 5 June 1835.
55. 3 H, 116:335, 29 Apr. 1851.

the reasonableness of rates, the appropriateness of authorizing competing lines, and the need to regulate finance, both to protect investors and to prevent upsetting the money market. In the early years of railroads, there were mutterings, in which several economists shared, that Parliament should take a more positive regulatory policy, but the first detailed parliamentary statement of an economist came from Morrison in 1836. He said that, as in canals and water supply, competition in railroads was not the way to serve the public: "It is plain from the facts now stated and I might have referred to fifty other similar instances, that competition in such cases is not to be depended upon as a means of reducing the exorbitant rates of charge which produce such extraordinary and unlooked-for profits."[56] Morrison also spoke of the wasteful investment in railroads, and moved that Parliament reserve the right to control rates and dividends.

Morrison was but the first of many economists to question the adequacy of competition in the railroad field.[57] Howick presented much the same picture a decade later in words that would not be out of place in modern economic theory. He said that a charter should be granted only after a decision that there was an economic basis for the line, as "the public cannot really obtain the benefits of competition by creating two lines of railway. The competing lines will probably carry on a ruinous competition for a certain time, and then come to some mutual understanding injurious to the public."[58] Perronet Thompson felt that free trade was not applicable to railroads: "Another point he must resist, was the doctrine that the House ought not to interfere in railway proceedings. On the contrary, he believed, that not a sparrow fell to the ground in railway matters for which this House was not held responsible whether for good or evil."[59] And J. L. Ricardo, than whom there was no more doctrinaire free trader in international trade or labor relations, regarded unregulated railroads as a monopoly.[60] Peel, however, argu-

56. 3 H, 33:981, 17 May 1836. This speech was published separately as a pamphlet. Morrison expressed much the same idea in 3 H, 55:931, 23 July 1840, and 88:845–46, 18 Aug. 1846.

57. Hume, 3 H, 21:1115–16, 1 March 1836; Grote, 3 H, 32:203–4, 11 March 1836; Poulett Thomson, 3 H, 46:1221, 27 March 1839.

58. 3 H, 77:264, 11 Feb. 1845.

59. 3 H, 110:67, 9 Apr. 1850.

60. 3 H, 110:1068, 1 May 1850.

ing as though competition were as applicable to railroading as to textile mills, said, "It was precisely by the vigorous, judicious, steady pursuit of self-interest, that individuals and companies ultimately benefitted the public at large," and argued that the real control came from holding out to the existing roads "the menace of competition."[61]

In the Commons the only opposition of economists, other than Peel, to railroad regulation related to safety regulation, and in varying degrees Peel,[62] Muntz,[63] and Lowe[64] either felt it was impracticable to legislate safety, or that the matter would correct itself by the public's refusing to travel on railroads with a bad record of accidents. In the Lords Brougham,[65] Ashburton,[66] and Monteagle[67] all spoke of the need to exercise more supervision of railroad finance. Although the economists were not in the forefront of action in the movement to regulate utilities and railroads, what they had to say was discriminating recognition of the peculiar economic problems of natural monopolies, and a voice well ahead of its time in urging government intervention.

61. 3 H, 72:250, 5 Feb. 1844.
62. 3 H, 60:175–76, 8 Feb. 1842; 64:179–80, 18 June 1842.
63. 3 H, 76:679–80, 16 July 1844.
64. 3 H, 142, 2092–2093, 27 June 1856.
65. 3 H, 79:225–29, 7 Apr. 1845.
66. 3 H, 79:231–33, 7 Apr. 1845.
67. 3 H, 109:632–37, 11 March 1850.

Chapter 6

Monetary and Banking Policy

Between 1780 and the outbreak of war with France in 1793 there
was little discussion of monetary and banking questions in Parliament, by economists or anyone else. Legally the standard was bimetallic at a ratio of 15.21:1, but as the market ratio had been for
nearly three-quarters of a century below this figure, the country had
a de facto gold standard. The Bank of England, established in 1694,
enjoyed important monopoly privileges in the London area and was
the financial arm of government, but it was not a central bank in
the modern sense. It has no national monopoly of note issue, it was
not the holder of the country's ultimate banking reserves, there was
no recognition of a responsibility as a lender of last resort. In England note issue outside of London was almost entirely in the hands
of private banks; the only incorporated banks in Britain were the
Bank of England and three chartered banks in Scotland; and the
Bank of Ireland was the only incorporated bank in that country.

Problems Following Outbreak of War with France

From the outbreak of war with France until the close of this study
there was almost continuous debate in the press, in brochures, and
in Parliament over monetary and banking policy. For nearly a decade the economists in Parliament played only a limited role in this
debate. Sinclair was a member of the Select Committee of 1793 on
the State of Commercial Credit,[1] which recommended the issue of
Exchequer bills to ease the crisis that followed close on the outbreak
of war, but there is no evidence that he played any important role in
the committee's work. In 1797 both the Bank of England and the
Bank of Ireland suspended cash payments. No economists were on
either the Commons or Lords secret committees that year to inquire
into the suspension of payments by the Bank of England, but

1. Reprinted in P.P., 1826 (23) III.

Thornton and Boyd were witnesses before both committees. Their evidence was notable in the emerging theory as to the responsibilities of the Bank of England. Thornton stressed the central role of the bank, and Boyd emphasized the need for the bank, when there was an internal run for cash, to ease credit rather than to restrict it.

Policy in the early years of the Restriction was all within the framework of war finance, and what parliamentary economists had to say was more by way of comment than a challenge to the continuing suspension of payments. Horner, Huskisson, Parnell, and Thornton, who in 1810 and 1811 were leading the parliamentary attack on the depreciation on the foreign exchanges and the rise in the price of gold, had little to say in the beginning years of the century. The most forthright attack on the wartime expansionist policy of the bank came from Lord King. More than anyone else he hammered on the idea that expansion of the note issue was the root cause of the depreciation of the notes of the Bank of Ireland and of the Bank of England,[2] but he was unsuccessful in attempts to limit the note issues of the Bank of Ireland,[3] and to require the Bank of England to publish quarterly statements of note circulation.[4]

Irish Currency Committee and Bullion Committee

In the early years of the Restriction the Bank of England note had not, except for brief periods, been depreciated below pre-Restriction figures either on the foreign exchange or on the gold market, and most of the discussion had centered on the Bank of Ireland, whose notes in 1803 were at a discount of almost 10 percent in terms of Bank of England notes. The result was the appointment by the Commons of a Committee on the Circulating Paper, the Specie, and the Current Coin of Ireland.[5] Petty, Rose, Sinclair, Thornton, and Vansittart were members of the committee, and there is circumstantial evidence that Thornton played an important role in the work of the committee and was responsible for at least

2. P.H., 36:1156–57, 22 Feb. 1803; l H, 1:153–55, 9 Dec. 1803.
3. P.H., 36:1247, 5 May 1803.
4. 1 H, 1:153–54, 9 Dec. 1803.
5. The report of the committee, selections from its minutes of evidence, and an introduction giving the background of the committee's work, and the results of its report, are in my *The Irish Pound, 1797–1826* (London: George Allen and Unwin, 1955; and Evanston, Ill.: Northwestern University Press, 1955).

part of the report. The report laid down what was in effect the cornerstone of British monetary policy from 1819 until 1914—a metallic standard, with the Bank of England assuming the responsibility for maintaining convertibility by appropriate credit policy and by use of its reserves.

This report had little immediate impact, because the Irish pound was nearly back at par with the British pound by the time the report appeared, and no parliamentary debate followed. But six years later, with the sharp increase in the price of gold, and the depreciation of the British paper currency on the foreign exchanges, the issue burst forth again, and for over a decade the parliamentary economists were in the center of the controversy. In February 1810 Horner moved for a committee—popularly known as the Bullion Committee—[6] to inquire into the cause of the high price of gold bullion. In its membership of twenty-one was a blue-ribbon group of economists: Alexander Baring, Giddy, Grenfell, Horner, Huskisson, Parnell, and Thornton, and its report was drafted in large part by Horner, Huskisson, and Thornton, with some contributions by Alexander Baring and Parnell. The report was adopted 13–5,[7] with all the economists in the majority except for Alexander Baring, who is generally believed to have supported the theory of the report but opposed its policy recommendation of a return to specie payments in wartime.

The ensuing debate on the Bullion Report, in which Horner, Huskisson, Parnell, and Thornton took a leading role in support, and Rose, Sinclair, Vansittart, and—with some reservations—Alexander Baring in opposition, involved a mixture of economic theory and public policy. The Bullion Report was two things: a theory of the operation of the gold standard,[8] and a policy recommendation that the gold standard be reestablished, even in wartime. So to discuss the support of and opposition to the Bullion Report is not a simple question. The economist authors of the report firmly believed in the power of the Bank of England to maintain a convertible

6. P.P. 1810 (349) III.

7. For a discussion of the vote in the committee, see my "The Politics of the Bullion Report," *Economica*, n.s. 26 (May 1959): 99–120.

8. Strictly speaking the Bullion Report supported a metallic standard, but not necessarily a gold standard, but as England had a de facto gold standard when specie payments were suspended in 1797, discussion of resumption of specie payments at that time generally tacitly assumed gold payments.

currency, and in 1802 and 1803 Horner, Parnell, and Thornton had in writings made important theoretical contributions to the subject. For them the report simply restated a theory of the monetary standard and of the foreign exchanges which they had expressed years before in a nonparliamentary setting. Applying this theory in wartime, in the face of warnings from government spokesmen that this would hamper the prosecution of the war, was another matter. Horner, both because he was a man of theoretical enthusiasms and also lukewarm about the war, probably was the most ardent supporter of resumption even in wartime. Fragments of circumstantial evidence suggest that Thornton, and particularly Huskisson, may have had reservations as to resumption in wartime, but were willing to support such a position as a protest against the official government view that the Bank of England policy and the money supply had no influence on prices or the foreign exchanges. Alexander Baring agreed with the theoretical concept of Horner, Huskisson, Parnell, and Thornton, but stopped short of their wartime policy recommendations. Horner's resolution laying down the principle of a convertible metallic currency was defeated 151–75; his resolution for resuming specie payments in two years was defeated 180–45, with no listing of individual votes on either resolution.[9]

Not until 1819 were effective steps taken for the resumption of specie payments, and in the intervening years the economists repeated what they had said in the Bullion Report and in the debates of 1811. With the end of the war Horner pressed for a speedy return to cash payments,[10] and Alexander Baring joined him.[11] Grenfell, whose opposition to inconvertible paper was strengthened by his feeling that the Bank of England had reaped large profits from the suspension of payments, put the case this way: "As long as he had the honour of a seat in the House, and God gave him health, he would enter his protest against a measure which he should always consider as one which took the money out of the pockets of those who could but ill afford it, and enriched those who had already amassed too great a wealth by usurious means."[12] Horner's motion calling for the restriction to end by 5 July 1818 was beaten 133–57,

9. 1 H, 29:1169, 9 May 1811.
10. 1 H, 34:139–48, 1 May 1816, and on other occasions.
11. 1 H, 34:161–63, 1 May 1816.
12. 1 H, 34:405–6, 8 May 1816.

with Althorp, Brougham, Finlay, Grenfell, Horner, and Parnell in the minority.[13] It is significant as showing the trend of economists' thinking that although economists were less than 2 percent of the membership of the Commons, they made up more than 10 percent of those voting for an early resumption.

Demonetization of Silver

Shortly after Waterloo parliamentary economists were also involved in the debate over demonetization of silver and the formal adoption of a single gold standard. Following the suspension of payments in 1797 the earl of Liverpool (formerly Jenkinson) as a member of the Committee on Coin took an action of great historic significance. The rise in the silver-gold ratio made it profitable in 1798 to bring silver to the mint for coinage. This was blocked by an order of the Privy Council Committee on Coin, of which Liverpool was a member, and this administrative action was, without debate, ratified by legislation,[14] pending a recommendation from the Lords of the Committee of Council on a permanent policy. Not until 1816 did the Lords present the report called for by the legislation of 1798, although in 1805 Liverpool in his *A Treatise on the Coins of the Realm* had spelled out the theory of a single gold standard, and recommended its adoption. For the next ten years, however, depreciated paper was a more pressing issue, and the *Treatise* aroused virtually no public discussion.[15] But the issue surfaced in 1816 in a form that could not be avoided. In the first place, there was by then a consensus that specie payments would be resumed, although when and in what form was not clear, and hence the issue of the legal basis of resumption had to be faced. Secondly, of less importance from the standpoint of national monetary policy, but of more concern to the man in the street, was the miserable situation, getting steadily worse, of the country's silver coinage.

On 10 April 1816 Grenfell had spoken of the "disgraceful state" of the silver currency, and said that "in change for a one-pound note persons usually received one half in French coin, and the other

---

13. 1 H, 34:250, 3 May 1816.

14. 38 Geo. III, c. 59.

15. I discuss this matter in *The Development of British Monetary Orthodoxy* (Cambridge, Mass.: Harvard University Press, 1965), pp. 57–58.

half perhaps in counterfeit coin made at home."[16] A few weeks later he recommended "that the new silver currency should be fabricated not agreeably to the existing law, but agreeably to the plan proposed by Lord Liverpool in 1805."[17] Alexander Baring reechoed Grenfell's proposal: "A measure which he should suggest, would be to alter the standard of the silver currency, so that it might not be carried out of the country on every slight variation of the price of that metal. No inconvenience would result from this, because gold should always be looked upon as the real standard of value."[18] Horner said that "it might be inconvenient to re-establish the old mint standard of silver."[19]

What went on behind the scenes, or what influence the words of Lord Liverpool or the urgings of Alexander Baring, Grenfell, and Horner may have had, we do not know. But on 21 May 1816 the Lords of the Committee of Council issued its long-overdue report. No witnesses were called, and the committee's terse report recommended that silver coins be fiduciary, legal tender only for two guineas or less.[20] The bill to implement these recommendations was government sponsored, and considering the historic significance of the decision made, provided little debate from economists or anyone else. Giddy and Huskisson had good words to say for the single gold standard;[21] but Alexander Baring, in a shift in position, suggested the resumption of cash payments could be effected more easily in silver;[22] and Horner, although not opposing the measure, thought it might be better to postpone action until the bank was prepared to resume payments.[23] In the Lords Lauderdale was the only economist to speak out against the gold standard, and in a protest made the theoretically sound point that a greater stability in the price of gold than in the price of silver did not prove that gold was a more stable standard than silver.[24] The gold standard was adopted in both houses without formal votes.

---

16. 1 H, 33:1148–49, 10 Apr. 1816.
17. 1 H, 34:239, 3 May 1816.
18. 1 H, 33:1149, 10 Apr. 1816.
19. 1 H, 34:147–48, 1 May 1816.
20. P.P. 1816 (411), 6:402.
21. 1 H, 34:964, 965, 30 May 1816.
22. 1 H, 34:964, 30 May 1816.
23. 1 H, 34:965, 30 May 1816.
24. 1 H, 34:1235–39, 21 June 1816.

Resumption Legislation of 1819

In 1819 both the Commons and the Lords appointed secret committees on the resumption of cash payments. Peel, as a freshman member of Parliament in 1811, had opposed the report of the Bullion Committee, but the accidents of politics made him chairman of the Commons committee of 1819. In the hearings and reports of these committees,[25] and in the extended debates that preceded passage of the resumption legislation, little new was added by economists to what they had already said in the Irish Currency Report, the Bullion Report, and the debates of 1811 and 1816. It was simply that a large part of Parliament had come to accept the economists' analysis that appropriate monetary policy could establish and maintain a fixed price of gold. This economic argument was strengthened by a mixture of sociopolitical arguments, in particular the idea that paper money encouraged forgery and the consequent wave of hangings;[26] the belief that inconvertible paper money gave too much power to a private corporation, the Bank of England; and an almost mystical feeling probably shared by many, but best epitomized in Peel, that entirely aside from economic analysis, stability in all forms was the cornerstone of the political and social order.

In addition to Peel as chairman, Grenfell, Huskisson, and Vansittart were members of the Commons committee, and Alexander Baring and Ricardo—not yet a member of Parliament—gave evidence. King, Lansdowne, and Lauderdale were members of the Lords committee, and Matthias Attwood, Baring, and Ricardo gave evidence. On only two points did economists make significant new contributions in the committee hearings or in the debates: Ricardo's proposal for redemption in gold ingots[27] and Baring's support of bimetallism. Baring as usual tempered his theoretical analysis with practical reservations about the dangers of deflation: he wished a resumption of cash payments but felt this should be done more gradually. Also he stated, with more assurance than in 1816, that bimetallism was preferable to a gold standard:

25. P.P. 1819 (202, 282, 324, 338), III; P.P. 1819 (291), III.
26. A fuller discussion of this point is in my *Development of British Monetary Orthodoxy*, pp. 71–73.
27. Ricardo had made such a suggestion as early as 1811 in *Observations on Some Passages in an Article in the Edinburgh Review*, later included as an appendix to *The High Price of Bullion*; and in 1816 in *Proposals for an Economical and Secure Currency*, but it was his lucid and forceful explanation in 1819 that gave general publicity to the idea.

I should prefer the mixed standard under either circumstances [coin, or bullion payments]: I was formerly always of a contrary opinion; but I have observed, during some time, that two metals circulate together with so much facility in France, that I have altered my opinion; and I think, although they never could be kept exactly at a par with each other, yet that the difference would be too inconsiderable to create practical difficulties.[28]

In the Lords Lansdowne rejoiced "on account of the sound principles of economy and legislation which it contained. It recognized a metallic standard as the only safe foundation for a circulating medium";[29] and King took the same view.[30] Lauderdale moved for bimetallism, but when that was turned down without a division,[31] he supported the resumption legislation, which was adopted in both houses without formal vote.[32]

Economists' Support of Bimetallism

The Act of 1819 was followed by full resumption of payments in 1821, and the abandonment of Ricardo's bullion plan, and from then on the gold standard withstood all parliamentary challenges. However, Alexander Baring to the end of his life continued to believe that bimetallism was preferable; and the Birmingham economists—the two Attwoods and Muntz—and the three unorthodox spokesmen for agriculture—Cayley, Davenport, and Western—made repeated but unsuccessful attempts to repeal the resumption legislation of 1819. Furthermore, although the point would be difficult to document with hard evidence, circumstantial evidence suggests that Alexander Baring, King, Lauderdale, Poulett Thomson, and Torrens, in principle supporters of a silver standard or of bimetallism and yet at the same time strongly opposed to inconvertible paper money, held back in pushing their intellectual beliefs when they realized that they had as unwelcome allies the inconvertible paper advocates who were willing to join in any attack, no matter what its source, that might discredit the resumption act of 1819. In a free-for-all debate in 1833, prompted by two resolutions by the brothers Attwood that on their face were simply requests for inquir-

28. Commons Committee, p. 191.
29. 1 H, 40, 1225, 21 June 1819.
30. 1 H, 40, 640–43, 21 May 1819.
31. 1 H, 40, 655–57, 21 May 1819.
32. 59 Geo. III, c. 49.

ies into the causes of the national distress but were regarded by the Whig government as an attack on the act of 1819, Alexander Baring indicated that he favored discussion of bimetallism, but made clear that he would in no way give support to inconvertible paper:

> He was of opinion, and many Gentlemen were of the same opinion, that at the time of settling the currency question the Legislature committed a great mistake in fixing upon a single standard, that of gold. He protested against our doing so at the time that the question was settled, and the gold standard determined upon. He was glad to find that the Governor of the Bank of England was now of the same opinion, and, he trusted, that the time was not far distant when such a remedy—a remedy to which he attached the greatest importance, in facilitating the circulation of the country, and rendering it secure against many dangers—would be applied to the existing state of things.[33]

The Commons finally adopted, 304–49, with the two Attwoods and Cayley the only economists in the minority, Althorp's motion opposing any alteration in the standard of value.[34] Two years later a motion by Cayley for a committee on agricultural distress and the silver standard was defeated 216–126, but had the support of Thomas Attwood, Cayley, Fielden, Pryme, and Scrope.[35] Lord Ashburton, in principle, continued to support bimetallism, although as a practical politician he did not use up his influence in a campaign for a lost cause. It is possible, although there is no direct evidence on the point, that, as suggested by Professor R. S. Sayers,[36] Ashburton's influence was responsible for the provision in the Bank Act of 1844 that one-fifth of the bank's reserve could be in silver. The continuing support of silver by Ashburton, and also the fact that by the late 1840s his views on silver were in the eyes of contemporary economists but a relic of an ancient controversy, is indicated by the remark of Wilson in his maiden speech in the Commons: "There is nothing in my estimation so astonishing as to find anyone with the experience in commercial life of large monetary transactions possessed by the noble Lord advocating the theory of a double standard of value."[37]

33. 3 H, 16:950, 21 March 1833.

34. 3 H, 17:586–91, 24 Apr. 1833. I give a more detailed account of these debates, in which Althorp, Baring, Peel, and Torrens played an important part, in *The Development of British Monetary Orthodoxy*, pp. 159–62.

35. 3 H, 28:337–38, 1 June 1835. By this time Alexander Baring and Torrens, who probably would have favored the motion, no longer were in the Commons: Baring had been raised to the peerage as Lord Ashburton and Torrens lost his seat in the 1835 election.

36. "The Question of the Standard, 1815–1844," *Economic History* 3 (Feb. 1935):100–101.

37. 3 H, 95:419, 30 Nov. 1847.

The California and Australian gold discoveries prompted only one economist to raise in Parliament their possible inflationary effects. In June 1852 Perronet Thompson, with a long history of concern about the ill effects of inflation, particularly for working men, moved twenty-one resolutions that the government take steps to protect the public against a depreciation in the purchasing power of gold.[38] There was no discussion, and the resolutions were turned down without a division. This was the last concern of parliamentary economists about the standard in the period of this study. The debate over bimetallism, with the great fall in the gold price of silver in the 1870s, was left for a new era and a new generation of economists.

The Role of the Bank of England

The role of the Bank of England presented a more complex issue than that of the standard, and for the half century from Waterloo to 1868 there was sharp division of opinion among parliamentary economists. The monetary standard fitted well into the framework of most economists' thinking: a metallic standard conformed with the idea that the forces of nature, and not political decisions, should determine the monetary supply. That is, it was sound economics. The Bank of England did not fit neatly into this framework. It was a private monopoly created as a financial arm of the Whig government of the 1690s. Adam Smith, more than eighty years after its founding, referred to it as "the greatest Bank of circulation in Europe" and a "great engine of state,"[39] but made no reference to its holding of the reserves of other banks, or its responsibility as a lender of last resort.

By the end of the Napoleonic wars it was evident that the Bank of England had a more complex role than in the time of Adam Smith, and more than a devotion to free trade and a dislike of private monopoly was needed to define a public policy vis-à-vis the bank. The situation was complicated by the fact that the bank, regardless of its functions, was a private stock company, whose stockholders wanted to maximize their returns, and whose management, as far as forms of law were concerned, were answerable not to the govern-

38. 3 H, 122:899–901, 17 June 1852.
39. *Wealth of Nations*, Cannan ed. (London: Methuen) 1:301, 303.

ment but to its stockholders. Developments after the outbreak of war with France in 1793 soon made it clear that the Bank of England was more than just a big private bank with some monopoly privileges. For the next eighty years economists were caught in a crossfire between their opposition to monopoly and economic decision making by government, and their observation of the economic facts of life. They came increasingly to recognize that free competition in the creation of money was not the same as free competition in the production of goods and services, and that with a fractional reserve banking system some discretionary authority was essential to prevent chaotic conditions in time of crisis. This rules vs. discretion controversy repeatedly split the ranks of parliamentary economists.

Until the final defeat of Napoleon this problem was overshadowed by the debate over the causes of exchange-rate fluctuations, and over the terms on which the bank granted loans to government to carry on the war. About the only point raised as to the philosophy of the bank's situation was the question of making its notes legal tender. The government at the time specie payments were suspended in 1797, and throughout the restriction, opposed this step, particularly because of the association in the public mind of legal tender with the depreciated *assignats* of revolutionary France. Almost the only member of Parliament to urge, in 1797, the realities of the situation was Francis Baring, who, close on the heels of the restriction, urged that bank notes be legal tender.[40] For this idea he received no support, and not until 1833 did Parliament accept the economic reality that bank notes were money.[41]

Economists took a leading role, beginning in 1812, in questioning the large profits of the bank, in demanding more publicity on its operations, and in stressing the public nature of its operations and the possible conflict between its obligation to its stockholders and its public responsibilities. In 1812 Lauderdale pressed for information about the bank's profits, dividends, and the price of its stock;[42] and his motion was supported by Lansdowne, who said that the "Bank

---

40. P.H., 33:330–31, 22 March 1797; 354, 27 March 1797.
41. I cover the legal tender situation in detail in "Legal Tender during the English and Irish Bank Restrictions," *Journal of Political Economy*, 58 (June 1950):241–53.
42. 1 H, 21:235, 8 Apr. 1812; 1131–32, 1 May 1812.

proprietors had an interest distinct from that of the public. When he saw a body of twenty-four men invested with such authority; when he felt that they must be divided between their duty to the public and to the individuals whom they represented, he thought the motion ought to be agreed to."[43] The motion was defeated. There may have been an element of Whig partisanship in what Lauderdale and Lansdowne said, but it was an idea whose time was coming. Grenfell, beginning in 1815, led a campaign for financial arrangements more favorable to the government, for more publicity on the bank's operations, and in general for a clearer recognition of the bank's public responsibilities.[44] No other economist spoke in support of Grenfell's motion, and Alexander Baring and Vansittart opposed it, but evidently there were many who agreed that the public was entitled to know more about the bank's operations, for one of his motions was defeated only 94–75.[45] Grenfell kept to the attack, with emphasis on the public responsibilities of the bank, and in 1818 asked whether the government had any plan "for securing to the public any share of the vast profits which the Bank of England received from this system [of inconvertible paper]."[46] The reply of Vansittart, then chancellor of the Exchequer, shows how much water has flowed over the dam since then on the relations of governments and central banks: " . . . it would not be consistent with the honour or welfare of the country, to make itself a partner in any profits which the Bank of England happened to derive from the restriction."[47]

Grenfell's campaign did not produce an immediate result in legislation or in a committee investigation, but he was a vigorous force in shaping public opinion to demand more information about the bank's operations, and in stressing the public responsibilities of the bank. Moreover, Grenfell's attack on the bank's profits had a specific important consequence: his conversation with David Ricardo in 1815, following his parliamentary attack on the bank, was the impetus to Ricardo's writing *Proposals for an Economical and Secure Currency*, which incorporated many of the ideas that Grenfell had expressed

---

43. 1 H, 22:1133, 1 May 1812.
44. 1 H, 30:871–74, 26 Apr. 1815, and on several other occasions.
45. 1 H, 30:669, 19 Apr. 1815. There is no record of individual votes.
46. 1 H, 37:1283, 10 Apr. 1818.
47. 1 H, 37:1284, 10 Apr. 1818.

in Parliament.[48] Even after resumption Grenfell continued his criticisms of the bank, and in 1822, in objecting to the extension of the bank's monopoly, he spoke of "their tyrannous conduct towards government and towards the public, exemplified by their letters to committees of the House of Commons in 1819."[49] Although this was not the first suggestion in Parliament that the bank's charter should not be renewed, it symbolizes the intensification of a controversy, latent for many years but until 1819 overshadowed by the immediate issues of fluctuating exchanges and the monetary standard, as to whether the Bank of England should have a monopoly, and if so what its responsibilities were.

The controversy continued until the passage of the Bank Act of 1844, and in the less clearly defined field of bank policy it lasted until the victory, in the 1870s, of the Bagehot principle that the Bank of England must be a lender of last resort. The problem had so many aspects that there was rarely a clear-cut confrontation between directly opposing views, but it was basically one of rules vs. discretion, complicated both by political overtones and by differences of opinion as to just how far discretion should go. By 1819 the decision had been accepted by the great majority of parliamentary economists that there should be no discretion in the monetary standard, and that it should be a fixed amount of a precious metal. Some of the most ardent supporters of a metallic standard, such as Ricardo, also felt that the Bank of England should have no discretion in monetary matters. The conflict between this view and the view that there was something peculiar about the extension of bank credit, that called for discretionary action by the bank, made its parliamentary appearance in embryonic form as early as Thornton's testimony before the secret committees of 1797. Thornton and Boyd had pointed out the special position of the Bank of England, and the need for it to expand credit in time of crisis, contrary to what a private bank would do. Similarly the Bullion Report of 1810, written almost entirely by economists, suggested the need for discretion-

---

48. For more details on the relation between Grenfell's parliamentary proposals and Ricardo's pamphlet, see "Note on 'Economical and Secure Currency'" in Ricardo, *Works*, 4:45–48.

49. 2 H, 7:760, 31 May 1822. Later in 1822, and several times in subsequent years, Grenfell returned to his criticism of the bank.

ary action by the bank.[50] Both Grenfell's criticism of the bank, and Ricardo's *Proposals for an Economical and Secure Currency* and his subsequent statement in Parliament: "If, during his continuance in office, the Bank of England should apply for a renewal of the charter, he hoped that the chancellor of the exchequer would be particularly careful that they did not overreach him,"[51] had suggested that the arrangements between the government and the bank were too favorable to the bank.

Hume went even further with a suggestion that the bank's charter should not be renewed, and a national bank should be established.[52] The proposal evoked no response from the economists other than Grenfell, who continued to stress the public nature of the bank and the need for more information on its operations. Parnell urged a full investigation of renewal of the bank's charter, "before any negotiation should be entered upon between the government and the Bank."[53] Alexander Baring, who never let theoretical doctrine stand in the way of what he thought was practical, not only took issue on several occasions with Grenfell's attacks on the bank but added: " . . . if any persons believed that the country would be able to get on without any such establishment as a Bank, or without an establishment a good deal like what the Bank was at present, he differed from such persons in opinion, and he thought that they would find themselves mistaken."[54]

The easy credit policy of the bank in 1823, 1824, and 1825, followed by the crisis of 1825 in which the bank at first played a vacillating role, suggested to many the need for more rules on the issue of money. Hume[55] and Parnell[56] repeated their attacks on the exclusive

---

50. The Bullion Report refers to "a distinction most important to be kept in view, between that demand upon the Bank for Gold for the supply of the domestic channels of circulation, sometimes a very great and sudden one, which is occasioned by a temporary failure of confidence, and that drain upon the Bank for Gold which grows out of an unfavourable state of the Foreign Exchanges. The former, while the Bank maintains its high credit, seems likely to be best relieved by a judicious increase of accommodation to the Country: the latter, so long as the Bank does not pay in specie, ought to suggest to the Directors a question, whether their issue may not be already too abundant" (p. 27).
51. 2 H, 8:138, 18 Feb. 1823. In Ricardo, *Works*, 5:247.
52. 2 H, 8:139, 18 Feb. 1823.
53. 2 H, 10:232–33, 19 Feb. 1824.
54. 2 H, 10:236, 19 Feb. 1824.
55. 2 H, 14:161, 9 Feb. 1826.
56. 2 H, 14:390–92, 14 Feb. 1826.

privileges of the bank. David Ricardo's posthumous *Plan for the Establishment of a National Bank* (1824) developed in detail the idea that the exclusive privileges be taken away from the bank, and the note issue be handled by a government agency.[57] In various forms the idea was mentioned repeatedly by economists in Parliament that limitations be placed on note issue, both of the Bank of England and of private banks. Whitmore, an ardent free trader, suggested that notes be issued on the deposit of gold at the Mint.[58] Hume, in the wake of heavy losses to note holders from bank failures in 1825 and 1826, wanted note issues of private banks to be backed by specific collateral.[59] He kept up his demands for more information from the Bank of England, for "he disliked the air of secrecy which was observed with respect to all the proceedings of the Bank of England."[60] Nothing specific emerged in the legislative field, but there was developing an idea in search of an occasion to dramatize it and a political leader to push it.

Bank Charter Investigation of 1832

The appointment in 1831 of the Bank Charter Committee, at the urging of Althorp, chancellor of the Exchequer, brought up for organized discussion many issues that previously had simply simmered beneath the surface. Althorp set the tone of the discussion when moving for the committee: "The issuing of money was the prerogative of the State, and, therefore, the Legislature had a right to say, on what conditions individuals should be allowed to issue money."[61] This view had been implicit in much that Grenfell, Hume, Parnell, Ricardo, and Whitmore had said, but such a categorical statement by the chancellor of the Exchequer marked the opening of a new chapter in the banking controversy. Eight of the committee's thirty-two members were economists—Althorp, Matthias Attwood, Alexander Baring, Graham, Morrison, Parnell, Peel, and

57. 2 H, 7:199–202, 29 Apr. 1822; and 761, 31 May 1922. The references in Ricardo, *Works* are 5:156 and 193. The *Plan* is in *Works*, 4:271–300.
58. 2 H, 14:574–76, 20 Feb. 1826.
59. 2 H, 14:878–81, 27 Feb. 1826.
60. 2 H, 14:1527, 26 June 1828.
61. 3 H, 12:1358, 22 May 1832.

Poulett Thomson—and among those who gave evidence were Thomas Attwood, soon to be a member of the first Reform Parliament, and Loyd, who had been a member in 1819–26, but did not stand for reelection in 1826.

The hearings revealed a wealth of information about the bank's operations, and in themselves were a victory for the position that the Bank of England was a public institution, not just a private monopoly. They produced little in the way of specific legislation, but did much to influence public thinking as to the future of the British banking system, and particularly the problem of rules vs. discretion in the management of the bank. The committee's report was noncommital as to policy, but the parliamentary debates that followed indicated the developing lines of thinking about the British banking system. The trend toward concentrating all note issues in a single institution was clear, although it offended the free-trade views of many economists. Althorp indicated that he would prefer that all paper money be issued by a single agency, but as a practicing politician he felt "certain that in the existing circumstances and state of the country it would be insanity to attempt to enforce such a system."[62] He wanted the bank's notes to be legal tender, but was against a government bank, as he felt "confident, that persons standing so prominent as the Bank Directors will be as completely controlled by public opinion as if they were acting under a legal responsibility."[63] On Althorp's attitude on a monopoly of the note issues, Alexander Baring's comment was a shrewd analysis, and a prediction of what time would bring: "Though the noble Lord deprecated the use of force towards the country bankers, he suspected that the noble Lord would not be unwilling to accelerate and extend Bank of England issues by a gentle shove, or a species of Quaker propulsion, which would effect the object the noble Lord had in view, and drive country bank paper out of circulation."[64]

Torrens's move to postpone action on renewal of the bank's charter was in its setting both a criticism of the bank, and a suggestion that the charter should not be renewed. Scrope seconded Torrens's motion: " . . . it was public only when it suited its purpose to be so, and

62. 3 H, 18:185–86, 31 May 1833.
63. 3 H, 18:169–87, 31 May 1833.
64. 3 H, 18:187, 31 May 1833.

private when it wanted to refuse to have its accounts investigated. . . . That the Government should, in this age, in the year 1833, continue this monopoly in the hands of a private company, was a most flagrant, a most crying public injury, a solecism in Government such as was nowhere else to be found."[65] Grote, Hume, and Parnell also criticized the bank, but Torrens only mustered 83 votes, including 6 other economists, against 316 in opposition.[66] A later motion to postpone for six months discussion of the Bank Charter bill—a parliamentary maneuver equivalent to rejection—was defeated 119–40, but the opposition included eight economists—Clay, Cobbett, Fielden, Gisborne, Hume, Parnell, Scrope, and Torrens.[67] In all, in speech or vote, eleven of the twenty-three economists in the Commons opposed, or wanted to delay, renewal of the bank's charter, or wanted terms less favorable to the bank, although the proposal for renewing the charter had the support of the Whig government, and was supported about three to one by the entire Commons.

The government's proposal to make the bank's notes legal tender revealed a similar hostility to the bank on the part of many economists, and unwillingness to go along with the views of the Whig government. Altogether thirteen economists opposed making the bank's notes legal tender,[68] although legal tender was carried in the entire Commons by a vote of close to two to one. Both the votes and the speeches suggest a relation between the rising strength of free-trade sentiment and this opposition, on one count or another, to the Bank of England. The idea of a privileged monopoly was offensive to free-trade principles, and only experience and time brought the majority of economists around to supporting the idea of a central bank with monopoly powers. Alexander Baring, probably better than any other economist who spoke, in his support of legal tender sensed the realities of the position of the Bank of England in a fractional reserve banking system, and that it had a responsibility in time of crisis that far transcended that of a commercial bank: "There was no practical man in all Lombard-street—and there were no more practical and respectable men in the Empire—who would not

65. 3 H, 18:1315–16, 28 June 1833.
66. Matthias Attwood, Cayley, Gisborne, Hume, Parnell, and Scrope. 3 H, 18:1353–54, 28 June 1833.
67. 3 H, 20:468, 9 Aug. 1833.
68. The votes in favor of legal tender were 274–156 (3 H, 18:1400–1401, 1 July 1833); 87–48 (3 H, 20:481–82, 9 Aug. 1833); and 82–35 (3 H, 20:782, 19 Aug. 1833).

tell the hon. Gentleman, that nothing would be more dangerous than for any banker to boast of being able to fulfill his engagements without the support of the Bank of England."[69]

Investigation and Debate, 1836–1841

In the decade following the renewal of the Bank Charter in 1833 there were no dramatic parliamentary confrontations on monetary and banking policy, but a series of investigations, in which economists played an important part, and occasional comments in debate, indicated a trend of thinking. Rice was chairman of the secret committees of 1836, 1837, and 1838 on joint stock banks, and six of the other members of the 1836 committee were economists, and the membership of the committees of 1837 and 1838 was essentially the same. Matthias Attwood, Clay, Gisborne, Graham, Grote, Hume, Morrisson, and Peel were members of the committee of 1840 on banks of issue; the same eight economists were members of the committee of the following year on banks of issue; and Cobden and Loyd were witnesses before the committee of 1840. The hostility to the bank shown in the debates of 1833, and along with it a feeling that the Bank of England or something similar was essential, continued, but no one was able to create from the crosscurrents of opinion an organized legislative program. The crisis of 1839, when the Bank of England turned to Paris and Hamburg for emergency help, contributed to the feeling that something was wrong about the Bank of England, but did little to clarify what that something was. Hume pressed unsuccessfully for an investigation of the Bank of England.[70] Clay, increasingly concerned with banking problems, although opposed to Hume's motion, made clear his feeling that the bank was a public institution: "He believed that the public were beginning to feel that a function as important as that of taking care of the currency, on the right discharge of which not only the prosperity of the country at large, but the fortune of every individual it might be said in a great degree depended, ought not to be left to any men or bodies of men, but ought to be left to the control of the supreme authorities."[71] Rice's remark, as chancellor of the Exchequer, indi-

69. 3 H, 18:1368, 1 July 1833.
70. 3 H, 49:3–37, 69–70, 8 July 1839.
71. 3 H, 49:63–64, 8 July 1839.

cated a hardening of the view that free-trade doctrines did not apply to the issue of money: "I deny the applicability of the general principle of the freedom of trade to the question of making money."[72]

Bank Act of 1844

The Bank Act of 1844 produced little debate from parliamentary economists. Peel, prime minister since September 1841, was no economic theorist, but a good broker in the economic ideas of others, which he would then interpret in the light of their political feasibility and his own conservative ideas. He had heard enough and decided that it was time to act, and his bill drew heavily on the ideas that Loyd and Torrens had put forward outside of Parliament. Bizarre as were its note-issue provisions in the light of modern central banking theory, Peel's bill provided a compromise on which an overwhelming majority of economists could agree, not as economic theorists, but as politicians: (1) monopoly by the bank of all additional note issues in England; (2) eventual elimination of all other note issues in England; (3) requirement of a 100 percent specie reserve against all note issues in excess of £14,000,000; (4) weekly publication of the bank's principal assets and liabilities.

Hume got in his message in opposition to restrictions on the note issue of commercial banks: "As to the regulation of the currency, he defied any legislation to regulate it. The operations of commerce must be its natural regulators, and, therefore, these restrictions upon the issues of private banks were impolitic and unnecessary."[73] Much as Hume and other economists may have disagreed with particular provisions in Peel's bill, they were prepared to accept it as an improvement on the existing situation. So when Muntz moved that the bill be deferred six months only eighteen members, of whom the only other economist was Gisborne, supported the motion, and 205 opposed it.[74] The spirit of political compromise that went into Peel's measure is indicated by Clay's mellow comment that he would accept Peel's judgment that the note issue provisions should not apply to Scotland and Ireland: "There were many obstacles that the philosopher might overlook in his closet, which no man engaged in

72. 3 H, 49:778–79, 25 July 1839.
73. 3 H, 75:834, 13 June 1844.
74. 3 H, 75:1319, 24 June 1844.

conducting the practical business of the world—least of all a Minister—could venture to disregard or neglect."[75]

In the Lords both Ashburton and Monteagle were critical of the provisions dividing the bank into an Issue Department and a Banking Department, and Monteagle in particular pointed out the difficulty that a fixed limit on fiduciary issues would create in case of an internal drain. But both supported the bill, which was approved without recorded vote.[76] As evidence of the surviving intellectual, but not political strength of the bimetallic sentiment, both Ashburton[77] and Monteagle[78] spoke favorably of it. They were unbending opponents of inconvertible paper money, and their statements—virtually silver's parliamentary swan song until the new conditions of the 1870s—emphasized a point that had characterized the support of bimetallism by parliamentary economists since 1816. Support had come from two divergent schools of monetary thinking: those, like the Attwoods and Muntz, who wanted inconvertible paper money but backed bimetallism as a more politically possible alternative that might accomplish, in part, their objective of higher prices; and those, like Ashburton, Monteagle, Poulett Thomson, and—at least for a time, Torrens—who were against inconvertible paper, but who favored bimetallism in the belief that this would be less restrictive and thus give greater strength to the metallic standard and make less likely the success of the efforts of the Birmingham economists.

Aftermath of Bank Act

The passage of the Bank Act of 1844, and the associated measures of 1845 on the Scottish and Irish banks, virtually ended the participation of the parliamentary economists in debate on monetary and banking issues. There followed a do-nothing legislative policy, with pressure for changes in policy and practice coming from the evidence and reports of parliamentary committees, and from brochures and periodical literature, rather than from talk or action in the halls of Parliament. The crisis of 1847 was followed by the suspension of the Bank Act. A secret committee of the Com-

75. 3 H, 74:1386, 20 May 1844.
76. 3 H, 76:711–33, 12 July 1844.
77. 3 H, 76:725–733, 12 July 1844.
78. 3 H, 76:723, 12 July 1844.

mons on Commercial Distress was heavily weighted with economists: Cayley, Clay, Cobden, Graham, Hume, Peel, J. L. Ricardo, and Wilson; and Ashburton was a witness. A secret committee of the Lords included Ashburton, Grey, Lansdowne, and Monteagle. There was a strong feeling in the committees that it was a mistake to have a fixed reserve requirement. The Commons committee recommended no change in the Bank Act of 1844, but only by a vote of 13–11 had it rejected Hume's motion: "That in the opinion of this Committee, the laws for regulating the issues of banks payable on demand aggravated the commercial distress in England in the year 1847." The vote of economists showed the strange alliance that political decisions can make: in the majority were Clay, Cobden, Graham, Peel, and J. L. Ricardo; in the minority Cayley, Hume, and Wilson. The Lords' report, drafted in large part by Monteagle, was highly critical of the rigid note reserve provisions of the Act of 1844: "The Inflexibility of the Rule prescribed by the restrictive Clauses of the Act of 1844 is indefensible, when equally applied to a State of varying Circulation."[79] The ensuing debate was limited, and brought no new ideas from the economists. No new legislation was passed, but the comment of Muntz is revealing as to the political prestige of Peel in putting through the Bank Act of 1844, and in defending it intact against criticism both in and out of Parliament: "[Peel] introduced the Bill now complained of with all that pomp of circumstance he so well knew how to assume."[80]

In 1857 a new Commons committee investigated the Bank Act, although the chancellor of the Exchequer, Lewis, an economist and member of the Political Economy Club, made clear that the government had no intention of proposing any change in the Bank Charter Act.[81] The following year, after the second suspension of the Bank Act, another Commons committee on the Act was appointed. Cayley, Graham, Hankey, Lewis, J. L. Ricardo, and Wilson were members of the committee of 1857, and John Stuart Mill, not yet a member of Parliament, gave evidence. The same members were on the committee of 1858. The noncommittal reports were not debated in Parliament, and the government opposed new legislation. It was becoming increasingly evident that banking legislation, like the

79. P.P. 1847–48, (565), 8, pt. 3:21.
80. 3 H, 96:856, 17 Feb. 1848.
81. 3 H, 142:277, 9 May 1856.

monetary standard, was passing outside the arena of parliamentary debate. The gold standard and the Bank had become institutional symbols of British greatness, vitually immune from economic analysis in Parliament. In the Lords Grey and Monteagle made clear their opposition to the rigid note reserve requirements in the Bank Act, but were not prepared to make a political issue of the matter. Their comments are worth quoting, as virtually the last parliamentary criticism by economists of the Act of 1844. As Grey put it: "His complaint against the Act was, that it was likely to place us in a situation in which some departure from the standard of value would be inevitable."[82] And Monteagle, in an analysis of the reserve provisions of the act, took issue with Overstone, whom he referred to as "the parent of the bill," and said, "He had stated his objection in the House in 1844. He had induced their Lordships to repeat it in their Report on Commercial Distress in 1848."[83]

The idea of having all note issues made by a government bank, along the lines of Ricardo's plan of 1824, was in the wind in the 1850s and 1860s, but never took the form of a legislative proposal. Grey said:

The Legislature allowed no money to be issued by trading persons; there was a Royal Mint only, which was open to all persons who chose to carry gold there to be coined. But to coin paper money was infinitely more dangerous than to coin gold; and, therefore, to carry out the principle of assimilation, what he would recommend was that they should put an end to all issue by the Bank of England. . . . [84]

But Grey never pressed the matter and the other economists in Parliament had nothing to say, one way or other, on the subject. One has the feeling that the economists in Parliament, much fewer in number than a couple of decades earlier, and in most cases more advanced in years than earlier generations of parliamentary economists, were not in the mood to lead any great causes, and in the banking field were prepared to let the Bank of England, delegations of country bankers, and the Treasury work things out. They had vitually nothing to say in Parliament on the responsibility of the Bank of England as a lender of last resort. In 1858 Hankey, a director of the Bank of England who had been elected to the Com-

82. 3 H, 148:73, 3 Dec. 1857.
83. 3 H, 148:32–85, 3 Dec. 1857.
84. 3 H, 148:541, 11 Dec. 1857.

mons in 1853, gave a lecture, published in 1867 in book form as *The Principles of Banking*, in which he attacked the idea that the responsibilities of the Bank of England were greater than those of other banks. This provoked a challenge from Walter Bagehot, editor of the *Economist*, who repeatedly in the columns of the *Economist* expounded the view, later published in his classic *Lombard Street* (1873), of the special responsibility of the bank to the money market. But the pages of *Hansard* reveal hardly a trace of this controversy.

Chapter 7

Taxation and Government Expenditures

Interest in the monetary standard might ebb and flow, concern over the working conditions of children might for some years be minimal, and the controversy over usury laws might end. But the parliamentary debate on power over the purse was never-ending: how much money should be extracted from the public, and of that how much should be borrowed and how much taken by taxation; what type of taxes should be used; for what purposes should the government spend money. Such issues have been at the heart of government since the beginning of organized society.

The most striking feature, from the vantage point of economics since Keynes, was the unquestioning acceptance by all economists—as by virtually all other members of Parliament—of a balanced budget in peacetime. In the Napoleonic and Crimean wars borrowing was recognized as an unfortunate necessity, but, aside from that, wide as the spectrum of economic opinion may have been on many topics, there was unanimous opinion that the budget must be balanced. Again and again, the argument against a tax change was that it might endanger the budget balance. There was no idea of functional finance or of "fine tuning," no belief that by fiscal policy the economy could be stimulated, although there were frequent suggestions that one type of tax rather than another was more conducive to a prosperous economy. Hume's statement, "A deficient revenue was too serious a matter to be trifled with,"[1] was no different in its thrust from those by men like Alexander Baring and Peel.

Sinking Fund

From 1800 to the late 1820s there was almost continuous debate over the sinking fund, a financial project introduced by Pitt in the

1. 3 H, 10:306, 13 Feb. 1832.

1780s with the idea that it would facilitate, in a painless way, the repayment of the national debt. A year's surplus revenue was to be turned over to a Board of Commissioners, who would then use the funds to buy up outstanding national debt. The purchased bonds were not to be redeemed, but the interest on them was to be used to buy up more debt, and the process continued until the entire debt was paid off. Many brochures, and hundreds of pages of parliamentary debates were devoted to the subject, but in retrospect it is often difficult to separate the economic analysis of the sinking fund from the mysticism and political emotions that often enveloped it; and also to see clearly, within the administrative complexities, the economic realities of the sinking fund. Frequently it is hard to say, when a member of Parliament like Alexander Baring defended the sinking fund against the criticism of the preponderance of economists, whether he is really defending the sinking-fund procedure, or simply saying that the term "sinking fund" is symbolically important as evidence of fiscal integrity.[2]

The developments of war finance made a farce of sinking-fund operations. With a surplus revenue, the sinking fund was an automatic, although administratively costly way of reducing the public debt. With large war borrowings what happened was that the commissioners went in the market and bought outstanding public debt for the sinking fund, and at the same time the Treasury went in the market and sold securities, although it would have been cheaper for the Treasury to have borrowed less, and instead of turning money over to the sinking fund, to have used it to meet current expenses. But the glamour of the name of Pitt, who, contrary to the judgment of history, is reported to have considered the sinking fund his greatest claim to fame, and the mystical idea that the mere existence of a sinking fund was a guarantee that the public debt would sometime be paid off meant that until several years after Waterloo there was little discussion of the theory of the sinking fund. With the final defeat of Napoleon, the failure of the government to reduce its public debt more rapidly gave rise to a wave of criticism of the govern-

---

2. For example, in his statement of 14 March 1823: "He was favourable to the principle of a sinking fund, but he could not see the justice or policy of making that sinking fund appear more than it really was" (2 H, 8:587, 14 Mar. 1823). Much the same situation is shown in the remark of Whitmore, who felt a sinking fund "absolutely necessary," but that the provisions of a bill continuing the fund were "one of the greatest juggles that was ever attempted to be practised in that House" (2 H, 8:580, 14 Mar. 1823).

ment's financial program in general, and of the sinking fund arrangements in particular. From economists came a succession of body blows against the theory, and even more the administrative arrangement of the sinking fund. It was not that the economists developed any new theoretical concepts—all they did was to apply the simplest economic analysis to a problem that had become enshrouded in political mysticism. They merely pointed out that the public debt could be reduced only by a surplus of receipts over expenditures, and that no administrative machinery, no matter how complex, could alter that fact.

In 1814 Grenfell, always on the alert for practices he felt costly to the public, stated that the practice of the government raising a loan at the same time that the sinking fund was buying government stock in the market "was a very circuitous way of going to work."[3] His motion that there be laid before the House information on the operation of the sinking fund since 1793 was carried without formal vote, but no further action was taken at the time.[4] Grenfell's motion had followed a conversation with David Ricardo, not yet in Parliament, and Ricardo had also advised Vansittart, chancellor of the exchequer, against such simultaneous creation and purchase of government debt. So it was no accident that when Grenfell returned to the attack with renewed vigor in 1819, Ricardo should have been a powerful ally.

After moving for a committee, Grenfell said: "This was creating a new debt for no other purpose than to destroy an old one: selling new stock cheap, in order to buy old stock dear; buying at a very high rate of interest to pay off a debt contracted at a very low one."[5] Ricardo joined in the criticism, and in addition brought out that under the existing practice the government could, without parliamentary authorization, borrow from the sinking fund, and thus the fund, instead of being a guarantee of debt reduction, sometimes enabled the government to spend beyond its tax receipts and authorized borrowing:

. . . he had already opposed the grant of 3 millions toward a sinking fund, because he did not wish to place such a fund at the mercy of ministers, who would take it whenever they thought that urgent necessity required it. He

3. 1 H, 27:579, 27 Apr. 1814.
4. 1 H, 27:641–42, 4 May 1814.
5. 1 H, 40:330, 11 May 1819.

did not mean to say that it would be better with one set of ministers than another; for he looked upon it that all ministers would be anxious, on cases of what they conceived emergency, to appropriate it to the public use.[6]

Both Vansittart and Huskisson opposed Grenfell's motion,[7] and it was defeated 117–39, with Althorp, Grenfell, Hume, and Ricardo in the minority.[8] Two years later Ricardo again attacked the sinking fund in a full-length speech, and said: "He [Ricardo] confessed he was one of those who thought a sinking fund very useless."[9] Hume reiterated the simple truth that the only way that a sinking fund could be effective was to have a surplus of tax receipts over expenditures,[10] and he continued to receive backing from Ricardo.[11] In varying degrees Alexander Baring,[12] Huskisson,[13] Parnell,[14] and Whitmore[15] made remarks that might appear to favor a sinking fund that would be an effective instrument of debt reduction, but were critical of a sinking fund that served as an instrument of financial manipulation. Hume's motion to abolish completely the sinking fund was lost 110–39, with Ricardo the only economist joining him in the minority.[16]

Time was running out for any defense of the sinking fund by economists. In the Lords both King and Lansdowne[17] criticized it when it was up for extension in a modified form in 1823, and King characterized even the bill that made some reform as "a Manifest delusion."[18] No economist had a good word to say for the way in which the sinking fund had worked in practice, and legislation of 1829[19] for all practical purposes abolished what has been referred to as "that glorious piece of nonsense."

6. 1 H, 40:40–41, 3 May 1819; and 1 H, 40:1022–24, 9 June 1819. In Ricardo, *Words*, 5:4–6, 20–22. The quoted passage is from his 9 June speech.
    7. 1 H, 40:353–55, 13 May 1819.
    8. 1 H, 40:360–61, 13 May 1819.
    9. 2 H, 5:1094, 1 June 1821; in Ricardo, *Works*, 5:117–18.
    10. 2 H, 8:91, 10 Feb. 1823; 8:352–57, 3 March 1823; 8:503–4, 6 March 1823; 8:580–82, 14 March 1823.
    11. 2 H, 8:219–21, 21 Feb. 1823; in Ricardo, *Works*, 5:248–51.
    12. 2 H, 8:587–88, 14 March 1823.
    13. 2 H, 8:585–87, 14 March 1823; 19:1704–8, 15 July 1828.
    14. 2 H, 8:536–38, 11 March 1823; 19:1674–82, 11 July 1828.
    15. 2 H, 8:579–80, 14 March 1823; 11:600–601, 7 May 1824.
    16. 2 H, 8:365, 3 March 1823.
    17. 2 H, 8:638–41, 21 March 1823.
    18. 2 H, 8:641, 21 March 1823.
    19. 10 Geo. IV, c. 27.

Criticism of Government Expenditures

Virtually all economists felt that expenditures should be kept to a minimum, and the great majority of economists came close to the view that government expenditures were nothing but waste. This view was strengthened by the feeling, expressed many times, that these expenditures were in large part to bolster the established social order. Virtually no national public expenditures were made for education or for social welfare—the poor law was handled by parishes—whereas there were large outlays for sinecures and pensions. On the other hand, the tax system during most of the period was regressive. So the practical situation—as distinguished from any theory of functional finance—was that increased government expenditures meant taking money from the poor to give to the rich, and particularly to the economically nonproductive rich.

Many economists were critical of large military expenditures. In 1783 in a debate on navy estimates, Jenkinson (later the 1st earl of Liverpool) considered the figures too high for peacetime;[20] and even during the war Sinclair asked for a smaller naval appropriation.[21] In 1810 Huskisson, a Tory, and Parnell, a Whig, pointed to unnecessary army expenditure;[22] and Alexander Baring several times criticized army and military expenses as excessive.[23] Horner, anticipating a criticism that Hume was to make repeatedly in later years, demanded more information about army estimates: "What had become of the functions of that House, if, when ministers demanded a large sum of money, gentlemen should be told that it was irregular to ask for what purpose it was wanted?"[24]

After Napoleon's final defeat Brougham attacked the peacetime military establishment as too large[25] and spending too much on display. Of the Guards he said: "The only end which their existence to so large an amount could answer, was the gratification of a childish and contemptible passion for military parade—childish it might be

20. P.H., 23:1216, 20 Nov. 1783.
21. P.H., 33:1562, 27 Nov. 1798.
22. 1 H, 15:617–20, 631, 26 Feb. 1810. Huskisson said much the same thing the following year, 19:377–78, 380, 15 March 1811; 22:302–3, 317, 318, 13 Apr. 1812; 22:1150–51, 1 May 1812, and on later occasions.
23. 1 H, 32:412, 11 Feb. 1816; 33:588–89, 25 March 1816; and on other occasions.
24. 1 H, 29:406, 21 Nov. 1814.
25. 1 H, 32:855–63, 26 Feb. 1816.

called, though not altogether contemptible, when its dangerous tendency was considered."[26] Althorp called for a smaller army,[27] and in the Lords Lansdowne said military expenditures should be reduced,[28] and criticized any expenditure without the sanction of Parliament.[29]

When Hume reentered Parliament in 1818 he began an attack on military expenditures that continued until his death nearly forty years later. The extent of Hume's opposition to government expenses in general, and to military expenses in particular, is indicated by his criticism of the education of officers at government expense at the Royal Military Academy at Woolwich: "So long as they remained pensioners of the State, by putting it to unnecessary expense for their education, he could not but call them paupers— he called all persons paupers who took the money of the State without giving value for it."[30] Hume was regularly defeated on his motions to eliminate items in the military and naval appropriations, but he received the strong support of economists. His motion for detailed ordnance estimates was defeated, 58–44, on 15 February 1821, but five other economists supported him: Brougham, Grenfell, Parnell, Ricardo, and Whitmore.[31] The following month seven economists—Althorp, Hume, Loyd, Parnell, Ricardo, Rice, and Western—were in the minority of 115 who voted to reduce the army.[32] The same pattern of voting appeared a score or more times in the 1820s.

Of Hume's efforts Alexander Baring, who on many issues was in head-on conflict with him, said that he was "never to be named without gratitude, for his efforts in throwing light on the enormous expenditure of the country."[33] Brougham said, after Hume had made a devastating attack on the accuracy of navy estimates: "And he hoped he would go on with the same persevering zeal for the public good, careless of the taunts of those who profited by abuses, forgetful of the neglect shown to his labours by the gentlemen opposite, thinking only of his country, dreaming only of his duty, and, great

26. 1 H, 33:146, 11 March 1816.
27. 1 H, 37:862–66, 6 March 1818.
28. 1 H, 33:305–20, 15 March 1816.
29. 1H, 33:979–80, 5 Apr. 1816.
30. 2 H, 24:310, 30 Apr. 1830.
31. 2 H, 4:472, 6 Feb. 1830.
32. 2 H, 4:1245, 14 March 1821.
33. 2 H, 4:1516, 30 March 1821.

as his services were to that country, still laying up additional claims to its gratitude."[34]

Rice, in a debate on navy estimates, was critical of the "overgrown establishments,"[35] and the vigorous young Poulett Thomson, elected in 1826 to the Commons in a campaign in which Jeremy Bentham had canvassed for him, said that there must be something wrong with the navy if it needed such large appropriations, and cited the efficiency of the American navy.[36] The only economist between Waterloo and the 1830s to put up a strong defense of existing military and naval outlays was Wilmot (from 1823 Horton), one of the few imperialists among the economists.[37]

On 29 March 1830 Graham's action to amend the ordnance estimates was defeated 200–124, but eleven of the eighteen economists were in the minority,[38] and in the 1830s and early 1840s similar proposals were defeated, with the economists well represented in the minority. In Cobbett's brief parliamentary career he turned his trenchant prose against large military outlays.[39] After Molesworth[40] and Cobden took their seats in the Commons, they joined their voices to the criticism of military outlays; and Cobden, with his eye for simple economic realities, after attributing much of the poverty of the Middle Ages to the monastic system, added: "But I wish to know the difference between keeping 2,000,000 or 3,000,000 of people in black cloaks in idleness in convents, and keeping 2,000,000 or 3,000,000 in red coats in barracks. In either case they must be supported."[41] Cobden made some telling criticisms of the navy's technical inefficiency, including the failure to recognize the coming of ironclads.[42] A strong case could be made that Hume and Cobden, in constant conflict with the military and naval establishments, were an influence increasing their fighting effectiveness.

The Select Committee of 1828 on Public Income and Expenditure, of which Parnell was chairman, included in its membership an impressive list of economists: Althorp, Alexander Baring, Horton,

---

34. 2 H, 6:798, 27 Feb. 1822.
35. 2 H, 16:348, 12 Dec. 1827.
36. 2 H, 19:343, 2 May 1828; 344–49, 5 May 1828.
37. 2 H, 7:1517–18, 5 July 1822, and several times later.
38. 3 H, 33:23, 21 Apr. 1836; 1004, 18 May 1836.
39. 3 H, 21:1003–5, 1008–9, 3 March 1834, and several times later.
40. 3 H, 97:1169–75, 31 March 1848, and on later occasions.
41. 3 H, 97:830, 20 March 1848.
42. 3 H, 159:1071–76, 1077–88, 5 March 1863.

Howick, Hume, and Huskisson. Their report, believed to have been written in large part by Parnell, was a powerful appeal, both for the reduction or elimination of needless expenditures, and for the reform of the tax system in the interest of administrative efficiency, greater equity, and stimulus to production. One of its passages, quoted by Sir James Graham in moving for a reduction in ordnance estimates, well epitomizes the view held by the great majority of parliamentary economists of the time: "No Government is justified in taking the smallest sum of money from the people, unless a case can be clearly established to show that it will be productive of some essential advantage to them, and one that cannot be obtained by a smaller sacrifice. The real wants of the people shall not be made to give way to any imaginary wants of the State, which arise from so many sources, that it is frequently very difficult to prevent the operation of an undue influence."[43]

Shortly thereafter Parnell published *Financial Reform*, incorporating many ideas from the committee report. This influential book went through three editions and was translated into French. Later Parnell made more specific his criticism of military expenditures: "He conceived there was an interest, to which the merely army interest was secondary, namely, the public interest; but the gallant officer [Captain Boldero], like most other military men, seemed to think there was no interest to be considered but that of the army. The Secretary at War should virtually be the trustee of the public, and as such, a check upon the tendency of military men to advance their own profession at the expense of the public."[44]

Sinecures and Civil List Pensions

Other expenditures which many economists were on the alert to reduce, if not eliminate, were sinecures and civil-list pensions, grants to the royal family, and payments in support of the Established Church. In the earlier years of the period covered by this study the British government organization was honeycombed with well-paid posts that involved virtually no responsibility, and which at best were given as a reward for public service, at worst were simply handouts to political favorites and impoverished aristocrats. Much the

43. 2 H, 23:1009, 29 March 1830.
44. 3 H, 11:1029, 28 March 1832.

same can be said of civil-list pensions. In Hume's blunt question: "When the poor of the country are starving, is it a time for giving a pension to the Master of the Hawks?"[45] lies a major explanation why classical economists were so opposed to government spending.

The economists, in 1807, led the attack on "offices in reversion," by which favorites of government were granted the right to a sine-cure, already held by someone, upon that person's death. Such "offices in reversion" had in many cases been granted under scandalous circumstances, and Giddy, Horner, Huskisson, Parnell, and Petty, and Lauderdale in the Lords, criticized the practice.[46] This same group of economists also kept up a criticism of sinecures. Thornton added a criticism that economists made constantly about all aspects of the financial operations of government: secrecy. Asking for more information about sinecures, he said: "The public could not longer be kept in ignorance, and from the diffusion of political knowledge, it was now necessary to have every thing clearly stated, that they might not appear to act from bad grounds and want of informa-tion."[47] Althorp, more than two decades later, expressed the same idea: "It was his opinion, that none of the regular expenses of the State ought ever to appear upon the Civil List, inasmuch as they ought to be under the constant and vigilant control of Parliament, and ought not to be voted permanently at the commencement of each reign."[48] Brougham enriched the controversy with the comment: "The ark itself did not contain a greater variety of beings than were to be found marshalled in the civil list."[49] Vansittart[50] and Rose,[51] both of whom held government appointments, were the only economists to defend the prevailing practice. Huskisson, however, urged re-straint in the investigation of what were, in form, royal grants, as "it would be most indecorous were the committee to extend its investi-gations into the private expenditure of the Royal Family,"[52] thus set-ting a pattern followed repeatedly in the next thirty years by those defending grants made nominally by the royal family.

45. 3 H, 1:452, 12 Nov. 1830.
46. 1 H, 9:182–83, 183–84, 185–86, 186–87, 24 March 1807; 1 H, 10:870, 1 March 1808, and on several other occasions.
47. 1 H, 14:425, 8 May 1809.
48. 3 H, 3:960, 25 March 1831.
49. 2 H, 1:117, 5 May 1820.
50. 1 H, 25:408, 29 March 1813.
51. 1 H, 33:770 and *passim*, 1 Apr. 1816.
52. 1 H, 30:635–36, 14 Apr. 1815.

That dominant opinion of economists in the early years of the century on sinecures and civil-list pensions was in conflict with prevailing parliamentary opinion is shown by votes on several measures. George Tierney's motion for a select committee on the civil-list accounts was defeated 213–122, with seven economists—Althorp, Alexander Baring, Brougham, Finlay, Grenfell, Horner, and Parnell—in the minority, and only Giddy and Huskisson in the majority.[53] The civil-list controversy was associated with the broader issue of the right of Parliament to know how money was spent. The problem was basically one of political theory and philosophy of government, but it was one on which the great majority of the economists had strong opinions. In 1812 came a debate on the Droits of Admiralty—revenues that automatically came to the crown without specific parliamentary authorization, and which the crown could spend without accounting to Parliament. Brougham summarized the issue: "Whether the crown had the power to use certain funds, certain enormous sums of money, without any grant from parliament, or even without its privity?"[54] In the Lords King[55] and Lansdowne[56] pressed unsuccessfully for more information on civil-list payments. Hume's motion for information on pensions on the civil list was defeated on 20 May 1828, 131–52, with six economists in the minority; Althorp, Alexander Baring, Howick, Hume, Poulett Thomson, and Whitmore.[57] The hardening sentiment, both among economists and others, against abuses of the civil list is shown by the vote of 15 November 1830, when Parnell's motion to create a select committee to examine the civil list was carried 233–204, with thirteen economists in the majority, and only Peel in the minority.[58] The vote led to the resignation of the Wellington ministry.

To ask for more information on the civil list or to dramatize particularly glaring abuses in sinecures was one thing; to abolish the whole system of civil-list payments and sinecures was a different matter. Hume's motion to abolish all sinecures, made early in the Reform Parliament, was defeated 232–138, with ten economists—Thomas Attwood, Cayley, Clay, Cobbett, Fielden, Gisborne, Grote,

53. 1 H, 34:299–302, 6 May 1816.
54. 1 H, 21:241, 21 Jan. 1812.
55. 2 H, 1:90–91, 4 May 1820.
56. 2 H, 1:86–88, 4 May 1820.
57. 2 H, 19:840, 20 May 1828.
58. 3 H, 1:549–55, 15 Nov. 1830.

Hume, Molesworth, and Pryme—in the minority, and six economists—Althorp, Graham, Howick, Rice, Poulett Thomson, and
Whitmore—in the majority.[59] Three years later a motion for a select
committee to examine the pension list was defeated 268–146, with
much the same lineup of economists.[60] And the following year, after
the accession of Victoria, Rice, as chancellor of the Exchequer, moved
for a select committee to investigate the pensions on the civil list.
The motion was passed 295–233, with eleven economists in favor,
and Matthias Attwood and Peel the only economists in opposition.[61]
The argument over the civil list almost faded away in Victoria's
reign, in part because many of the more flagrant abuses were elimi-
nated, in part because the popularity of the young Queen dulled a
criticism which, although founded on economic grounds, also had
represented in some degree a dislike of the reactionary politics and
extravagances and personal scandals of some members of the royal
family.

Grants to Royal Family

Much of the same argument arose in connection with direct
grants to the royal family. With the exception of Muntz—and he
only in a mild way—no economist was critical of the institution of
monarchy, but for the quarter-century before Victoria came to the
throne grants to the royal family were under continuous attack, and
repeatedly economists asked for smaller grants. The idea of income
distribution—i.e., taxing the poor to support a free-spending royal
family—came up a number of times. The cautious Thornton put it,
in connection with a proposed grant to the royal princesses: "Some
enquiry ought to take place, proving the necessity of throwing such
an additional burden on the people."[62] In 1815 a grant to the unpopular duke of Cumberland upon his marriage was defeated 126–
125, with Alexander Baring, Finlay, Giddy, Grenfell, Parnell, and
Western in the majority, and the four Tory economists Huskisson,
Peel, Rose, and Vansittart in the minority.[63] With the death in child-
birth in 1817 of Princess Charlotte, the House of Hanover was left

59. 3 H, 15:713–16, 14 Feb. 1833.
60. 3 H, 32:1240, 19 Apr. 1836.
61. 3 H, 34:933–37, 8 Dec. 1838.
62. 1 H, 22:141, 23 March 1812.
63. 1 H, 31:1080–82, 3 July 1815.

without heirs other than the childless royal dukes—the sons of George III. Hence the government proposed increased grants to the unmarried royal dukes to induce them to make appropriate unions to carry on the Hanoverian succession. The duke of Kent, the future father of Victoria, had his annual grant increased to permit him to abandon his mistress of many years to marry a widowed German princess. These grants touched off a general criticism of the size of royal grants. In the Lords Lansdowne said: "The marriage of any member of the royal family ought always to be a subject of joy and congratulation with the whole nation; but it would cease to be so, if upon all occasions such an event was to be attended with new and grievous impositions."[64]

Criticism in the same spirit continued, with the majority of the economists almost always on the losing side, but providing votes for economy far out of proportion to their numbers. The reactionary political views of the duke of Cumberland, who but for the birth of Victoria would have come to the throne in 1837, made him a particular target. Criticism of his grant stepped up when, in 1837, the crowns of the United Kingdom and Hanover were separated, and he became king of Hanover. The annuity was never suspended, but as late as 1843 a motion to that effect, although defeated 197–91, received the support of six economists—Cobden, Gisborne, Hume, Morrison, Muntz, and J. L. Ricardo—with only Graham and Peel in the majority.[65] In addition to expenditures for the army and navy, for the royal family, and for the favorites of government, the expenditures of the Established Church also came under attack, but as these expenditures were closely associated with the larger question of the relation of church and state, discussion of them is postponed until chapter 10.

Views on Taxation

The emphasis in the economists' discussion of public finance was on expenditures rather than on taxation. Expenditures were, in their minds, in large part a waste, and their concern was more in eliminating the waste than on figuring out how to pay for the waste. Close to the surface in some discussions was the idea that elimina-

64. 1 H, 38:64, 15 Apr. 1818.
65. 3 H, 70:531–33, 30 June 1843.

tion of wasteful expenditures would pretty much dispose of the problem of taxation. Nevertheless taxation was under continuous debate by economists. At one time or another they raised four general policy questions: incidence of taxation between rich and poor; the related subject of direct vs. indirect taxation; taxation of property vs. labor income; taxation of business income as compared with funded income.

Before the Napoleonic wars there was a small land tax, but revenue came largely from indirect taxes: import duties, and a wide variety of excise taxes, which in addition to those universal sources of revenue—tobacco and alcohol—hit such diverse sources as salt, servants, horses, newspapers, and windows. It is hard to identify any theoretical underpinning for these indirect taxes beyond the age-old one of avoiding taxes that arouse organized protest from powerful groups. The financial demands of war shifted taxation to the center of the political stage, and in 1799 Pitt put through his first income tax. But even before that bill discussions of other tax proposals foreshadowed the emerging theoretical issues. The earl of Liverpool "thought a tax on capital bad, because it tended to check the sources of industry. A tax upon expenditure was the only one which he considered eligible."[66] And Sinclair, always the spokesman for agriculture, in opposing a tax that he thought would burden land, expressed a view that was to reappear repeatedly in the next seventy years: "The best judges, the truest patriots of all countries, have been of opinion, that of all taxes, that upon immoveable goods, that upon lands and houses, ought to be the last resource."[67] Francis Baring, when the income tax was proposed, favored taxation of income rather than of capital, and said, representing a mercantile rather than an agricultural point of view: "There was nothing that should have a stronger claim on the protection of government, than creative talents in mercantile pursuits."[68]

This argument that some taxes were more discouraging to economic activity than were others reappeared in many forms, and although a head-on clash rarely emerged, was in conflict with another idea that was to gain increasing favor among economists—that taxation should be equitable as between rich and poor, and that funded

66. P.H., 33:1282, 9 Jan. 1798.
67. P.H., 33:1444, 9 May 1798.
68. P.H., 34:95, 14 Dec. 1798.

property income should be taxed more heavily than business or professional income. But the idea of progressive taxation smacked too much of revolutionary France for even the liberal-minded Petty, then chancellor of of the Exchequer, to accept. He favored exemption of lower incomes from the property duty tax—essentially an income tax—but "he objected to the idea of taking a greater percentage from the rich than from the poor, since its tendency was to alter the order of society."[69] Shortly thereafter he put the same idea in even stronger language:

Of all the dangerous doctrines that could possibly be held out in a legislative assembly, there was not one that could possibly be more mischievous in its tendency, than that of equalizing all ranks of society by reducing the higher orders to a level with those of a different class, and depriving them of every comfort which they had a right to expect from their exalted situation.[70]

The conservative Vansittart viewed with alarm increased taxation of the rich, as it would cause them to cut down expenses "and the evil would thus be communicated from the most exalted to the lowest members of the community."[71] Grenfell, however, suggested that if the property tax were extended lower incomes should be taxed at a lesser rate than higher incomes—the earliest parliamentary support by an economist of progressive taxation.[72] Likewise Althorp, also no radical, was concerned about taxes whose impact was particularly hard upon the poor, and this was his reason for opposing the leather tax.[73]

Changing Views on Income Tax

Pitt's income tax of 1799, discontinued during the peace of Amiens, and then reintroduced, was a subject of full-scale, acrimonious debate after Napoleon's defeat at Leipzig. It came under widespread attack from several parliamentary economists. Their opposition was based on a number of grounds, not always consistent or buttressed by any well thought-out economic analysis. But of compelling importance was an idea that, regardless of the theory of the

69. 1 H, 6:920–21, 25 Apr. 1806; 7:55, 7 May 1806.
70. 1 H, 7:218–19, 15 May 1806.
71. 1 H, 23:790, 26 June 1812.
72. 1 H, 29:338–39, 18 Nov. 1814.
73. 1 H, 26:233–34, 18 May 1813.

tax, it was bad because it would permit the government to continue unnecessary military and naval expenditures and sinecures, pensions, and civil-list outlays. As Alexander Baring put it, "This tax came with very bad grace after the vote declining to make any inquiry into the lavish expenditure of the Civil List. . . . He for one should for ever oppose the tax as a permanent source of revenue in time of peace."[74] After Waterloo criticism became even stronger. Althorp, Alexander Baring, Brougham, Finlay, Grenfell, Horner, and Western joined in the attack. Brougham called it "the worst and most odious of all taxes—that tax which even necessity could scarcely justify—that most inquisitorial and most oppressive, and most intolerable tax, the property tax, as it is falsely called, being in fact a tax upon income."[75] In the Lords Lansdowne criticized the tax.[76] So many Tories turned against the government on this issue that the tax went down to defeat 238–201, with the only economist support coming from Giddy and the Tory politicians Huskisson, Peel, Rose, and Vansittart.[77]

The debate on the income tax sharpened up a point that had been raised earlier, and was to figure prominently in the parliamentary economists' debates of the next thirty years—the relative burdens on agriculture, and on business and commerce. The argument at this moment centered on taxation, but later was to extend to the Corn Laws and to tithes. As Alexander Baring, at this time a spokesman for commerce, put it: "What he objected to was, a bill which would disregard the other classes of the community, and enact a more lenient rate to the agricultural interest at their expense."[78] A few days later he reiterated the idea: "A number of candid [sic] gentlemen thought that when they were taking care of the landed interest, all the other classes might be trodden down at pleasure."[79]

With the income tax out of the way until its restoration by Peel in 1842, discussion of taxation was in large part absorbed into problems of import duties, and particularly the Corn Laws, already discussed in chapter 3. On domestic taxation the discussion was

74. 1 H, 30:716, 20 Apr. 1815.
75. 1 H, 32:810, 22 Feb. 1816.
76. 1 H, 33:517–18, 22 March 1816.
77. 1 H, 33:451–55, 18 March 1816.
78. 1 H, 32:1133, 5 March 1816.
79. 1 H, 33:218, 13 March 1816. Presumably "candid," as given in *Hansard*, is a misprint for "country."

principally on individual taxes, no one of which was of great fiscal importance but frequently involved important economic issues. A large part of the economists in Parliament, aside from the three diehard Tories—Peel, Rose, and Vansittart—were intellectual children of the Enlightenment. Basic to their thinking was the idea of change in all fields, of the adjustment of men to external economic conditions, in contrast to a structural and stabilized society, in which status and tradition, not economic forces, determined men's actions. The defenders of a status-oriented society may have recognized what today would be called price elasticity of demand, but they rarely if ever mentioned the idea. On the other hand, several economists, and notably Althorp,[80] Howick,[81] Hume,[82] and Poulett Thomson,[83] repeatedly stressed the effect of tax changes on individual products upon consumption and hence upon tax receipts.

The idea that taxation should not place a heavy burden on the poor, and the idea that taxation of the rich was bad because it reduced the funds for the maintenance of labor, seemed at times to be at war with each other, even in the mind of the same economist. Sometimes the issue was bypassed by the view that a reduction in expenditures was more important than any argument as to how to finance unecessary expenditures, as in Parnell's statement: "The object of the Legislature should be to remove all the obstructions to the operations of industry, and one material obstruction was taxation."[84] Even the radical Hume criticized overtaxing the rich: "But what was the best way of promoting the employment of the working classes? It was, in his mind, by not taking money out of the pockets of those who afforded them employment."[85]

Hume's remark, in the same speech, that he would support the reintroduction of a property tax, was symptomatic of a shifting attitude, particularly among the more radical parliamentary economists, toward the income and property tax. The opposition in 1816 by economists was not so much to the income tax as such, but as a

80. 2 H, 23:336–38, 15 March 1830.
81. 3 H, 61:875–96, 18 March 1842.
82. 2 H, 10:950–52, 12 March 1824; 22:480–99, 15 Feb. 1830; 3 H, 33:673–76, 6 May 1836; 48:1375–82, 5 July 1839.
83. 3 H, 2:496–98, 14 Feb. 1831.
84. 2 H, 23:911, 25 March 1830.
85. 3 H, 32:572, 24 March 1836.

symbol of the inquisitional powers of government, and as an instrument for financing what they considered the extravagances of government. By the 1830s emotions had cooled, and it became increasingly clear that in the absence of an income tax government must increase its receipts from indirect taxes. So, although it was the conservative pragmatist Peel who brought back the income tax in 1842, primarily to insure a balanced budget, it was the radical economists, in the decade preceding, who helped to create a more favorable parliamentary climate. Perronet Thompson said: "The cause of the resistance to a property tax, was in the desire of the rich to throw a fair share of the burthen from themselves; and he believed it would never be a 'merry England,' till the taxation was laid on the property of the rich, and not on the consumption of the poor."[86] Three years later Fielden said, in connection with Thomas Attwood's motion to go into committee on the Chartist position: "Let them enact an equitable property tax, by which the rich would be made to support the burthens of the State."[87] Muntz had much the same view.[88]

Several economists opposed reintroduction of the income tax in 1842, but without the fervor with which economists had attacked it in 1816, and possibly more from opposition to tax collectors than to the theory of the income tax.[89] Lansdowne, although on other points favorable to lightening taxation on the poor, still had the view, probably bolstered by touches of the wage-fund theory, that an income tax, even though paid by the rich, hurt the poor by decreasing capital for productive use. His idea was that an income tax had no effect on the consumption of the rich, but only on their savings. The notion that labor income should be taxed less than property income was urged by Brougham.[90] Scrope felt the rate should be less on income from "productive industry" and pointed out the need for making allowance for depreciation in the case of professional incomes.[91] Matthias Attwood said that to tax business profits as highly

86. 3 H, 32:579, 24 March 1836.
87. 3 H, 49:226, 12 July 1839.
88. 3 H, 57:558–59, 23 March 1841.
89. Brougham, 3 H, 61:509, 14 March 1842; Howick, 61:875–96, 18 March 1842; Clay, 61:962, 21 March 1842.
90. 3 H, 61:508, 14 March 1842.
91. 3 H, 61:995–96, 21 March 1842.

as "the owners of fixed property and of permanent annuities was manifestly unjust,"[92] and Hume "thought the principle of taxing incomes arising from capital and landed property, and yearly incomes arising from trades and from professions at the same rate percentage was manifestly unjust."[93]

So many considerations went into the position of economists on Peel's income tax bill, as finally amended, that not too much importance should be attached to the vote on the measure, which was carried 255–149 with a strange collection of bedfellows. Graham, Muntz, and Peel were the only economists to vote for it, whereas Clay, Cobden, Fielden, Howick, and Hume opposed it.[94] Similarly in the Lords, in two crucial votes on the income tax, Bexley, Brougham, and the bishop of Llandaff supported it, and Lansdowne, Monteagle, and Western were in opposition.[95]

The income tax was here to stay, but debates continued, with the issue of the relative importance of direct and indirect taxes, and the broader question of the distribution of tax burden between rich and poor, to the fore. Remarks from several economists indicate the crosscurrents that operated to produce the final policy judgment: they may have disapproved in principle of an income tax, but felt it necessary because indirect taxes had reached their equitable—or politically acceptable—limit. For example, Lansdowne in 1853 defended a plan of phasing out the income tax as the "succession"— i.e., inheritance—tax came to yield more revenue: "He was not enamoured with this tax, nor with the income tax; but the adoption of both was founded on the belief that it was not expedient to carry indirect taxation further."[96] Butt said that "nothing but the strongest necessity would reconcile him to the reimposition of the income tax,"[97] yet a few weeks later voted for a continuation of the tax.[98] Monteagle, in the forefront of reform on so many issues, both economic and political, with advancing years became an outspoken critic of the income tax, and particularly of progressive taxation, and his

92. 3 H, 61:1156, 23 March 1842.
93. 3 H, 62:1257, 29 Apr. 1842.
94. 3 H, 63:1048–54, 31 May 1842.
95. 3 H, 54:83, 17 June 1842; 339, 21 June 1842.
96. 3 H, 129:735, 25 July 1853.
97. 3 H, 126:957, 2 May 1853.
98. 3 H, 127:1212, 6 June 1853.

statement, when the income tax came up for extension in 1853, well summarized the economic issue:

The great battle now to be fought out was that between direct and indirect taxation: and if Parliament allowed itself to be tempted to substitute for the most part direct for indirect taxation, the public credit of the country and its social state would both be brought into the greatest peril.... He held that the rate ought to be the same upon all incomes, and he felt considerable alarm at the admission of the contrary principle. The new principle, begun in injustice, might lead to socialism and confiscation.[99]

There was an anachronistic flavor to Monteagle's speech, for his statement, true as it might have been twenty years before, did not correctly picture the situation as of when he spoke. The issue between direct and indirect taxation had been virtually decided by 1853, the issue still to be decided was the specifics of direct taxation. Brougham, when Crimean War financing was under debate, thought the income tax was the worst of all taxes, but then drove a big wedge through this statement by adding "with the exception of taxes upon food, taxes upon knowledge, and taxes upon the administration of justice."[100] Muntz, who had voted for the income tax, said that he opposed it in principle, but that it was better than increasing taxes on the necessities of the poor.[101]

Proposals for Overhaul of Tax System

Parnell, in the committee he headed in the late 1820s, and in his influential book based on the committee report,[102] had urged a thorough overhaul of the tax system. The small progress toward a goal that a majority of economists approved and that also had increasing support from the Commons at large, is to be explained largely in terms of political infighting.[103] In 1833 F. J. Robinson's motion for a committee to consider revision of the tax system was defeated 221–155, but the minority included nine economists—all with more

---

99. 3 H, 127:799–801, 27 June 1853.
100. 3 H, 132:1045, 1 May 1854.
101. 3 H, cxxxxi, 640–44, 8 Apr. 1856.
102. See pp. 117–18.
103. F. Shehab, in *Progressive Taxation* (Oxford: Clarendon Press, 1953), in chap. 4 traces the development in economic thought and political controversy that led to Peel's reintroduction of the income tax in 1842.

radical leanings: Thomas Attwood, Clay, Cobbett, Fielden, Gisborne, Grote, Hume, Molesworth, and Torrens.[104]

In 1851, when the income tax was to expire, there was a burst of parliamentary oratory, of which the economists contributed their share, and Hume sponsored a motion that it be extended for only one year. This was carried 244–230, in a vote that reflected the many considerations that evidently influenced the voting of economists, with long-time allies on tax questions on both sides of this motion. Only Muntz and J. L. Ricardo voted with Hume, while against him were seven economists, several of whom had heretofore consistently voted with Hume on tax matters: Clay, Cobden, Lewis, Molesworth, Scrope, Perronet Thompson, and Wilson.[105] Hume then secured the appointment of a Select Committee on Income and Property Tax,[106] of which he was chairman. Cobden, J. L. Ricardo, and Wilson were members, and John Stuart Mill, not yet a member of Parliament, gave testimony. The committee simply reported the minutes of evidence, as Hume was unable to convince his fellow committee members to sign his draft report, supporting "capitalization," a plan by which the tax on a given income varied with its present capitalized value.[107]

In 1859 John Gellibrand Hubbard, who had previously written on the income tax, was elected to Parliament as a Conservative and soon mounted a criticism on the tax in its then existing form, in particular the taxing of annuities, and the failure—in his mind—to make proper allowance for business expenses, depreciation, and depletion.[108] His views on many details differed from those of Hume, who had died in 1855, but he replaced the driving force of Hume in urging that the income tax, if it were to be a permanent part of the tax system, be overhauled to remove its many anomalies. On 9 March 1861 he moved for a Select Committee on Income and Property Tax. He was chairman; the other members were Lowe, Northcote, and J. L. Ricardo; and he and John Stuart Mill were witnesses. Disagreements within the committee led to the rejection both of Hubbard's ideas for a rate schedule more favorable to earned in-

104. 3 H, 16:1118, 26 March 1833.
105. 3 H, 116:496–99, 2 May 1851.
106. 3 H, 116:732, 8 May 1851.
107. This is discussed in Shehab, pp. 106–11.
108. 3 H, 155:227–28, 21 July 1859; 156:624–36, 19 Feb. 1861.

come, and the taxation of net rather than gross income, and of Lowe's draft report, supporting a uniform rate and opposing more favorable treatment of savings.[109] The inconclusive report was not followed by legislative action, and it was not until the closing years of the century that a new generation in Parliament made any important overhaul of the income tax. But the efforts of Hubbard, Hume, and Lowe, supplemented by the testimony of John Stuart Mill, had stimulated a discussion that laid the groundwork for later reform.

Window Tax and Salt Tax

Aside from the broader question of tax policy, the controversy over indirect and direct taxes, and over the economic efforts of taxing low incomes as compared with high incomes, there were a number of recurring debates over individual taxes, notably the window tax, the salt tax, and taxes on publications. The window tax was of many years' standing in 1780, but not until the 1820s did the economists discuss it in Parliament, and their attitude was overwhelmingly critical—partly on grounds of health, partly on grounds of equity between rich and poor. In 1821 David Ricardo was joined by Grenfell, Parnell, Rice, and Western in support of a motion, defeated 109–83, to repeal the house and window tax.[110] The following year Hume urged repeal of the house and window tax, but Vansittart opposed repeal.[111] Hume was not one to give up easily, and nearly a quarter of a century later he was campaigning against the window tax, which he said was injurious to health, and "most unequal in its operation—pressing most heavily upon those who were least able to bear such a burden—and its collection was also attended with great difficulties."[112] And then in 1848 he called the window tax "one of the most mischievous of taxes,"[113] but his motion to bring in a bill for its repeal was defeated 160–68, with only Perronet Thompson voting with Hume, and the economists' opposition coming from Cayley, Graham, Lewis, Peel, and Scrope.[114] Charles Wood included in his 1850 budget repeal of the window tax, and so it died, without a

---

109. See the discussion in Shehab, pp. 141–57.
110. 2 H, 4:1122, 1127–28, 6 March 1821. Ricardo's speech is also in his *Works*, 5:79–80.
111. 2 H, 7:1491–93, 1495–97, 2 July 1822.
112. 3 H, 78:1078–79, 18 March 1845.
113. 3 H, 96:1269, 24 Feb. 1848.
114. 3 H, 96:1297–99, 24 Feb. 1848.

ripple of discussion from the economists, who for three decades had said so many harsh words about it.

The salt tax had a similar history. It was of long standing and too easy and sure a source of revenue for those in power to give up lightly. In 1805 Rose felt an increase in the salt tax essential,[115] and Huskisson supported him.[116] In 1817 Vansittart, then chancellor of the Exchequer, opposed a motion for a committee on the salt duties.[117] The motion was defeated in a thin house, 79–70, with Brougham, Grenfell, and Parnell in the minority.[118] Grenfell, in 1819,[119] urged the repeal of the salt duty, but got no support. And in 1822 a motion to introduce a bill for gradual reduction of the salt duties was defeated 169–165, with the familiar picture of the Tory economists in government opposing any change, and Althorp, Brougham, Hume, Ricardo, Rice, and Whitmore favoring the reduction.[120] The government's support of the salt duties had been on grounds of fiscal necessity rather than economic theory, and with the budgetary situation better the government reversed its view, and the salt tax ended in February 1825.

Newspaper Tax

The newspaper tax had much the same history, as far as the economists were concerned, as did the window tax and the salt tax. The economists of the Tory government defended it, primarily on the ground that it was needed for budgetary balance; but occasionally suggesting that such a tax helped to hold down that potent revolutionary force—the printed word. In 1797 the rate had been raised to 2½ d. for each four-page sheet, and Smart said of the situation in 1800: "Few persons below the middle rank of life could afford to buy a newspaper regularly."[121] In 1819 Vansittart, for the Tory government, urged a tightening of the newspaper tax,[122] and was supported by the recently elected Wilmot, an economist with con-

115. 1 H, 3:568, 19 Feb. 1805. Rose also defended the salt duties on later days: 3:702–3, 4 March 1805, and 3:789, 7 March 1805.
116. 1 H, 3:790, 7 March 1805.
117. 1 H, 35:1326–28, 25 Apr. 1817.
118. 1 H, 35:132, 25 Apr. 1817.
119. 1 H, 34:1036, 18 March 1819.
120. 2 H, 6:860–62, 28 Feb. 1822.
121. 1:41.
122. 1 H, 41:575–76, 1 Dec. 1819.

servative political views. Wilmot stated bluntly what many other political conservatives undoubtedly felt: " . . . it was to check that source of sedition and blasphemy whose contaminating waters were spreading around their pollution, that he gave his vote in support of the measure."[123] A motion to go into committee on the bill—equivalent to its support—was approved 222–76, with six economists—Althorp, Brougham, Graham, Hume, Parnell, and David Ricardo, in opposition.[124] The bill was passed without formal vote in either the Commons or Lords.[125] In the following years, in addition to Brougham and Hume, Davenport and Grote spoke against the newspaper tax, with Peel the only economist to defend it, principally on the ground that it was a help in controlling a seditious press.[126] Where Peel saw danger in the freedom of the printed word, Torrens saw it as giving stability to society: " . . . the only way to prevent the working classes from being imposed upon and influenced by injurious doctrines was, to counteract the effect of those doctrines, by rendering knowledge cheap. . . . If the people had knowledge, they would see that their interests were dovetailed in with the interests of society . . . by the present system, the people were kept in ignorance of the very first principles of political science."[127] Grote buttressed his support of repeal by an argument that reads strangely in the light of history—that it was important that workers have access to literature that would explain the evils of trade unions.[128]

The days of what critics called "taxes on knowledge" were numbered, and only a combination of inertia and supposed fiscal necessity was preserving them. In 1836 the Commons voted 241 to 218 to reduce sharply the duty on newspapers to a figure which enabled the lower middle class and better-paid workers to buy copies, and fourteen of the nineteen economists in Parliament supported the reduction.[129] Economists had won their main objective, and criticism of the small remaining tax was dulled. Not until 1855 was the tax effectively repealed, but before that it provided Cobden an occasion to get in a word for three of his favorite themes: abolition of the tax,

123. 1 H, 41:1360, 20 Dec. 1819.
124. 1 H, 41:1366, 20 Dec. 1819.
125. 60 Geo. III, c. 9.
126. 3 H, 4:426–29, 28 June 1831.
127. 3 H, 6:12, 15 Aug. 1831.
128. 3 H, 23:1221–22, 22 May 1834.
129. 3 H, 34:663–67, 20 June 1836.

the advantages of education, and the progressive spirit of America. He reported that the visitor in New York would see "among the first sights that met his eye, the cabmen (and they were all either Irishmen or blacks, for no American citizen would condescend to be a cabman), each with his small paper in his hand; and the same was to be seen among the porters waiting to be hired."[130]

Predominant Economists' View on Fiscal Policy

On no economic issue, with the exception of the Corn Laws, was there such uniformity of opinion among economists as on issues of fiscal policy. On the role of the Bank of England, on the legal tender, even on regulation of the hours of labor, there were so many differences of opinion among economists that it is not possible to speak of them as representing a school. But on fiscal policy there was close to unanimity on most major questions. It is true that on the broad issue of a balanced budget there was little difference of opinion between the economists and other members of Parliament, but on the question as to how that balance should be maintained the majority of economists differed from the predominant parliamentary opinion. The economists were in the forefront in bringing simple financial realities into the discussion of the sinking fund, as a corrective to mysticism that so often dominated the discussions. The economists continually pressed searching questions on the purposes of government expenditure. Although much of what they said was on its face opposition to all government expenditures, the wellspring of their opposition was the fact that much government expenditure was in effect handouts, relief payments, and unemployment benefits for a privileged aristocracy. Hume was the most persistent critic of expenditures, but at the same time he spoke for other less vocal but like-minded economists, and probably convinced others of the need to curb abuses in expenditures. Alexander Baring said, after Hume's exposé of an outlay for a staff of a garrison where there was no garrison: "His hon. friend the member for Montrose, might possibly diminish his influence in the House by the manner in which he objected to every vote. It was, however, unquestionable, that his vigilance had seen an insuperable obstacle to

130. 3 H, 125:1182, 14 Apr. 1853.

many objectionable practices and designs."[131] Many economists opposed continuing the income tax in 1816, but their hostility seems to have been based more on the feeling that the income tax would provide more funds for government extravagance than on any theory of taxation. When it became clear that an income tax was the only realistic alternative to indirect taxes on consumption goods, the predominant economist opinion was in favor of an income tax. Although economists did not develop any modern concept of capacity to pay, and showed little enthusiasm for progressive taxation, many of their statements showed glimmerings of modern tax theory in their opposition to the regressive taxes on windows, salt, and newspapers.

131. 2 H, 16:598, 20 Feb. 1827.

Chapter 8

Education

Most of the economists were spiritual children of the Enlightenment, and this orientation revealed itself many times in their debates on education. It was not merely how much national income was to be devoted to education, or how education was to be financed, but also such broader questions as to whether it was sound policy to educate the lower classes, whether the Church of England should control education, whether nonadherents of the Church of England should be allowed to obtain university degrees, and whether public money should be used for Protestant proselytizing in Ireland.

Educational Setting of 1780

In 1780 England and Ireland had no educational system, and practically no government financial support went to education at any level. The Universities of Oxford and Cambridge were endowments of the Established Church, and education was limited to adherents of the Established Church, and was almost untouched by the scientific spirit or the winds of the Enlightenment. Readers of Adam Smith and Edward Gibbon know their low opinion of Oxford of the mid-eighteenth century. The Scottish universities and Trinity College, Dublin, were less church dominated, and there the spirit of inquiry had freer scope. In Scotland the local governments had established primary schools, and the literacy rate was higher than in England or Ireland. In those two countries government took no responsibility for elementary education. The aristocracy and upper middle class received their early education at home, or at private schools usually run by clergymen, and later at the so-called public schools. Whatever education the poor received was largely a matter of chance—either from a local philanthropic endowment or from a public-spirited clergyman. As late as 1829 Brougham said that in two thousand English parishes with a total population of 578,000 there were no schools of any sort.[1] There were frequent charges, from 1800 on, that many educational endowments were abused, and were not providing the education that their donors had intended. South of the Tweed and west of the Irish Channel, establishment thinking of 1780 was that literacy for the lower classes had dangerous overtones for social and political stability.

Plans for Elementary Educational Reform

In 1807 Samuel Whitbread, as part of a broad plan for reforming the Poor Laws, included voluntary national education with religious instruction. The attacks on the educational provisions from Rose and Giddy are suggestive of the establishment view. Rose feared that education of the "labouring poor" for more than two years "would . . . tend rather to raise their minds about their lot in life";[2] and went on to say: "He had no doubt that the poor ought to be taught to read; as to writing, he had some doubt, because those who had learnt to write well, were not willing to abide at the plough, but looked to a situation in some counting house."[3] Giddy, at that time a political reactionary, who later mellowed from age or from the shifting winds of public opinion, was if anything more extreme than Rose in opposing education for "the labouring classes of the poor":

. . . it would in effect, be found to be prejudicial to their morals and happiness; it would teach them to despise their lot in life, instead of making them good servants in agriculture, and other laborious employments to which their rank in society has destined them; instead of teaching them subordination, it would render them factious and refractory, as was evident in the manufacturing counties; it would enable them to read seditious pamphlets, vicious books, and publications against Christianity; it would render them insolent to their superiors.[4]

The education provisions of Whitbread's bill received no attention from other economists, other than Petty, who "expressed his difference in opinion from those gentlemen who apprehended that danger might result from carrying the education of the lower orders too far, as they expressed it."[5]

1. 2 H, 21:1762, 5 June 1829.
2. 1 H, 9:539, 24 Apr. 1807.
3. 1 H, 9:800, 13 July 1807.
4. 1 H, 9:798–99, 13 July 1807.

The first economist to urge positive action on education was Brougham, who in 1816 brought to parliamentary attention a life-long mission to improve education at all levels. He spoke of the deplorable educational situation among the poor of London, of the misuse of the funds of educational endowments, and of the need for parliamentary aid for education; and secured the appointment of a committee "to inquire into the education of the lower orders in the metropolis."[6] In addition to Brougham as chairman, Horner, Parnell, and Rose were members of the committee. The committee was renewed in 1817 and 1818, with Brougham and Parnell again members. In view of later developments in British education, it is noteworthy that Brougham's stress was on the private financing of education, in particular by a correction of the abuses of existing educational endowments.[7] The idea that education was injurious to work habits was strong at this time, and Brougham was not the last to cite American experience in refutation:

America affords another instance which deserves to be cited as a triumphant refutation of the whimsies of ingenious men, who fancy they can descry something in education incompatible with general industry. That is surely the last country in all the world, where idleness can expect to find encouragement. The imputation upon it has rather been that the inhabitants are too busy to be very refined. An idler there is a kind of monster; he can find no place in any of the innumerable tribes that swarm over that vast continent. In the rapid stream of its active and strenuous population it is impossible for any one to stand still a moment; if he partakes not of its motion he will be overwhelmed or dashed aside. Yet such is the conviction there, that popular education forms the best foundation of national prosperity, that in all the grants made by the government of their boundless territory, a certain portion of each township, I believe the twentieth lot, is reserved for the expense of instructing and maintaining the poor.[8]

Brougham's committees produced comprehensive reports, devastating in their criticism of English education,[9] and in 1820 Brougham sponsored a bill for the better education of the poor in England and

5. 1 H, 9:805, 13 July 1807.
6. 1 H, 34:633–36, 21 May 1816.
7. 1 H, 37:817, 5 March 1818.
8. 1 H, 38:594, 8 May 1818.
9. P.P. 1816 (427, 469, 495, 497, 498) IV; 1817 (479) III; 1818 (136, 356, 426, 427, 428) IV.

Wales. The bill provided, probably against Brougham's own preference but in recognition of the existing power structure of the country, that the Church of England was to control the schools, and that all teachers must be members of the Established Church. The bill aroused the opposition of Catholics; and of Dissenters, of whom there were few in Parliament but who in many areas were a political power at the hustings. It died, and from then until 1868 the religious situation colored every parliamentary consideration of education.

One of the few parliamentary appropriations for primary education was an annual grant, dating back many years, to the Irish Protestant Charter Schools. Hume objected to this grant as the use of government money for religious proselytism. His motion to reduce the grant was defeated, 74–33, but economists—two of them Irish Protestants—accounted for five of the minority: Althorp, Hume, Parnell, Rice, and Western.[10] Two years later Hume and Rice were again critical of the use of government money for the support of Protestant education in Ireland,[11] and in the Lords King and Lansdowne took the same view.[12] Torrens "considered it most unfair to tax Catholics for the support of a system of education they disliked."[13]

Education was temporarily put in the background by the battle over Catholic emancipation and over parliamentary reform, but with these issues settled for the time being by the legislation of 1829 and 1832, the education controversy resumed in the early 1830s. Grote urged the government to do something for education;[14] Althorp, while not opposed to the extension of popular education, said that Parliament "ought to consider whether they could not acquire education for the people without the immediate and direct interference of the Government."[15] He opposed compulsory education, as did Peel.[16] At this time not a single economist favored compulsory education, which was frequently referred to in a derogatory way as Prussian, and alien to British ideas of personal liberty and the economic doctrine of free choice.

10. 2 H, 10:1046, 15 March 1824.
11. 2 H, 15:2–10, 27–28, 20 March 1826.
12. 2 H, 15:34–36, 21 March 1826.
13. 3 H, 4:1255, 14 July 1831.
14. 3 H, 20:166–67, 30 July 1833.
15. Ibid., p. 168.
16. 3 H, 20:172–73, 30 July 1833.

From several economists came an idea with a utilitarian flavor, that as the people were more educated they would be more rational, politically more enlightened, and less prone to crime. A dissenting opinion came from Cobbett, that master of the purple language, a political radical whose nostalgic devotion to an agricultural England that was passing sometimes led him to agree with reactionaries on particular issues. He "could not consent to take from the people one single farthing in the way of taxes, directly or indirectly, in order to teach the working classes reading and writing. . . . education had been more and more spread, but what did it all tend to? Nothing but to increase the number of schoolmasters and school-mistresses—that new race of idlers. Crime, too, went on increasing. If so, what reason was there to tax the people for the increase of education?"[17]

It appeared that every economist, with the exception of Gisborne and Cobbett, believed in popular education, but only on his own terms. In the Lords Brougham and Lansdowne pressed for education bills in 1837, but both made clear their opposition to compulsory education.[18] Clay, a supporter of a more active program of national education, said in discussing the topic:

It was extremely unfortunate that no subject could be debated in that House without appeals being made to the religious feelings of some portion of the people. Whether the measures under consideration had reference to the granting of municipal corporations to Ireland, or whether they had reference to any other portion of the policy of the country, still those measures were discussed with reference to the effects which it was argued they would have upon the religion of some particular portion of the people.[19]

In 1833 the Commons, in a thin house in which economists' participation was high in relation to their number, had voted 50–26 an appropriation of £20,000 in support of private plans to educate children of the poor. Six economists supported the appropriation—Althorp, Graham, Pryme, Rice, Scrope, and Torrens—and Cobbett, Fielden, and Hume opposed it.[20] In 1839 a measure to increase the annual appropriation for education to £30,000 was passed 275–273, with all sixteen economists voting, and only Matthias Attwood,

17. 3 H, 20:734–35, 17 Aug. 1833. He made much the same point the following year: 24:131–33, 3 June 1834.
18. 3 H, 39:425–27, 432–64, 1 Dec. 1837.
19. 3 H, 43:725, 14 June 1838.
20. 3 H, 20:736–37, 17 Aug. 1833.

Fielden, and Graham opposed.[21] In the Lords Lansdowne, in supporting the measure, spoke of the low quality of English elementary education: " . . . excluding Spain and Russia and taking only the central states of Europe, England would come last in the scale, both as to the quantity and the quality of its secular education." And he denied that the Established Church had any right to control the education of those who were not its adherents.[22] The annual appropriations in aid of private education were subsequently increased, but this was as far as Parliament was prepared to go in support of a national system of education, despite the increasingly favorable attitude toward the principle.

Religious Issue and National Educational Policy

The religious issue continued to be the stumbling block to any national educational program. Molesworth wanted the national government to play a role, but felt education "ought not to be placed under the exclusive control of the clergy of the Established Church."[23] In 1843 a resolution "that in no plan of education maintained and enforced by the State, should any attempt be made to inculcate peculiar religious opinions" was defeated 156–60, with Fielden, Gisborne, Hume, and J. L. Ricardo favoring the motion, and Graham and Peel the only opponents among the economists.[24] Despite his extreme laissez-faire views on many issues, Hume, like Adam Smith, made an exception of education, and in 1844 urged it be compulsory: "He did not think it an invasion of liberty to compel parents to bring up their children so as to perform their duties as men, and their duties to the state."[25] Howick felt it "not desirable to make education completely governmental," as there was not sufficient toleration among the various religious sects.[26] Brougham in the Lords continued his opposition to compulsory education, and added a comment that is further evidence of the religious issue as a barrier to a national educational system: "Both Church and sects loved edu-

21. 3 H, 48:793–98, 24 June 1839.
22. 3 H, 48:1255–74, 5 July 1839.
23. 3 H, 24:130–31, 3 June 1834. He expressed the same view thirteen years later: 3 H, 91:1183–95, 22 Apr. 1847.
24. 3 H, 69:565, 18 May 1843.
25. 3 H, 70:1344, 25 July 1843.
26. 3 H, 76:1077–81, 19 July 1844.

cation much; but there was one thing which both the Church and the Dissenters loved more, and that was controversy, which made them neglect the great object of education, and made them prefer more than anything else—victory; they lost sight of the main object in the glory of the victory: that was what he universally found."[27]

The Russell government's proposal in 1847 of limited aid to education, but with provisions for church control, precipitated a debate over religion rather than education. Gisborne, taking over the role of Cobbett as a belittler of education, ridiculed its advantages and poked fun at the situation in Prussia and in Scotland, which others had held up as models.[28] Hume, after criticizing Gisborne, said: " . . . in the United States, where education was widely diffused, the morality was very high, and the females were remarkable for the purity and virtue of their lives."[29] Clay,[30] Molesworth,[31] and Muntz[32] all favored a national system of education, but objected to control by the Church of England. As Muntz put it: "He thought the Government as much bound to provide the means of educating those who were not able to educate themselves, as to collect the taxes," but wanted the education to be secular.[33] The 1847 budget included an education grant of £100,000, and such grants were continued, but the religious issue prevented, until after 1868, any comprehensive program of national education.

Cobden, ardent free trader though he was in most fields, agreed with Hume that the government should furnish compulsory education, but without religious instruction.[34] After they had passed from the scene Henry Fawcett in 1867 preached the same message of state-financed compulsory education: " . . . the state was performing one of its clearest and most undoubted duties when it rescued a child from a grievous and irreparable injury."[35] Hubbard and Lowe, although not opposed to government education, proposed conditions that in the political setting of the time hindered positive action.

27. 3 H, 89:869–77, 5 Feb. 1847.
28. 3 H, 111:1066–74, 20 Apr. 1847.
29. 3 H, 111:1171–75, 22 Apr. 1847.
30. 3 H, 111:1158–67, 22 Apr. 1847.
31. 3 H, 111:1183–95, 22 Apr. 1847.
32. 3 H, 111:1280–81, 23 Apr. 1847.
33. 3 H, 111:1280–81, 23 Apr. 1847.
34. 3 H, 116:1282–89, 22 May 1851; 132:276–83, 12 May 1854; 139:1415–18, 26 July 1855.
35. 3 H, 185:1067–68, 26 Feb. 1867.

Lowe felt that education should be voluntary, and although willing to give some government assistance, hoped that the desire for education would become so great that such financial aid would no longer be necessary,[36] and Hubbard poked fun at the idea of compulsory education, and at the same time stressed the importance of having religious education.[37]

Religious Discrimination at Universities

In 1825 Brougham worked, in and out of Parliament, for the founding of University College, London, later to become part of London University, both to provide higher education at less cost than at Oxford and Cambridge, and to provide it for those who could not subscribe to the religious tests of Oxford and Cambridge.[38] The establishment of London University was originally supported by Hume, but he showed his devotion to the market principle in higher education by later resigning from its Council: "The reason of his declining any further connexion with the London University was, because the Council would give salaries."[39] An incident that reflected the opposition of Hume and Brougham both to expenditures in general and in particular for unpopular members of the royal family, came in connection with a debate over educating abroad the young son of the reactionary Duke of Cumberland. *Hansard* reports Hume's remark: "At all events, let the young prince be brought to this country. He would undertake for 100 £ a year to get him a better education than he could get abroad for 6000 £. [Mr. Brougham said, in a low tone, 'Aye, at the new University.'] Aye, resumed Mr. Hume, at the new University."[40] The grant was approved 120–97, but seven economists were in opposition—Alexander Baring, Brougham, Grenfell, Hume, Parnell, Rice, and Western.[41]

Whereas the parliamentary history of the economists and primary education was largely that of attempts, wrecked on the shoals of religious controversy, to establish a national education, at the uni-

36. 3 H, 151:148–50, 21 June 1858.
37. 3 H, 192, 1994–97, 24 June 1868.
38. 2 H, 13:840–41, 26 May 1825; 1033–36, 3 June 1825.
29. 3 H, 4:986, 8 July 1831.
40. 2 H, 13:913, 27 May 1825.
41. 2 H, 13:951–52, 30 May 1825.

versity level, aside from the foundation of the University of London, it was largely a matter of attacking the privileges of Oxford and Cambridge. This again was in large part a religious issue, but colored by opposition to taxing the poor to subsidize the education of the rich. Hume objected to parliamentary grants for salaries at Oxford and Cambridge: "Oxford was rich enough, and ought to support its own Professors. Those who went to Oxford should pay for their own education. Why should the people of England be required to assist in paying for the education of the sons of noblemen, and other gentlemen of great wealth?"[42] But few if any economists shared Hume's feeling. Rice defended the grants: "The Universities were not devoted exclusively to the highest classes of society; many of the humblest received the benefit of education in those venerable institutions."[43] The grant was approved 203–15, with Hume the only economist in opposition.[44]

In 1834 both Rice and Pryme, sitting for Cambridge borough, urged that Cambridge degrees not be limited to adherents of the Established Church.[45] Peel, at his reactionary worst, would have none of such an idea: " . . . the demand on the part of the Dissenters, to be admitted to degrees in the Universities of England, is, as a claim of abstract right, without exception, the most extravagant demand which has been advanced in modern times."[46] The Commons then passed a bill, 164–75, to admit Dissenters to universities but not to grant them degrees, with nine economists in favor, and three—Matthias Attwood, Alexander Baring, and Peel—in opposition.[47] The Lords defeated the bill, 187–85, with Brougham and Lansdowne supporting it, and Bexley and the bishop of Llandaff opposing.[48]

Breaking down the privileged position of the Established Church at the universities was an idea whose time was coming; the only question was how long the forces of reaction could postpone that time. It was not only the university religious tests that bothered

42. 3 H, 4:982, 8 July 1831. Much the same point was made the following year, 12:477–78, 13 Apr. 1832.
43. 3 H, 4:982, 8 July 1831.
44. Ibid., p. 988.
45. 3 H, 22:569–87, 597–98, 24 March 1834.
46. 3 H, 22:704, 26 March 1834.
47. 3 H, 25:653–55, 28 July 1834.
48. 3 H, 25:886–88, 1 Aug. 1834.

many economists, but also the attitude of university spokesmen that they were purely private institutions, and that the government had no right to inquire into their administration or use of their endowment. Brougham and Hume had, to no avail, challenged that view in the 1820s, and now new voices of criticism were added in Pryme,[49] Rice,[50] and Perronet Thompson. In 1845 Hume called for an investigation of Oxford and Cambridge: "It had been said that they were private property; now, if that were the case, they belonged to the Catholics; but if they were public property transferred to their present possessors by the authority of Parliament, then they came within the range of Parliamentary inquiry."[51] Thompson's attack, five years later, on the exclusion of Dissenters from the universities did not crack the defenses of the establishment, but it was a good statement of what was to come: "He did believe that this was a point on which, without the smallest unfriendliness, he was justified in saying the Universities must in the end give way, simply because it was not just and in accordance with the events that were taking place in the world."[52] Only four years later, by a vote of 252–161, the Commons approved that for matriculation at Oxford no oath be required except the oath of allegiance. The strength of economists' feeling is evidenced by the support of seven—Butt, Cayley, Clay, Cobden, Hankey, Muntz, and J. L. Ricardo—and opposition only by Graham.[53] The same day a motion that went further, to have the elimination of oaths apply also to recipients of degrees, was defeated 205–196, with the same lineup of economists as in the previous motion.[54]

Further legislative action against university test oaths received strong support from Goschen, who wanted a bill "to get rid of a system [of oaths] which distressed conscience, promoted dishonesty, impeded learning, discouraged theological study at the university, and on the whole was unjust, intolerant, and inquisitorial."[55] The

49. 3 H, 38:509–12, 4 May 1837.
50. Ibid., pp. 517–20.
51. 3 h,79:440, 10 Apr. 1845.
52. 3 H,110:746, 23 Apr. 1850.
53. 3 h,134:585-88, 22 June 1854.
54. Ibid., pp. 590-92.
55. 3 H, 174:155, 16 March 1864. He made remarks to the same effect on 24 June 1863 (171:1394–96); 1 June 1864 (175:1033–36), and 14 June 1865 (180:185–207).

only other economists who spoke on the subject were Fawcett, who shared Goschen's view,[56] and Hubbard and Northcote, who wanted to maintain the tie between Oxford and Cambridge and the Established Church.[57] Though other economists said nothing in support of the Goschen-Fawcett position, their votes left little doubt that the maintenance of Oxford and Cambridge as preserves of the Established Church had little support among the declining ranks of parliamentary economists. (Only eight were in Commons in the 1865–68 Parliament.) In 1866 the Commons approved, 245–172, a measure whittling down still further the oath requirement at Oxford, with five economists—Fawcett, Goschen, Hankey, Lowe, and John Stuart Mill—in the majority, and only Northcote in the minority (Hubbard and Scrope did not vote).[58] The following year a motion to eliminate the oath provision at Cambridge was approved 253–116, with practically the same lineup of economists.[59] But legislation to implement these motions was a casualty of political infighting, and was withdrawn in 1868. Only in 1872 was legislation passed outlawing all test oaths at Oxford, Cambridge, and Durham.[60]

56. 3 H, 187:1248–51, 29 May 1867.
57. 3 H, 182:671–82, 21 March 1866; 192, 230–32, 13 May 1868.
58. 3 H, 184:341–46, 13 June 1866.
59. 3 H, 186:1443–46, 10 Apr. 1867.
60. 34 & 35 Vict., c. 26.

Chapter 9

Relief of Poverty: Poor Laws
and Emigration

The economists' views on education involved little economic theory in the narrower sense, but in large part reflected their social philosophy, a philosophy in many cases influenced by utilitarianism. On the other hand, the debate over the relief of poverty raised some fundamental principles of classical economics, in particular population theory and wage theory, although this theory was sometimes colored by emotionalism based on political and social considerations.

Poor Relief under Old Poor Law

In 1780 there was no uniform system, in England and Wales, for relief of destitution, whether the result of old age, illness, or incapacity, or the inability of the able-bodied to secure employment. Relief, which was governed by legislation that went back to the reign of Elizabeth I, was handled entirely by the parishes, which enjoyed a high degree of autonomy in interpreting and administering the laws. Although practices varied as between parishes, in general there was little if any distinction between situations calling for "indoor relief" to the elderly, the blind, the crippled widow with six children, and "outdoor relief" to the able-bodied man without employment. The costs were met by "poor rates," which were in effect real estate taxes, fixed by the poor law wardens of each parish at the figure necessary to cover relief needs.

There had always been criticisms of the operation of the Poor Laws, both by those seeking relief, and by those who paid poor rates. The criticism was endemic, but beginning around 1780 it increased and became more specific. The percentage of the population in receipt of poor relief became greater; at the four dates from 1688 to 1776 for which there are estimates, the highest figure was 3.8, and then rose steadily until in 1818, in the post-Napoleonic depression, it was 13.2, and in 1834, at the time of the enactment of the new Poor Law, it was 8.8.[1] Similarly, the approximate per capita poor rate rose from 2s.6d. in 1688 to 5s. in 1784, 8s.3d. in 1801, 13s.3d. in 1818, and in 1834 was 9s.1d.

The principal criticisms related to:

1. The failure to distinguish between "indoor relief" and "outdoor relief," and the feeling, particularly on the part of those who paid poor rates, that many on outdoor relief were shiftless loafers who preferred handouts to hard work.

2. The increase in poor rates, and in some cases the great difference in rates among parishes. This criticism was bolstered by a widely held belief that industrial areas, with a working population drawn in large part from agriculture and which returned to their place of origin in times of distress, put the burden of relief on agricultural landowners.

3. The "law of settlement" by which those applying for relief were sent back to the parish in which they were born, or in which they had previously lived for a given number of years. This law aggravated the situation, indicated in 2 above, of agricultural areas having to finance poor relief of persons thrown out of employment elsewhere.

4. The introduction in 1795 of what came to be known as the Speenhamland system by which in some parishes payments from the poor rates supplemented wages, which, because of rising prices, were not adequate to meet minimum family needs.

The rapid population expansion in the last quarter of the eighteenth century, the increase in enclosures, and the rise in the cost of food in the late 1790s all contributed to make matters worse. Almost everyone, in and out of Parliament, felt that something ought to be done about it, but few had any specific proposals. The publication in 1798 of Malthus's *Essay on the Principle of Population* gave a new dimension to the situation, by adding intellectual respectability to the idea that too liberal relief might be worse than useless by simply

---

1. Sidney and Beatrice Webb, *English Poor Law History: Part II: The Last Hundred Years* (London: Longmans, Green and Co.; New York: Toronto, 1929), Appendix 2, "English Poor Law Statistics," pp. 1036–55. As the Webbs point out, these figures are not exact, but they are a useful indication of the order of magnitude, and particularly of change of magnitude.

adding to the numbers applying for relief. The idea that a tougher poor law—tougher both toward able-bodied workers who preferred relief to work, and tougher toward those who, in or out of wedlock, were increasing the population with the assurance that the poor rates would take care of them and their offspring—was needed appeared repeatedly in parliamentary debates after 1800.

In Ireland there was no poor law before 1838. Those who were not taken care of by private benevolence of the church, a patron, or relatives, died, became wandering mendicants, or moved across the Irish Channel and there depressed wages and in some cases shared in English poor relief. In Scotland the administration of the Poor Law was under the control of the Church of Scotland, and was financed in large part out of voluntary contributions by the Church. Furthermore, under the Scottish system it was much less common to give any relief to an able-bodied adult, even if completely destitute. This largely voluntary system continued in Scotland until 1844.[2]

Proposals for Reform of Poor Law

In 1807 Samuel Whithead proposed wide-ranging reforms in the Poor Laws, including the establishment of schools for poor children, referred to in chapter 8, and a change in the law of settlement, but his bills died and the Poor Laws remained unchanged. Few economists in Parliament showed interest, one way or the other, in any move at this time to amend them, although Giddy, reflecting his then conservative views, "was of opinion, that the whole of the poor laws should be repealed."[3] Horner, however, objected to a more rigorous law of settlement "as condemning as vagrants and criminals, persons who might be legally entitled to a settlement."[4]

Giddy continued his criticism of the Poor Laws.[5] In 1812 he "thought the whole system of the poor laws required alteration,"[6] and six years later, when about one person in seven was on poor relief, he expressed the fear: "Unless some limit were set to the rapid progress of the poor-rates, the ruin of the country was inevi-

---

2. This summary description of the Irish and Scottish situation is based on the Webbs, 2:Appendix 2, "The Irish and Scottish Poor Laws," pp. 1025–35.

3. 1 H, 11:423, 10 May 1808.

4. Ibid., 423–24.

5. 1 H, 19:515, 26 March 1811.

6. 1 H, 21:1261, 13 March 1812.

table."[7] Horner spoke up against provisions which he felt too severe on recipients of relief,[8] and Lansdowne objected to a proposed amendment in 1818 on much the same grounds.[9]

In 1819 a Poor Rates Misapplication Bill, which was intended to ease the standards for granting relief, particularly to women with illegitimate children, met the full blast of Hume's rugged individualism and Scottish morality.[10]

He disapproved of the bill. Until the country looked the evil fairly in the face, and taught the labourer to depend more on himself, no adequate remedy could be supplied. This measure, if passed into a law, would increase the evil. He wished a course to be taken in this country, similar to that which had been adopted in Scotland, where, if a woman had an illegitimate child, she was obliged to maintain it. What followed? She was careful not to repeat the fault she had committed, lest she should bring into the world a second. In England, women frequently threw two, three, or four children on the parish. He had hoped the hon. gentleman, in bringing in this bill, would have gone the length of declaring, "that from and after the passing of this act, no child legitimate or illegitimate should be entitled to a maintenance from the parish." Such a course, if taken, would strike at the root of the evil, and such a measure he still hoped to see introduced.

Lansdowne objected to the bill on the grounds that it would help the children of improvident families at the expense of children of parents "who struggled to bring up their families in decent and moral habits."[11] David Ricardo's first speech in Parliament was in opposition to the bill.

. . . the two great evils for which it was desirable to provide a remedy, were the tendency towards a redundant population, and the inadequacy of the wages to the support of the labouring classes; and he apprehended, that the measure now proposed would not afford any security against the continuance of these evils. On the contrary, he thought that, if a provision were made for all the children of the poor, it would only increase the evil; for if parents felt assured that an asylum would be provided for their children, in which they would be treated with humanity and tenderness, there would then be no check to that increase of population which was so apt to

7. 1 H, 37:735, 3 March 1818.
8. 1 H, 27:278–80, 13 Dec. 1813; 28:31, 8 June 1814.
9. 1 H, 38:915–16, 25 May 1818.
10. 1 H, 40:472, 17 May 1819.
11. Ibid., p. 1514, 5 July 1819.

take place among the labouring classes. With regard to the other evil, the inadequacy of the wages, it ought to be remembered, that if this measure should have the effect of raising them, they would still be no more than the wages of a single man, and would never rise so high as to afford a provision for a man with a family.[12]

The bill passed the Commons but died in the Lords.

With the temporary improvement of economic conditions in the 1820s, and the concentration of public concern on Catholic Emancipation and Parliamentary Reform, there was little parliamentary discussion of the Poor Laws. But, as the Webbs have pointed out,[13] three ideas were influencing public thinking on the Poor Laws:

1. Public relief of destitution by tax funds degraded the character of recipients and induced bad behavior.

2. Operation of the Malthusian principle of population—of the first edition of the *Essay*—made relief of poverty futile, and only increased the number of destitute.

3. The national government should impose more uniform standards upon local Poor Law authorities.

The feeling that something ought to be done about the Poor Laws was given added stimulus by rural insurrections in southeast England in the latter part of 1830, followed by executions and wholesale imprisonment or transportation to Botany Bay. In 1832 Althorp, the leader of the Commons, speaking for the Whig government, which had been spurred on by two other economist members, Howick, under-secretary for the colonies, and the activist Brougham, recently raised to the peerage and now lord chancellor, announced that the government would appoint a Royal Commission on the Poor Laws. The recommendations of the Commission[14] covered some 150 pages, and their main thrust was: (1) abolition of outdoor relief to able-bodied persons or their families, and relief to them to be given only in "well regulated workhouses"; (2) creation of a Central Board for control and administration of local Poor Law authorities; (3) tightening of the law of settlement; and (4) stricter rules governing relief to mothers of illegitimate children.

12. 1 H, 39:1158–59, 25 March 1819. In Ricardo, *Works*, 5:1.
13. 8:7.
14. P.P. 1834 (44), 17. The recommendations are summarized by the Webbs, 8:58–61.

New Poor Law of 1834

Althorp moved to introduce a bill for the amendment of the Poor Laws,[15] and economists who were far to the left on most political and economic issues joined Tory reactionaries in favoring a more restrictive Poor Law. Clay, Grote, Hume, Scrope, and Torrens supported the motion, although not approving every detail of the bill.[16]

There was little dispute in principle over indoor relief, except where illegitimate children were concerned. Outdoor relief invoked a wide range of opinion, even among economists who were in agreement on most other issues. At one end of the spectrum was the view, of which Hume was the leading spokesman, that unemployment was the fault of the individual—a job was almost always available to the man of enterprise, and in any short periods of unemployment the provident man could be expected to support himself out of savings. Relief should be given to such persons only if they first became inmates of a workhouse, where the barest means of subsistence would be provided, and living conditions would be unpleasant. At the other end of the spectrum was the view of Scrope—that unemployment was in large part the result of the economic system and of misguided economic policy, and no persons should be forced into a workhouse simply because society could not provide employment. He wished to see the Poor Laws reformed, but he felt that they should do more than take care of the infirm and incapacitated. He said in criticism of the recommendations of the Poor Law Commission to stop outdoor relief:

So preposterous a recommendation, he could scarcely have expected to proceed from some juvenile theorist—some raw tyro in political economy, unacquainted with the state of the working classes of England, and the spirit or operation of the Poor-laws, but, disposed to dogmatize on the subject, and eager to administer some universal miracle-working specific, to fit all possible cases; and careless of the cost, the injustice, and the danger of applying his violent and experimental nostrum.[17]

Thomas Attwood[18] and Cobbett[19] agreed with Scrope's view.

---

15. 3 H, 22:874–89, 17 Apr. 1834.
16. 3 H, 22:890–91, 892–93, 897, 17 Apr. 1834; 23:812–16, 821–22, 9 May 1834; 23:1320–34, 1345, 26 May 1834.
17. 3 H, 23:1326, 26 May 1834.
18. 3 H, 23:1337–38, 26 May 1834; 24:314–15, 6 June 1834.
19. 3 H, 23:1335–37, 26 May 1834; 24:309–11, 6 June 1834; 24:324–27, 9 June 1834.

Alexander Baring[20] and Whitmore[21] approved the general principle of the new legislation; Whitmore believed that surplus population was the cause, and "that it had been brought about by the maladministration of the Poor-laws, which had operated as an encouragement to the increase of population." Torrens, never one to be doctrinaire when human suffering was involved, nevertheless "looked upon the Poor-laws in their present shape as the most crying evil under which the country laboured; and unless they were checked by arresting pauperism in its progress, they would, in a little time, absorb the entire rental of this country."[22] Brougham took a hard line on unmarried mothers—the woman should bear the penalty for her bastard children.[23] He left no doubt about outdoor relief: " . . . just in proportion as persons, from the nature of a charity, were enabled to look forward to it—were enabled as it were to depend on it beforehand, just in that proportion it was bad, because it encouraged idleness."[24] And he even went so far as to suggest that it might be better to let private charity take care of "the sick, the aged, and the impotent."[25]

The motion that the bill be read a third time was carried 187–50, with Matthias Attwood, Thomas Attwood, Cobbett, and Fielden in the minority.[26] The bill was amended slightly in the Lords, and when it came back to the Commons Thomas Attwood restated his opposition to the draconian provisions of the bill: "The people had a right to claim relief if they could not obtain employment—as good a right as the noble lord [Althorp] had to the hat on his head. If the people were prevented from living honestly, they would be justified in living dishonestly."[27] The bill was finally passed without recorded vote.

The position of parliamentary economists on the Poor Laws may to the present-day reader appear a paradox. The great majority of economists in the late 1820s, 1830s, and 1840s were in the forefront of radicalism, both political and economic. They wanted reform of

20. 3 H, 24:923–24, 27 June 1834.
21. 3 H, 24:1037–39, 1 July 1834.
22. 3 H, 23:973, 14 May 1834.
23. 3 H, 25:604–10, 28 July 1834.
24. 3 H, 25:437, 24 July 1834.
25. 3 H, 25:219, 21 July 1834.
26. 3 H, 24:1061, 1 July 1834.
27. 3 H, 25:1224, 11 Aug. 1834.

Parliament; removal of discrimination against Catholics, Dissenters, and Jews; reform of a tax system that weighed heavily on the poor; reduction or elimination of the privileges of the Established Church; freedom of trade in production and shipping; and the breakdown of monopoly in all fields. Yet their position on the Poor Laws has frequently been regarded as hardhearted and reactionary. By implication, if not specifically, the attitude of a number of modern writers has been that their views represented classical political economy at its worst—a blind application of economic theory with little consideration of the human consequences. Yet it seems clear that to such economists as Brougham, Grote, Howick, Hume, Poulett Thomson, and Torrens there was no inconsistency in pressing for the removal of economic and political abuses, and supporting the Poor Law changes of 1834. There are two plausible explanations of what to those of today may seem a bizarre association of radicalism and reaction. In the first place, Malthusianism in some degree affected the thinking of almost every economist, not the fatalism of Malthus on the first edition, but a belief that population if unchecked could defeat any hope of economic improvement. Hence it was not to grind the faces of the poor that so many economists wanted tougher Poor Law but to stop what they thought was a policy that stimulated population growth. Less obvious, but probably an element in the thinking of some, was the belief in the ability of men to respond to challenge, and to improve their situation if there were rewards for efforts and penalties for inertia. To those who wanted to reform Parliament, remove religious discrimination, shift tax burdens from the poor, and to repeal the Corn Laws, it was not, in the setting of the times, inconsistent to support a tougher Poor Law, although on this issue they were lined up with men who opposed almost all political and economic reforms.

Poor Law Controversy: 1834–68

In the years through 1868 there were no changes of significance in the English Poor Laws. The predominant opinion of the economists in Parliament seemed to be that although details of the new law might be wrong, and that hardship resulted in individual cases from the severe limits on outdoor relief, the overall results were a great improvement over the old situation. Lansdowne said: "The poor were much better off, and the expense to the parishes was considerably less than it had been before."[28] Brougham,[29] Howick,[30] and Hume[31] defended the new Poor Law, and Fielden[32] and Thomas Attwood[33] continued their criticism. The predominance of economists' thinking is shown by the vote on a parliamentary move to repeal the new Poor Law. It was defeated 321–13, with twelve economists, including Thomas Attwood and Fielden, in the majority, and no economists in the minority;[34] later the same day Thomas Attwood was the only economist to join Fielden in support of the latter's motion to bring in a bill to amend the Poor Law. The motion was defeated 309–17.[35] Muntz, the Birmingham manufacturer elected to fill the vacancy left by Thomas Attwood's resignation in 1839, continuing in his town's tradition of economic heterodoxy, protested "against adding this insult to exasperate the poor, already irritated and exasperated by distress and want of food."[36] By others the old arguments were repeated, with Scrope stressing the need to put able-bodied persons in productive work such as "reclaiming waste lands, making roads, arterial drainage, or other permanent improvements."[37] More than any other economist in Parliament, Scrope saw the fundamental economic issues involved: the need to distinguish between the incapacitated and the able-bodied unemployed, and the recognition that any system of relief to the able-bodied was only dealing with symptoms, and that the real problem was to have the able-bodied in socially useful employment. Further evidence of the general attitude of economists that it was better not to alter the new Poor Law legislation was the vote on a motion of Disraeli to go into committee "to take into Consideration such Revision of the Laws providing for the Relief of the Poor of the United Kingdom of Great Britain and Ireland as may mitigate the Distress of the Agricultural Classes." The motion was defeated 273–252, with Cayley the only economist supporting it, and ten economists opposing it.[38]

28. 3 H, 30:1316, 3 Sept. 1835.
29. 3 H, 38:1652–55, 27 June 1837.
30. 3 H, 50:106–8, 8 Aug. 1839.
31. 3 H, 36:1048–52, 24 Feb. 1837.
32. 3 H, 36:1012–19, 24 Feb. 1837.
33. 3 H, 34:1290–91, 6 July 1836.
34. 3 H, 40:1413–16, 20 Feb. 1838.
35. 3 H, 40:1416, 20 Feb. 1838.
36. 3 H, 65:501, 22 July 1842.
37. 3 H, 110:851–53, 26 Apr. 1850.
38. 3 H, 118:1272–75, 21 Feb. 1850.

Poor Law for Ireland

The proposal to introduce a Poor Law in Ireland produced a more complicated issue, in some of its aspects involving the special political status of Ireland, the lower living standards in Ireland, and—at least in the minds of some persons—the supposed aversion to work of the Irish. As early as 1806 Parnell supported a measure to increase the authority of Irish grand juries to assess cities to build "houses of industry" for the "correction of vagabonds and sturdy beggars" and "relief of the needy poor." He said that "it was impossible to travel over the high roads in Ireland, without being sensible of the necessity of this measure."[39] The bill was read the first time, and that was the last heard of it.

In 1822, when distress in Ireland was acute, the prime minister, Lord Liverpool, opposed any relief to the poor on the ground that it would interfere with the operations of the market, but two economists in the Lords took a less doctrinaire view. Lansdowne, while agreeing in principle with Liverpool, "was still of opinion, that the case of the suffering poor, in the part of Ireland [Clare] alluded to, formed an exception to any general rule, and that it was incumbent upon their lordships to take care that every thing was done that could be done for the relief of the unhappy sufferers."[40] King, in supporting even more relief than Lansdowne proposed, criticized the Irish landlords, the "rapacity of the church of Ireland, and of the government of Ireland."[41]

With continuing economic distress and political unrest in Ireland, Poor Laws for that country were under almost continuous debate for a decade, beginning in 1828. Rice "was convinced, that the introduction into Ireland of Poor-laws would lower the rate of wages in that country, and complete the misery and distress of the people."[42] Horton, the great sponsor of subsidized emigration (see below, pp. 161–64), was lukewarm about an Irish Poor Law, but was receptive to an idea of coordinating such a law with a public works program and emigration.[43] Torrens, with his facility for using florid language to get

---

39. 1 H, 7:844, 26 June 1806.
40. 2 H, 7:472, 10 May 1822. See also 7:727–28, 23 May 1822; 7:1047, 14 June 1822.
41. 2 H, 7:726, 23 May 1822.
42. 2 H, 21:1142–43, 7 May 1829; 3 H, 6:847–51, 29 Aug. 1831.
43. 2 H, 18:1419–20, 1 Apr. 1828; 21:742, 13 Apr. 1829; 21:1131–36, 7 May 1829.

at the heart of an economic question, favored relief for "impotent poor" in Ireland but was against relief for "ablebodied labourers":

The labouring classes composed the great bulk of every community; and a country must be considered miserable or happy in proportion as these classes were well or ill supplied with the necessaries, comforts, and enjoyments, of life. The study of political economy teaches us the way in which labour may obtain an adequate reward; and, if it did not teach us this, it might, indeed, serve to gratify a merely speculative curiosity, but could scarcely conduce to any purposes of practical utility.

He defended the "principles of political economy," which he said "is not, as has been erroneously stated, the appropriate or exclusive science of the Statesman and the legislator; it is emphatically the science of the people." And then he delivered the *obiter*: " . . . benevolence and charity, when not under the guidance of economical science, might become the involuntary instrument of mischief, aggravating the evils they endeavoured to remove, and resembling in their effects those splendid but baleful meteors, which shed a deceitful lustre on the disorder they created."[44]

Althorp felt that the effect of Poor Laws in Ireland "would be to induce the poorer classes in that country to be even less provident than they are said to be at present,"[45] and Hume, opposing any Poor Law for Ireland until the English Poor Laws were reformed, in the spirit of Adam Smith said: "It was the disposition of all classes, high as well as low, to indulge themselves at the expense of others."[46] Clay[47] and Thomas Attwood[48] favored a Poor Law for Ireland, and Scrope brought in a bill that died without debate.[49] Scrope said that the views of those who wanted a Poor Law for Ireland "were discountenanced by the then reigning school of political economy, which had espoused the doctrine of Mr. Malthus, that poverty was solely the consequence of excess of population; that any relief to the poor only led to an increase of their numbers, and consequently to an increase of pauperism and misery." But he added that there was a change in opinion "even by the most bigoted political economists."[50] Whether

44. 3 H, 6:818–25, 29 Aug. 1831.
45. 3 H, 17:869, 2 May 1833.
46. 3 H, 17:887, 2 May 1833.
47. 3 H, 17:891–92, 2 May 1833.
48. 3 H, 29:342, 8 July 1835.
49. 3 H, 31:429–30, 15 Feb. 1836.
50. 3 H, 33:590–98, 4 May 1836.

the cause was declining faith in the more rigid form of Malthusian population thought, or the stark realities of Irish misery, the prospect of a Poor Law for Ireland was looming constantly larger on the political horizon. In 1837 both Howick[51] and Peel[52] gave restrained approval to the idea, and they, as well as Scrope, felt that emigration might be coordinated with a Poor Law. The following year a Poor Law bill for Ireland, making no provision for outdoor relief, was passed 234–59. The bill, although apparently not completely satisfactory to all economists, received their almost unanimous support, and only Pryme opposed it.[53] The bill passed the Lords 93–31, with Ashburton, Bexley, and Lansdowne voting for it, and Brougham, still implacable on the subject, the only economist in opposition.[54]

Famine conditions in Ireland in 1846 revived the same issues that had run through the earlier debate on the English and Irish Poor Law. Those, or their doctrinal heirs, who had felt that outdoor relief was but a means of subsidizing indolent Irish seemed to be strengthened in their beliefs; those who felt that able-bodied unemployed were entitled to relief when work was not available saw in the failure of the potato crop an additional argument to support their view. Graham was against any change in the Poor Law to give outdoor relief, although he favored a government public works program.[55] Hume questioned the advisability of distributing food: "In the case of public societies which gave relief to the entirely destitute, they had ample proof how very rapidly the number of claimants increased, and how unworthy of relief the parties were."[56] Gisborne did not think the Irish situation called for any policy other than "unshackled free trade."[57] Scrope brought out that relief by mendicancy was a wasteful use of human resources,[58] and stressed the importance of having outdoor relief, but for productive work.[59] In the Lords Brougham, the flaming liberal of so many causes, opposed any aid to the able-bodied poor: "He wished to record anew his objection to any measure of relief that proceeded on the assumption of the doc-

51. 3 H, 36:492–97, 13 Feb. 1837.
52. 3 H, 36:497–504, 13 Feb. 1837.
53. 3 H, 42:715–18, 30 Apr. 1838.
54. 3 H, 42:28–29, 9 July 1838.
55. 3 H, 83:729–30, 11 Feb. 1846.
56. 3 H, 84:984, 13 March 1846.
57. 3 H, 84:1036, 13 March 1846.
58. 3 H, 85:1007–10, 24 Apr. 1846.
59. 3 H, 95:1425, 20 Dec. 1847; 97:343–45, 9 March 1848.

trine, that it was part of the duty of any Government whatever to feed the people of any country, or to provide food, wages, or labour for the people."[60] Lansdowne,[61] Monteagle,[62] and Archbishop Whately[63] all expressed their opposition in principle to outdoor relief in Ireland." Lansdowne, while against "an indiscriminate right to outdoor relief in Ireland," nevertheless sponsored on behalf of the government a bill for temporary outdoor relief in Ireland. He said:

I am deeply sensible that I am inviting your Lordships to follow me in a path which is beset with difficulties and with danger, and that we are about to embark in a navigation in which, although it is clear to what port we ought to steer, yet that our arrival at that port must be through rocks and shoals, which it will require all the care of your Lordships, and all the care which the best exertions of goverment can bestow upon the administration of this law, to steer clear of, so as to make it finally effective and secure.[64]

The bill passed the Lords, 33–10, with Grey, Lansdowne, and Monteagle in the majority, and Brougham the only economist in opposition.[65]

Early Debates on Emigration

The controversy over emigration raised some economic issues similar to those in the Poor Law controversy. Up to the close of the Napoleonic wars, there was little if any discussion of emigration as a means of dealing with economic distress. Religious differences, political difficulties, and restless ambition in manifold form had been the great driving forces for movement to the new British lands beyond the seas. Furthermore, with the economic thought dominant up to Malthus, government support of emigration would have been regarded as contrary to national interest, and until Napoleon's final defeat industrial and military manpower needs ruled it out, even by those who had approvingly savored Malthusian ideas. The only mention of emigration by a parliamentary economist before the end of the Napoleonic wars, and probably representative of public opinion at that time, was a question by Horner as to whether the govern-

60. 3 H, 89:1329, 15 Feb. 1847.
61. 3 H, 92:60–75, 29 Apr. 1847.
62. 3 H, 91:418–44, 26 March 1847; 92:94–104, 29 Apr. 1847.
63. 3 H, 91:484, 26 March 1847.
64. 3 H, 92:61, 29 Apr. 1847.
65. 3 H, 94:327–28, 15 July 1847.

ment was planning to promote emigration from Scotland. In the
context, it was clear that Horner did not approve of such a policy.[66]
But with mass unemployment after 1816, and rising poor rates, the
possibility of relieving distress by assisted emigration was seriously
proposed. Malthus in his fourth edition of 1817 had in reserved
language suggested emigration as a temporary relief when population increased rapidly "while the means of employing it and paying
it have been essentially contracted." The same year Torrens, shortly
before he made his first unsuccessful bid for a seat in Parliament,
had recommended emigration in a brochure, *A Paper on the Means
of Reducing the Poors Rates and of Affording Effectual and Permanent
Relief to the Labouring Classes.* Not until 1819 did parliamentary
economists get into governmental policy toward emigration, when
Vansittart urged a grant of £50,000 to send emigrants to South Af-
rica.[67] He found an ally in Hume, who in supporting the idea said
that if persons on relief refused to migrate "it might even be advis-
able to transport them without their consent."[68] The grant was
approved.

Any program to relieve poverty, or to reduce the poor rates by
emigration had theoretical nuances that would provide materials for
many meetings of an advanced economic seminar. An obvious point
was that if one accepted the more draconian version of Malthusian
doctrine of the first edition, emigration was no permanent solution.
Insofar as it temporarily raised the condition of workers, this would
cause a population increase which would again bring people to the
subsistence level, with just as many demands on the poor rates as
before the emigration. Any theoretical case for publicly assisted emigration required a shift to Malthusiam doctrine of the second edition, bolstered by analysis of the relation of the factors of production.
If one could show that a reduction in labor in relation to land or
capital would reduce unemployment and raise return to labor, and
moral restraint would prevent a new population increase, then a
sound theoretical case could be made for financing emigration from
the poor rates or from taxation. Further theoretical niceties were
introduced if the proposal was to have the emigrants, after they

66. 1 H, 30:52–53, 8 March 1815.
67. 1 H, 40:1549–50, 12 July 1819.
68. 1 H, 40:1550, 12 July 1819.

were settled in their new homes, reimburse those who had financed their emigration.

Robert Wilmot Horton's Emigration Plan

The economist in Parliament who did most to urge subsidized emigration and to press home the theoretical issues at stake was Wilmot, who assumed in 1823 the name of Horton. Horton is known to the literary world as the representative of Lord Byron's estate who took the responsibility for the burning of the poet's memoirs, and whose wife was the subject of Byron's line "She walks in beauty." In his political attitudes Horton was a conservative but a strong supporter of Catholic emancipation, and although he wanted the lower classes to respect authority and to stay in their place, he wanted their place to be comfortable. For several years after his first election to Parliament in 1818 he had an amateur interest in economic theory and an upper-class concern about the conditions of the poor. In 1822 he had distributed a memorandum urging that the poor rates be mortgaged to finance emigration. He sent a copy to David Ricardo—and presumably to others in public life—and Ricardo replied on 19 January 1823, commenting favorably on the proposal:

The plan would be economical; it would enable us to get rid of the most objectionable part of the Poor-laws, the relieving ablebodied men; and, what is to me by far the most important consideration, it would not fail to make the wages of labour more adequate to the support of the labourer and his family, besides giving him that as wages, which is now given to him as charity.[69]

Horton then moved for a grant of £15,000 to support subsidized emigration to Canada, and this bill was adopted without a recorded

69. The full text of the letter, and comments on it, are given by Lionel Robbins in "A Letter from David Ricardo," *Economica*, n.s. 23 (May 1956): 172–74. The letter is also in Ricardo, *Works*, 11:15–16. The original of the letter is in the Horton papers in the Derby Public Library, along with some twenty letters bearing on emigration from Torrens, and others from Alexander Baring, Thomas Chalmers, Howick, Malthus, McCulloch, James Mill, Parnell, James Pennington, Nassau Senior, and Thomas Tooke. R. N. Ghosh has published two articles based on these letters: "Malthus on Emigration and Colonization: Letters to Wilmot-Horton," *Economica*, n.s. 30 (Feb. 1963), pp. 45–62; and "The Colonization Controversy: R. J. Wilmot-Horton and the Classical Economists," *Economica*, n.s. 31 (Nov. 1964): 385–400.

vote. Ricardo, in the next-to-last speech he made in Parliament, gave restrained approval to Horton's motion, saying that "he should not, however, object to the present grant by way of experiment, and to show the people of Ireland that Parliament was anxious to afford them whatever assistance was possible," but added that "he could not consent to any large grants for the purpose hereafter."[70]

In 1825, when distress in Ireland was particularly acute, Horton again proposed that a grant be made to assist emigration from Ireland to Canada,[71] and Parliament approved £30,000 to assist emigration from the South of Ireland.[72] The next year Horton secured the appointment of a select committee. He was chairman, and the other economist members were Althorp, Hume, Parnell, Peel, and Rice. The committee was reappointed the following year, with Hume no longer a member, but Graham and Torrens added to the membership. Rice gave evidence before the 1826 committee, and he and Parnell gave evidence before the 1827 committee.[73]

Hume, although approving of a committee, suggested that it might be better for the government to spend money in developing employment opportunities in Ireland.[74] This suggestion raised a theoretical point that was rarely brought up specifically but was just below the surface in much discussion of subsidized emigration— comparison of the marginal return from investment in public works in Ireland, and from investment in transporting unemployed to the resource-richer British possessions. Horton had the idea that emigration, financed in the first instance by government but eventually to be on a self-supporting basis from repayments by emigrants, would shift employment of labor from zero or very low marginal return to a higher return.[75] Torrens had a similar thought, and gave

70. Horton's motion and Ricardo's speech are not reported in *Hansard* or the Ricardo *Works*, but are in the *Morning Chronicle*, 24 June 1823, and the Belfast *News-Letter*, 1 July 1823. I am indebted to Professor R. D. C. Black for calling the references to my attention and furnishing me with a copy of the Belfast item. A fuller discussion of Horton's activity on behalf of emigration is given in Black's *Economic Thought and the Irish Question 1817–1870* (Cambridge: Cambridge University Press, 1966), pp. 206–15; in Helen I. Cowan, *British Emigration to British North America* (Toronto: University of Toronto Press, 1961; original ed., 1928), rev. and enlg. ed., chap. 4 and 5; and in H. J. M. Johnson, *British Emigration Policy 1815–1830* (Oxford: Clarendon Press, 1972). The grant of £15,000 is in 4 Geo. IV, c. 100.

71. 2 H, 12:1358–59, 15 Apr. 1825.

72. 6 Geo. IV, c. 134.

73. The hearings and report of the 1826 committee are in P.P. 1826, 4 (404); of the 1827 committee in P.P. 1826–7, 5 (88, 237, 550).

74. 2 H, 14:1364, 14 March 1826.

75. 2 H, 16:475–89, 15 Feb. 1827.

his colleagues a lecture on economic theory. As against the idea that capital investment in Ireland would increase employment opportunities there, Torrens, in supporting a motion for renewing the emigration committee,[76] replied that in a country such as Ireland with limited agricultural land, increased investment might simply make it profitable to cultivate the land with less labor:

... where there were not fertile lands on which capital could be applied, it might happen, that in one and the same country both capital and labour might be redundant.... England had a redundant capital, and a redundant population; Ireland had a redundant population, and in the colonies land was redundant. Emigration, therefore, was merely the application of the redundant capital and population of the united kingdom to the redundant land of the colonies

And in the best Torrensian style, in his peroration he said

that the measure which was contemplated by the present motion, was a great measure, pregnant with mighty results, and founded upon the best and soundest principles of political economy—that it would combine those productive elements of wealth and power, which, uncombined, were fruitless ... and ... that it would spread the British name, the British laws, and British influence throughout all climes of the world

With the exception of Graham,[77] no economist expressed outright opposition to emigration, but many had reservations as to how much government aid, if any, should be given, with the result that their statements brought out important theoretical points, but produced no consensus on positive action. Alexander Baring opposed any idea of trying to get repayments from Irish emigrants to Canada: "From his knowledge of the settlers, they were not persons much given to the payment of money.... It was always impolitic to give to a whole people an interest to throw off allegiance; and in this case, perhaps, to turn their shillelaghs against us on the other side of the Atlantic."[78] The legislative result of Horton's campaign, except for the small grants of 1823 and 1825, was nil. Despite the almost unanimous opinion that some sort of emigration, under some circumstances, would be good, the members of Parliament prepared to support further government-financed emigration were few. Hor-

---

76. 2 H, 16:492–95, 15 Feb. 1827. This was Torrens's last speech in this session before he was unseated on charges of irregularities in his election.

77. 2 H, 16:299–300, 7 Dec. 1826.

78. 2 H, 16:504, 15 Feb. 1827.

ton's several motions calling for positive action were either with-drawn or defeated.

In 1831 Howick, Horton's successor as under-secretary of the Co-lonial Office, moved to introduce a bill along the lines of Horton's effort, for parish aid to emigration.[79] Showing that he had not forgot-ten the economics he had learned from McCulloch, Howick stressed the economic importance of emigration in bringing about a better distribution of population in relation to resources in both the mother country and the colonies. The bill received the support of Althorp,[80] and restrained approval of Alexander Baring.[81] The Commons agreed to the introduction of the bill, and that was the last heard of it.

Horton left Parliament in 1830 to become governor general of Ceylon. Shortly after his departure the focus of emigration discus-sion shifted from what has sometimes been called "shoveling out paupers" to looking on emigration as a means of developing colo-nies as self-governing parts of a greater Britain. The impetus to this new approach came in large part from the writings and activity of Edward Gibbon Wakefield. In his *Letter from Sydney*, published in 1829, Wakefield, with an array of economic analysis, had urged that Australian land be sold at a price that would prevent new settlers from immediately becoming landowners, and thus secure the bene-fits of concentration of population, and also provide funds for fi-nancing free emigration. Several parliamentary economists, includ-ing Clay, Grote, Molesworth, Torrens, and Whitmore, were active in the organization in 1834 of the South Australian Association for fostering free emigration to Australia along the lines of Wakefield's proposals. Parliament took no positive measures to advance Wake-field's plans, but he was influential in getting Molesworth to oppose the transporation of convicts to Australia. In 1839 Molesworth made an extended speech in favor of a resolution supporting the Wake-field plan of settlement.[82] The resolution was withdrawn, not so much because of opposition to its main economic and political thrust, but because of doubts about jurisdictional matters. But the spirit of the Wakefield plan continued to receive support from Molesworth's op-position to the transportation of convicts and his support of colonial

79. 3 H, 2:875–80, 905–6, 22 Feb. 1831.
80. 3 H, 2:884, 22 Feb. 1831.
81. 3 H, 2:895–98, 22 Feb. 1831.
82. 3 H, 48:869–88, 25 June 1839.

self-government, a position in which he had allies in Grote, Bishop Whately, Lord Lansdowne, and finally Hume after a change in his views.[83]

Regulation on Emigrant Ships

The one aspect of emigration that received further attention from parliamentary economists was the regulation of sanitary and living conditions on emigrant ships, where mortality had been running high. Their remarks illustrate that even the most dedicated free-market economist, when faced with a specific abuse, was apt to come out for regulation. Hume, tempering his economic theory to the realities of human distress, early favored some regulation,[84] and Lansdowne supported government action to reduce the mortality rate on emigrant ships.[85] Alexander Baring's remark, facing both ways, is a good example of the dilemma of a man caught between his belief in the market mechanism and his concern about a particular abuse; he "thought that interference in such matters was not desirable except, where, from peculiar circumstances, it became indispensable."[86]

---

83. A more detailed account of the position of parliamentary economists on the transportation of convicts is given in chap. 12, pp. 192–94; their position on colonial self government in chap. 13, pp. 205–9.

84. 3 H, 26:1237, 19 March 1835; 96:1024–25, 21 Feb. 1848.

85. 3 H, 54:1373–78, 22 June 1840.

86. 3 H, 26:1237–38, 19 March 1835.

Chapter 10

Church and State

The influence of religion on the long debate over a national educational policy was but a limited sector of the larger problem of the relation of Church and State. A summary, both of the relation of Church and State at the beginning of the period covered by this study, and of the religious orientation of the economists in Parliament, will put these controversies in perspective.

Relation of Church and State in 1780

In England and Wales there was the Established Church of England. Its wealth consisted in large part of the properties confiscated by Henry VIII from the Church of Rome, and administered by the Church of England free from direct government control. In addition the parishes collected church rates, which were in effect real estate taxes imposed on all land owners, including Dissenters and Catholics, and used for the repair and maintenance of church property. Furthermore, in each parish the clergyman of the Established Church had a tithe right to one-tenth of the gross produce of crops and livestock. This was usually, but not invariably, collected from the occupier of the land, even if he were only the tenant. In Ireland, the Church of Ireland, which was the Irish arm of the Church of England, held a similar position. In England tithes and church rates had long been a source of festering discontent, but as the majority of those paying them had been adherents of the Established Church, there had been few organized refusals to pay, and the situation was not politically explosive. In principle the same situation existed with the Established Church in Scotland (Presbyterian), but this never provided a parliamentary controversy involving economists. In Ireland, where barely a fifth of the total population were Protestants, and of the Protestants less than a half were adherents of the Church of Ireland, the opposition to tithes and church rates was deep-seated and belligerent.

The wealth of the Established Church in England and Ireland, and the tithes and church rates channeled to the Church, were only part of a monopoly power structure against which the economists of the time reacted. More than one comment from economists in Parliament linked monopoly in trade, monopoly in government, and monopoly in religion as enemies of progress. But the power of the Established Church lay not only in the wealth and revenue that it controlled, but also in the patronage it dispensed. Rectories, bishoprics, and archbishoprics were all too frequently given like any other political patronage, and a large proportion of the economists regarded many of the practices of the Established Church in the same light as the Corn Laws and the rotten boroughs of the unreformed Parliament. In contrast to the favored situation of the Church of England, the Church of Ireland, and the Church of Scotland, no government aid went to any other church, with the exception of a small annual grant to the Catholic theological seminary at Maynooth, Ireland.

Religious Affiliations of Economists

No economist member of Parliament was of the Catholic or Jewish faith. As far as I can find out, John Fielden, of a Quaker family, who became a Unitarian, was the only member of a dissenting church, although David Ricardo, raised in the Jewish faith, married a Quakeress, registered some of his children at Quaker meeting, and occasionally attended the Unitarian church; and James Wilson, raised as a Quaker, appears to have had only a nominal church association after giving up the religion of his earlier years. Lord Lansdowne, and possibly others, had leanings toward Unitarianism, without joining that church. The only ones outspokenly antireligious were Molesworth and John Stuart Mill, but it is evident that several, including Brougham, Gisborne, Hume, Muntz, and Lord King, had no burning religious faith. Henry Thornton was an ardent Evangelical and the author of a well-known volume, *Family Prayers*. Both of Torrens's grandfathers were clergymen, and a religious note is apparent in some of his writings. But most of what economists had to say about the church had nothing to do with religious faith but with the church as a citadel of economic and political power. On the other hand, the defenders of the Established Church—and in particular Graham, Northcote, and Peel—had little if anything to say about religious doctrine but much about the importance of maintaining the Church of England and the Church of Ireland as bulwarks of the established order.

Early Discussion of Irish Tithes

It was not until well into the Napoleonic wars that economists made more than passing remarks about church problems. Parnell, the Irish Protestant who on so many occasions did legislative battle on behalf of Irish Catholics, in 1809 raised the question of Irish tithes, following the receipt of many petitions against the existing method of collecting them.[1] Parnell's opposition was not to tithes as such, but to the method of assessing them, and he quoted Adam Smith's criticism that the tithe "is always a discouragement both to the improvements of the landlord, and to the cultivation of the farmer." Parnell cited many examples of the arbitrary assessment of tithes, and asked rhetorically: "Is it wonderful that a succession of outrage and insurrection should have disgraced the page of Irish history?" He moved to bring in a bill to permit the clergy "having a right to Tithes in Ireland, to demise the same for a term of twenty-one years." The government opposed the motion, which was then defeated 137–62, with no recording of individual votes.[2] Parnell's subsequent attempts to reform Irish tithes received little support, and from the scanty total of votes cast it is evident that tithes were not in the forefront of parliamentary interest during the war years. In 1812 Parnell's motion that the Commons "take into its most serious consideration the state of the laws relating to tythes in Ireland" was defeated by only three votes, 39–36, with four economists in the minority—Alexander Baring, Grenfell, Horner, and Parnell;[3] and ten years later Hume's motion, critical of Irish tithes and the

1. 1 H, 14:625–35, 19 May 1809.
2. 1 H, 14:628, 624–35, 648, 19 May 1809.
3. 1 H, 23:732, 23 June 1812.

Church of Ireland, was defeated 72–65, with six economists in the minority—Brougham, Hume, Parnell, David Ricardo, Rice, and Western.[4]

Moves for Abolition of Irish Tithes

Hume's motion, and the debate that preceded it, in which Brougham, Hume, and Rice urged action and Peel was the only economist to defend the existing situation, marked a new turn in the economists' attitude toward the Church of Ireland and the Church of England. Up to this time the criticism had been aimed at the administration of tithes in Ireland; from now on the continuation of tithes in Ireland, and even in England, was on the economists' reform agenda, and the very idea of an established church in Ireland was increasingly a target. The following year Hume's motion for a select committee on the state of church establishment in Ireland—a more ominous threat to the Church of Ireland than his previous motion—was defeated 167–62, with Ricardo the only economist joining Hume in support of the motion; but it was the handwriting on the wall of what was to come after both Ricardo and Hume had passed from the scene.[5] In 1823 the government sponsored a bill[6] for the voluntary composition of Irish tithes, which several economists opposed—principally on the ground that unless composition were compulsory the reform would be meaningless. A few years later King left no doubt as to his view of all tithes: "All lovers of abuses could find something of good to be attributed to every abuse, however gross, except to tithes. They said that the Corn-laws worked well—that Colonial Slavery worked well—and that corrupt Parliaments and heavy Taxation worked well—but none of them would go so far as to pretend that tithes worked well."[7]

The refusal of many Irish to pay tithes in large part shifted the battle from the halls of Westminster to the hedgerows of Ireland, where peasantry and tithe collectors carried on guerilla warfare. In the Lords, Lansdowne, on behalf of the Whig government, intro-

4. 2 H, 7:1197–99, 19 June 1822.
5. 2 H, 8:416, 4 March 1823.
6. 4 Geo. IV, c. 99.
7. 3 H, 1:1109, 14 Dec. 1830.

duced resolutions calling for the "complete extinction of tithes," which passed without formal vote.[8] Torrens, after a discriminating analysis of the economic effect of tithes, shifted the issue to its religious aspect: "The grievance of Ireland was not so much that tithes were paid, as that they were paid in a wrong direction; that they were paid by a Catholic people to a Protestant Church."[9]

What emerged was a government-backed law, permitting the voluntary composition of Irish tithes,[10] but it did little to quiet the unrest of the Irish or the criticism of parliamentary economists. The following year Gisborne, in discussing a bill to make temporary loans to titheowners to cover the tithes the Irish, in mass revolt, were refusing to pay, put his finger on the basic tithe problem: "The real and substantial grievance was, that the people of Ireland were compelled to pay their money, to support a Church of which they did not approve, and that grievance, the present measure would not cure in the slightest degree. The proposition of the Government was merely a miserable temporary palliative."[11]

The bill caused a rift among the economists who had been critical of Irish tithes and of the Irish church establishment. Some felt that it represented an improvement by providing a temporary truce in the Irish tithe war and should be accepted; others felt that it left untouched the principle of taxation to support an alien church. Representing the second view was Grote, who said that the bill did not go "to the length that the people expected it to go in rectifying the great ecclesiastical enormity of Europe—the Irish Church."[12] A move to kill the bill was defeated 109–53, with seven economists in the minority and seven in the majority, with the lineup apparently determined in large degree by judgment as to whether part of a loaf should be accepted rather than to hold out for the full loaf.[13] The bill became law 29 August 1833.[14]

In 1835 Lord John Russell made a motion, calling for the giving up of all tithes in Ireland. This was approved, 285–258, with fourteen economists in the majority and only four—Matthias Attwood,

8. 3 H, 10:1269–82, 1291–92, 1303–5, 8 March 1832.
9. 3 H, 11:1378, 6 Apr. 1832.
10. 2 & 3 Will. IV, c. 119, 16 Aug. 1832.
11. 3 H, 18:830, 14 June 1833.
12. 3 H, 18:1093, 21 June 1833.
13. 3 H, 20:560–61, 12 Aug. 1833.
14. 3 & 4 Will. IV, c. 100.

Alexander Baring, Graham, and Peel—in the minority.[15] It became evident, however, that although a majority of Parliament were in principle opposed to the Irish tithe situation, no majority could agree on a specific plan to end tithes. The only legislation that emerged was the act of 1838, which made the owner of land and not the occupier, as heretofore, responsible for paying tithes.[16] This simplified the administrative problem of tithe collection and stopped the hedgerow warfare between peasants and tithe collectors, but left untouched the larger political and economic question of taxation to support a church of which only some 10 percent of the country— and in many localities less than 1 percent—were adherents. The law was approved in the Commons 148–30, and the economists' vote again showed a split, based more on political judgment than on economic analysis. The six economists who voted for the bill—Graham, Howick, Peel, Rice, Scrope, and Poulett Thomson—included both those who had previously criticized Irish tithes and those who had defended them. The three in opposition—Fielden, Grote, and Hume—were opponents of tithes who apparently were not prepared to support anything short of abolition.[17]

Grant to Maynooth Catholic Seminary

From then until the disestablishment of the Irish church in 1869, the tithe issue was quiescent, but debates on the broader issue of the Irish church were, if anything, intensified. Aside from head-on criticism of the Church of Ireland was a lesser issue, but one on which the majority of economists had strong feelings—the annual grant which had been started by the Irish Parliament before the Union, to the Catholic theological seminary at Maynooth. In 1808 a motion by Parnell to increase the grant was defeated 93–58, with Alexander Baring, Parnell, and Petty in the minority.[18] Following Catholic emancipation the grant came under attack from the extreme anti-Catholic faction, and Hume, Rice, and Torrens came to its defense. And Peel, whose respect for law and order, or his sense of political realism, was even greater than his anti-Catholic feelings, said that a

---

15. 3 H, 27:969–74, 7 Apr. 1835.
16. 1 & 2 Vict., c. 109, 15 Aug. 1838.
17. 3 H, 44:693–95, 26 July 1838.
18. 1 H, 2:98, 29 Apr. 1803.

discontinuance of the grant would be a breach of public faith.[19] In the Lords, Lansdowne and Monteagle supported a continuance of the grant.[20]

In 1845 Peel, then prime minister, favored an increase in the Maynooth grant, and the debate and votes that followed showed that most economists felt that the grant to Maynooth should continue. Other economists supporting the grant were Clay, Cobden, Graham, Archbishop Whately, Earl Spencer, and Earl Grey; and the only ones to speak against it were Muntz and the bishop of Llandaff, Muntz because he was opposed to all religious grants,[21] Llandaff because he opposed any aid other than to the established church.[22] As Muntz, never one to mince words, put it: " . . . if the Irish people want priests, and well educated priests, why don't they educate their own priests, and why not pay for their education?"[23]

An amendment to restrict the grant was defeated in the Commons 317–184, with the strange coalition of Clay, Cobden, Graham, Hume, and Peel against the amendment, and only Fielden and Muntz supporting it.[24] And in the Lords a similar crippling amendment was voted down, 155–59, with six economists, including the archbishop of Dublin, in the majority, and only Bexley and the Bishop of Llandaff supporting the amendment.[25] The Maynooth grant continued to be a subject of debate, with the dominant opinion of economists favorable to its continuation. The final attempt in 1863, in the form of a motion for a committee to consider repeal of the Maynooth grant, was defeated 198–100, with Butt, Cobden, Hankey, and Lowe opposing the motion, and no economist in the minority.[26]

Attacks on Church of Ireland

Tithes and the Maynooth grant were but minor skirmishes in the larger battle over the continuance of a Protestant state church in

19. 3 H, 55:55–58, 23 June 1840.
20. 3 H, 73:845–57, 858–60, 12 March 1844.
21. 3 H, 79:949–55, 18 Apr. 1845; 134:926–28, 2 March 1853.
22. 3 H, 81:550–54, 16 June 1845.
23. 3 H, 69:953, 15 Apr. 1845.
24. 3 H, 80:744–48, 21 May 1845.
25. 3 H, 81:116, 4 June 1845.
26. 3 H, 171:259–61, 2 June 1863.

Ireland. Initially the attack concentrated, not on the total disestablishment of the Church, but on curtailing its revenues and its patronage. In 1834 a motion "that the temporal possessions of the Church of Ireland, as now established by law, ought to be reduced," was seconded by Grote,[27] and Clay in supporting the motion said: " . . . the people of England would not consent to make Ireland a vast camp or a great garrison, to force upon a reluctant people the abomination of a Church Establishment to which they were not attached."[28] The motion was overwhelmingly defeated, 396–120, but was supported by ten economists—Thomas Attwood, Clay, Cobbett, Fielden, Gisborne, Grote, Hume, Molesworth, Morrison, and Parnell.[29] In 1844 a motion for a committee of the whole "to consider the present state of the Temporalities of the Church of Ireland," generally considered critical of the Church of Ireland's financial operations, was defeated 274–179, but was supported by eight economists—Clay, Fielden, Howick, Hume, Gisborne, Muntz, J. L. Ricardo, and Scrope—and opposed only by those consistent defenders of the Irish church—Graham and Peel.[30] In the late 1860s Howick, now in the Lords as Earl Grey, resumed his criticism,[31] and was joined by new voices in the Commons of Goschen, Lowe, and John Stuart Mill. Lowe said that "it has an Establishment altogether so superfluous and so monstrous as if it was intended to point and give sting to the inequality that already existed. . . . The Irish Church is founded on injustice; it is founded on the dominant rights of the few over the many, and shall not stand."[32] It was evident that the days of the established church in Ireland were numbered. Finally in 1868 the defenders of the Church of Ireland were beaten, 330–265, with five economists in the majority—Fawcett, Goschen, Hankey, Lowe, and Mill—and Hubbard and Northcote standing by the church establishment.[33] The bill was killed in the Lords, 192–97,[34] and only in 1869 was the Church of Ireland disestablished.

27. 3 H, 23:1397–1400, 27 May 1834.
28. 3 H, 24:73, 2 June 1834.
29. 3 H, 24:86–87, 2 June 1834.
30. 3 H, 75:667–71, 12 June 1844.
31. 3 H, 132:358–82, 16 March 1866.
32. 3 H, 191:729, 747–48, 2 Apr. 1868.
33. 3 H, 191:1675–79, 30 Apr. 1868.
34. 3 H, 193:298, 29 June 1868.

Criticism of English Tithes

The issue of church and state in England never aroused the bitterness that it did in Ireland, partly because it was not tied to an explosive political situation and partly because a majority of English were, at least nominally, adherents of the Established Church. But a high proportion of the economists in Parliament were opposed to tithes and church rates, and the political power of the Established Church, although on grounds of political expediency they may have been restrained in criticism. In 1816 Brougham defended tithes on principle, but his qualification that tithes, like all property rights, "could be regulated by the legislature when the general welfare demanded its interference,"[35] was a harbinger of stronger language to come from economists. In 1828 a bill, in retrospect innocuous, to permit the commutation of tithes aroused the fears of Peel that it was "pregnant with injustice to the church of England,"[36] but Alexander Baring, Davenport, and Hume supported it.[37] King attacked the abuses of tithes;[38] Hume suggested that tithes be abolished and the clergy of the Church be paid directly by the government;[39] and Torrens, who never let his parliamentary associates forget that he was an economist, spoke favorably of a commutation of tithes, "the effect of which would be, that the revenue of the Church would no longer be, as it now was, a tax on capital."[40] In 1836 a bill for the compulsory commutation of tithes was approved on second reading 300–261, with every economist voting: sixteen in favor, and only the triumvirate of conservatism, Matthias Attwood, Graham, and Peel, in opposition.[41] The bill became law after it passed the Lords without recorded vote.[42] It removed English tithes from political controversy for over half a century.

Other Criticism of English Church Establishment

Tithes were but one of several grounds on which economists had criticized the church establishment, but it was not until the 1830s,

35. 1 H, 34:693, 22 May 1816.
36. 2 H, 18:1151–53, 17 March 1828.
37. 2 H, 18:1156–59, 17 March 1828.
38. 3 H, 15:1133–36, 1139–41, 25 Feb. 1832; 15:1175–78, 27 Feb. 1833.
39. 3 H, 17:281–82, 18 Apr. 1833.
40. 3 H, 17:389, 18 Apr. 1833.
41. 3 H, 34:117, 122, 3 June 1836.
42. 6 & 7 Will. IV, c. 71, 13 Aug. 1836.

partly as a result of new voices in the Reform Parliament, that the economists' attack on Church of England practices became a continuous and organized movement. Althorp, Brougham, Cayley, Clay, Cobbett, Gisborne, Grote, Howick, Hume, Rice, and Lord King were in varying degrees critical of the financial arrangements of the Established Church. Lord King in particular criticized pluralities, by which a clergyman would hold several livings and performed few or no duties at some, and said that they "converted the profession of minister of the Gospel into a trade, which had the lucre of gain for its object,"[43] and asked the rhetorical question: "Was it not true that there was a great concentration of the good things of the world in the clergy?"[44] Cobbett, never one to understate his criticism, said of the clergy: "And should they not be punished? Yes, they should, for very soon must Parliament take from them the fleece and the fat. Not much longer would they have the fat and the fleece to live upon, and that would be to them a sore punishment."[45] In the 1830s three attempts to remove the bishops from the House of Lords were soundly beaten, although they were supported by about half of the economists.[46]

Repeatedly the argument was made by economists that property rights of the established churches of England and Ireland were not absolute, and that the churches were in effect trustees for the public and hence the government could determine the use to which their property was to be put. Brougham stated their view in succinct form in 1832, and in the next thirty-five years he and other economists were to ring the changes on the theme: "The peculiar circumstances which distinguished Church property from any other kind of property was this, that the Legislature could interfere with it so far as to enforce the performance of the duties, for the performance of which that property was enjoyed."[47] Hume, in answer to criticism that the Whig government's proposal in 1837 to abolish church rates was taking the church's property, asked: "What property? The right of putting their hands into the purses of Dissenters for their own purposes."[48] In this debate Peel, in the Commons, and the bishop of

43. 2 H, 10:1046, 15 March 1824.
44. 3 H, 16:1228, 29 March 1833.
45. 3 H, 16:116, 4 March 1833.
46. 3 H, 22:153, 13 March 1834; 30:320, 26 Apr. 1836; 36:630, 16 Feb. 1837.
47. 3 H, 11:804, 23 March 1832.
48. 3 H, 36:1268, 3 March 1837.

Llandaff in the Lords were the only economists to put up an outright defense of the existing system. The ministerial resolution was carried, 273–250, with sixteen economists in the majority, and only Graham and Peel in the minority,[49] but no action followed.

Time was running out on the defenders of church rates. Hume's motion of 1840 to bring in a bill to relieve only Dissenters of church rates split the ranks of those who had wanted the abolition of church rates—it was defeated 117–62, with Hume, Molesworth, and Pryme supporting the motion, and Clay, Graham, Parnell, and Peel opposing.[50] In 1849 Clay, Cobden, and Perronet Thompson renewed their criticism. Clay said:

He would frankly confess that, as a member of the Church of England, he was ashamed of the thing. He was ashamed that the members of the most richly endowed Church in the world, which comprised within its ranks the wealthiest among the higher and even the middle classes of society, should apply to the poor Dissenting shopkeeper to furnish the sacramental bread and wine, to pay for the warming and lighting of the church, and the washing of the clergyman's surplice.[51]

Perronet Thompson took issue with the argument that church rates were no burden on the landowner because they had been taken into account in the price of the land, and then shifted from the slippery ground of incidence of taxation to an ad hominem argument: "Doubtless they were legal, but that was not the question. All the heretics burnt in Smithfield were burnt legally."[52]

For years Clay had criticized church rates, and when in 1855 he introduced a bill for their abolition Muntz expressed a view that was held increasingly by economists, even though they may have stated it in more restrained language: "It was disgraceful to the Church of England to ask a Dissenter to pay church rates. Why, one man might as well ask another to pay for his washing and lodging."[53] The bill was approved by the Commons on the second reading, 217–189, with six economists supporting it, and no economist opposing it.[54] The government, however, refused to back the bill, and Clay, as a private member, decided not to push it.

49. 3 H, 37:550–54, 15 March 1837.
50. 3 H, 52:116, 11 Feb. 1848.
51. 3 H, 103:660, 13 March 1849.
52. 3 H, 103:656, 13 March 1849.
53. 3 H, 137:1365, 29 March 1855.
54. 3 H, 138:692, 16 May 1855.

Clay failed to be reelected in 1857, but others carried on his crusade. Not only an overwhelming majority of economists, but a majority of all members of the Commons had come to the conclusion that church rates belonged to the past. A bill to abolish them passed the Commons in 1858 by a vote of 266–203, with six economists—Hankey, Lowe, J. L. Ricardo, Scrope, Perronet Thompson, and Wilson—in the majority, and only Cayley and Lewis in the minority;[55] but died because of opposition in the Lords. In 1866 a bill for abolishing church rates passed a second reading 285–252, with every economist voting, but the bill got no further. The six in favor were a distinguished group: Fawcett, Goschen, Hankey, Lowe, John Stuart Mill, and Scrope; Hubbard and Northcote were opposed.[56] Compulsory church rates were finally abolished in 1868, following a debate in which economists took no part, and their abolition received royal assent[57] on the last day of John Stuart Mill's short parliamentary career.

55. 3 H, 150:1727, 8 June 1858.
56. 3 H, 181:1691–95, 7 March 1866.
57. 31 & 32 Vict., c. 109.

Chapter 11

Civil Rights and Religious Disabilities

In the early years covered by this study individuals not of the Established Church—or more strictly speaking, anyone, even an adherent of the Established Church, who was not prepared to take certain oaths—were seriously limited in civil rights. For example, no Catholic could be Lord Lieutenant of Ireland. No one of the Catholic or Jewish faith could sit in Parliament. No one could be a local magistrate, take a degree at Cambridge University or Oxford University, or even be enrolled at Oxford, unless he subscribed to the tenets of the Established Church.

Suspension of Civil Rights

In addition to religious discrimination, there were temporary restrictions on the liberty of the subject based on the theory that they were necessary to maintain the security of the state. Economists were involved in the parliamentary argument over all such restrictions: (1) the Seditious Meeting bill and similar legislation during the Napoleonic wars, aimed at persons considered infected by the ideas of Revolutionary France; (2) the so-called Six Acts, of the years shortly after Waterloo, when many conservatives believed that there was danger of domestic internal revolution, suspending the long-accepted legal protection of individuals; and (3) the suspension of such legal protection in Ireland at times of disturbance in that unhappy country. The last situation will be covered in chapter 13.

The split of economists on the Seditious Meetings bill and similar proposals in the 1790s was along party lines. Lauderdale, that crusty Scottish Whig, opposed the easy suspension of habeas corpus,[1] and

1. P. H., 31: 1280, 3 Feb. 1795.

regarded the Seditious Meetings bill and the Treasonable Practices bill as infringements on the liberties of the people.[2] Western opposed the former bill as "subversive of the fundamental principles of the constitution";[3] and in the Lords young King, in his second parliamentary speech, began his long campaign in defense of civil liberties by opposing the continued suspension of habeas corpus.[4] The Tories Rose[5] and Lord Hawkesbury defended such legislation. In Hawkesbury's words, "those restrictions were necessary in order to preserve the rest of the constitution entire."[6] in 1798 the habeas corpus suspension bill was passed overwhelmingly, 96–6, but with Francis Baring and Western in the minority.[7] Petty,[8] Horner,[9] Brougham,[10] Althorp,[11] and Alexander Baring[12] in several debates between 1805 and 1817 took what today would be called a civil liberties view. Other than the members of the Tory government, the only economists to support the suspension of habeas corpus were Finlay,[13] the politically independent but conservative Glasgow textile manufacturer, and Grenfell, of Whig orientation.

In the wake of widespread popular discontent and fears of an uprising, the Tory government late in 1819 introduced the notorious Six Acts aimed at suppressing sedition. Of these probably the most severe in its effects was the Seditious Meetings Prevention Act. David Ricardo expressed his opposition in language that would rank high as political theory, and used the occasion as a springboard to support parliamentary reform.

If they could not meet in such numbers as to make them be respected, their petitions would have no effect. At the same time, he admitted, that those meetings were attended with very great inconvenience. It could not be denied that circumstances might arise when the government should be fairly administered, and yet distress might arise from causes which the government could not control, and wicked and designing men might pro-

2. P. H., 32: 245–46, 6 Nov. 1795; 32: 546–47, 9 Dec. 1795.
3. P. H., 32: 507, 10 Dec. 1795.
4. P. H., 34: 1484–85, 27 Feb. 1800.
5. P. H., 31: 526, 17 May 1794.
6. P. H., 32: 550, 14 Dec. 1794.
7. P. H. 34: 125, 21 Dec. 1798.
8. 1 H, 3: 473–76, 14 Feb. 1805.
9. 1 H, 28: 714–15, 10 July 1814.
10. 1 H, 35: 653–54, 25 Feb. 1817.
11. 1 H, 35:727–28, 26 Feb. 1817.
12. 1 H, 35: 857–58, 3 March 1817.
13. 1 H, 35: 1096, 14 March 1817.

duce a great degree of mischief; it did not appear to him that such meetings were the sort of check which ought to exist in a well-administered
government; but it was necessary to have some check, because if they left
men to govern without any control in the people, the consequence would
be despotişm. The check which he would give, could be established only by
a reform of parliament.[14]

The bill passed the Commons 265–69 with six economists—Althorp, Brougham, Graham, Hume, Parnell, and Ricardo—opposing it.[15] In the Lords that triumvirate that had voted together on so
many issues—King, Lansdowne, and Lauderdale—were on the losing side of a motion, 135–38, to limit the duration of the law.[16]

A number of other issues on civil rights arose in the 1820s, with
essentially the same picture—the economists providing opposition,
well out of proportion to their numbers, to restraints that received
overwhelming approval of the entire Parliament. David Ricardo
spoke in support of a petition from Mary Ann Carlile, asking for
partial mitigation of her imprisonment for blasphemous libel:

He must now inform the House, that after a long and attentive consideration of the question, he had made up his mind that prosecutions ought
never to be instituted for religious opinions. All religious opinions, however
absurd and extravagant, might be conscientiously believed by some individuals. Why, then, was one man to set up his ideas on the subject as the
criterion from which no other was to be allowed to differ with impunity?
Why was one man to be considered infallible, and all his fellow men as frail
and erring creatures? Such a doctrine ought not to be tolerated: it sa-
voured too much of the Inquisition to be received as genuine in a free
country like England. A fair and free discussion ought to be allowed on all
religious topics. If the arguments advanced upon them were incorrect and
blasphemous, surely they might be put down by sound argument and good
reasoning, without the intervention of force and punishment.[17]

In contrast was Peel's defense of Mary Carlile's continuing imprisonment: "The law of the country made it a crime to make any attempt to deprive the lower classes of their belief in the consolations
of religion."[18] The suggestion of a connection between free-trade economics and free trade in other fields came in William Wilberforce's

---

14. 1 H, 31: 769–70, 6 Dec. 1819. This speech is in Ricardo, *Works*, 5: 28–29.
15. 1 H, 41: 1090–91, 3 Dec. 1819.
16. 1 H, 41: 1296, 17 Dec. 1819.
17. 2 H, 8: 722–24, 26 March 1823. The speech is in Ricardo, *Works*, 5: 280.
18. 2 H, 8: 724, 26 March 1823.

comment that Ricardo "seemed to carry into more weighty matters those principles of free trade which he had so successfully expounded."[19] Ricardo's last speech in Parliament came in seconding a petition from Christian ministers and members of their congregations asking for freedom of religious expression. He said: "No man had a right to say to another, 'My opinion upon religion is right, and yours is not only wrong when you differ from me, but I am entitled to punish you for that difference.' Such an arrogant assumption of will was intolerable, and was an outrage upon the benignant influence of religion."[20]

Repeal of Test and Corporation Acts

The most important, and certainly the politically most explosive issue of civil rights involved discriminations against Catholics, Dissenters, and Jews. The Test Act had a long history, and had been modified several times, but as it stood in 1780 it barred from holding public office anyone who was not prepared to take the sacrament according to the rites of the Established Church. In practice the Test Act was not as draconian as it appeared on its face, for it was possible to refuse to take the sacrament in the expectation of securing relief under the Indemnity Act which was passed annually by Parliament for offenses against the Test Act. It was this provision that enabled David Ricardo to sit in Parliament without taking the sacrament.[21] Similar in their effect were the Corporation Acts which, without benefit of an Indemnity Act, virtually excluded, particularly in Ireland, those not adherents of the Established Church from participating in local government.

In 1828 Lord John Russell brought forward a bill for repeal of the Test and Corporation Acts. It passed the Commons 237–193, with twelve economists in the majority, and Matthias Attwood, Huskisson, and Peel in opposition.[22] In the Lords amendments limited

19. 2 H, 8: 729, 26 March 1823. In less charitable tone was Wilberforce's entry in his diary, which despite the editor's deletion of the name before publication, evidently referred to Ricardo: "I had hoped that ——— had become a Christian; I see now that he had only ceased to be a Jew." Quoted in Ricardo, *Works*, 5:280.

20. 2 H, 9: 1387, 1 July 1823. The speech is in Ricardo, *Works*, 5: 326.

21. Sraffa, in Ricardo, *Works*, 10: 42–43, tells of Ricardo's personal problems with the Test Act.

22. 2 H, 18: 781–84, 26 Feb. 1828.

the liberalization of the bill, and the watered-down bill was approved in the Lords 150–52, with four economists in favor and only Bexley opposed.[23] The Lords version was passed in the Commons without recorded vote.

Campaign for Catholic Emancipation

Almost simultaneously with the repeal of the Test Act and the liberalization of the Corporation Acts, the controversy over the repeal of Catholic disabilities, in which economists had played a long and honorable role, provoked a political crisis. Whereas Dissenters, or those like David Ricardo with no formal church membership, could by the provisions of the Indemnity Act hold public office, the oath required of a member of Parliament effectively barred Catholics—even Lords—from sitting in Parliament. There were other disabilities covered by the campaign for Catholic Emancipation, but membership in Parliament became the symbol of the Catholic grievances. King George III, in his lucid moments, was adamant against Catholic emancipation—he is reported to have said: "I shall reckon any man my personal enemy who proposes any such thing,"[24] —and he was able, in the years of war, to maintain the principle that he would not permit any ministry that even suggested Catholic emancipation. It was the economists who for years were in the forefront of opposition to this view, and gave their votes in fruitless attempts to break the anti-Catholic front. In 1805 Lord King supported a motion for committee on the Catholic claims, which went down to overwhelming defeat.[25] In the Commons Brougham, Parnell, and Petty on a number of occasions spoke on behalf of Catholic claims, as did Petty after he went into the Lords as Marquess of Lansdowne. In 1815 Parnell, at the request of Daniel O'Connell, presented a series of resolutions for the removal of all Catholic disabilities,[26] but his petition for going into committee on the laws affecting Catholics was defeated 228–147, with six economists—Althorp, Finlay, Grenfell, Horner, Huskisson, and Parnell—in the minority.[27]

23. 2 H, 19: 229, 1 May 1828.
24. Smart, 1:46.
25. 1 H, 4:829, 843, 13 May 1805.
26. O'Connell's letter asking Parnell to present the motion and Parnell's memorandum relating to the matter are in the Parnell papers in the possession of the present Lord Congleton.
27. 1 H, 31: 524, 30 May 1815.

Parnell continued to press for the removal of Catholic disabilities. In 1821 a private member's motion favorable to Catholic claims was approved 227–221, with eleven economists, including Loyd, who rarely voted on any measure, favoring it, and Matthias Attwood, Gilbert, Peel, and Vansittart in opposition.[28] The Commons bill was thrown out by the Lords, 159–120, with no economists in the majority and King, Lansdowne, and Lauderdale in the minority.[29] Lansdowne spoke eloquently in a noblesse oblige defense of the bill: "Were the privileges of their lordships held for their own sakes only? Could it be reasonably supposed that the eligibility of the superior orders to offices of honour and distinction would not be gratifying to persons of inferior station?"[30]

There was little change, in the years immediately following, in the views or votes of economists on several measures involving the civil rights of Catholics. King continued his campaign, and in answer to the charge of the bishop of Chester that he was not a friend of the Church of England, King countered: "He was not a friend to the Church of England whilst it encouraged intolerance, and pluralities, and non-residents, and all the other abuses which at present existed in it."[31] In 1825 a private member's bill for removal of Catholic disabilities passed the Commons 248–227, with thirteen economists in favor and Peel the only economist in opposition.[32] Again the Lords defeated the bill, 178–130, with the familiar lineup of the economists King, Lansdowne, and Lauderdale supporting the bill, and Bexley opposing it.[33] Pressures for reform continued, and it was but a question of time before the defenses of the Protestant Church Establishment would be breached. The following year Lansdowne, in a powerful speech, stressed the notion of liberty as an idea that embraced both religion and economics.[34] Torrens, always one to paint on a broad canvas of social and political philosophy, in answer to

---

28. 2 H, 4: 1030–34, 28 Feb. 1821. David Ricardo was known to favor the Catholic claims, and it is not clear whether he was absent at the time of voting, or whether there was a mistake in the tally. For a discussion of this matter, see Ricardo, *Works*, 5: xxii–xxiii. The only other economists not recorded in the vote were Brougham and Graham, both of them favorable to Catholic Emancipation.

29. 2 H, 5: 356–59, 17 Apr. 1821.
30. 2 H, 5: 347–48, 17 Apr. 1821.
31. 2 H, 12: 1275, 29 March 1825.
32. 2 H, 13: 558–62, 10 May 1825.
33. 2 H, 13: 766–68, 17 May 1825.
34. 2 H, 15: 224–46, 17 Apr. 1826.

the claim "that the Catholics could give no security which would render it safe to make any further concession to them," said: "What security was required? If the legislature gave them political power, would not their love of that power induce them to retain it by their conduct?"[35] And King said, presenting a petition from Catholics: "It contained as strong expressions of loyalty as if it had been drawn up by the learned lord on the wool-sack, and had more charity than if it had been drawn up by the whole bench of bishops."[36] Again in 1828 the Commons, by a vote of 272–266, approved a motion favorable to Catholic emancipation. It was the old story again. Every economist but Grenfell voted, and they supported the motion 15–2, with only Matthias Attwood and Peel in opposition.[37] In the Lords a similar motion was defeated, 181–137, with that trio that had voted together on so many questions—King, Lansdowne, and Lauderdale—supporting it, and Bexley and the Bishop of Llandaff opposing.[38]

In the meantime the situation in Ireland, spurred on by the oratory of Daniel O'Connell, was becoming increasingly serious. Matters were brought to a head by the Clare election of 1828. William Vesey-Fitzgerald had sat for Clare since 1818. He was a landlord well liked by the Irish peasantry, and a strong champion of Catholic claims. That year he was appointed to the presidency of the Board of Trade, and hence was required to resign his seat and again stand for Parliament. His reelection seemed certain, but O'Connell, after the repeated rebuffs in Parliament of the Catholic cause, although ineligible to sit in Parliament, announced his candidacy. In an election that marked the beginning of active participation by priests in Irish elections, O'Connell won an overwhelming victory. Catholic emancipation seemed the only alternative to chaos in Ireland, and the duke of Wellington, then prime minister, and Peel in a four-hour speech of explanation, went back on years of promises that they would never yield on the Catholic question. The Roman Catholic Relief bill passed the house, 320–142, with fifteen economists supporting it, and no economist opposing it;[39] and the Lords, follow-

35. 2 H, 16: 286, 6 Dec. 1826.
36. 2 H, 16: 1013–14, 8 March 1827.
37. 2 H, 19: 675–80, 12 May 1828.
38. 2 H, 19: 1294–97, 10 June 1828.
39. 2 H, 20: 1633–38, 30 March 1828.

ing Wellington's lead, approved the bill 203–109, with the veteran trio of liberalism—King, Lansdowne, and Lauderdale—joined by the bishop of Llandaff, heretofore an opponent of Catholic emancipation, in the majority,[40] and Bexley the only economist in the minority. Little was said by economists in either House that had not been said before, but the speech of Western, a long-time supporter of Catholic Emancipation, was a good summary of the consensus of economists: " . . . having sat in that house nearly forty years, he had never given a vote with greater pleasure than that when he should give that night in favour of the measure before the House, which he firmly believed would have the effect of effacing from our Statute-book those penal laws which were a disgrace to them."[41] A few disabilities on Catholics remained for some years, but the back of the penal laws had been broken.

Removal of Civil Disabilities Against Jews

The move to get rid of similar civil disabilities against Jews became active some years later than the move on behalf of Dissenters and Catholics, but it had much the same history. In 1830 Lord Bexley, although a last-ditcher on the removal of Catholic disabilities, in presenting a petition on behalf of Jewish civil rights spoke of "prejudices which he had once entertained in common with others, though he had now brought his mind to think that the claims of the Jews ought to be conceded."[42] Brougham, Alexander Baring, and Huskisson, and Lansdowne in the Lords, all spoke in favor of civil rights for Jews. The only economists in the 1830s to oppose the idea were Peel[43] and Cobbett—the latter often in the forefront of reform, but at other times showing the prejudices of an English yeoman, who "wished to ask the hon. Member who said of the Jews that they were one of the most industrious classes of his Majesty's subjects, whether he could produce a Jew who ever dug, who went to plough, or who ever made his own coat or his own shoes, or who did anything at all, except get all the money he could from the pockets of the people?"[44]

40. 2 H, 21: 694–97, 10 Apr. 1829.
41. 2 H, 20: 1108, 17 March 1829.
42. 2 H 32: 924, 25 Feb. 1830.
43. 2 H, 24: 802–7, 17 May 1830.
44. 3 H, 16: 937, 21 March 1833.

Even more than on the Catholic question the Commons was eager to end Jewish disabilities, but the Lords was the roadblock. In 1833 a "bill for the relief of the Jews" was approved in the Commons on second reading, 159–52, with seven economists in the majority, and no economist in the minority.[45] The Lords killed the bill, 104–54, with five economists—Bexley, Brougham, the Archbishop of Dublin, Lansdowne, and Western—in the minority supporting the bill and only the bishop of Llandaff opposing it.[46] In 1836, on a motion to take up the subject again, Rice said: " . . . having removed from the statute book all religious disabilities except this, would the Legislature leave that one spot as a mark of the foul cancer which had so long gnawed and defaced our Constitution?"[47] And Perronet Thompson had the "hope that the time was not distant when we should get rid of the stigma of having in that House placed any man under political disabilities on account of his religious creed."[48]

The issue came to a head in 1847 with Baron Rothschild's election to Parliament from the City of London. He refused to take the customary member's oath on the Bible, "On my true faith as a Christian," but was prepared to put his hand on the Old Testament and swear, "So help me God." He was denied his seat. Again came the same series of arguments, and the same pattern of voting: approval by the Commons, with virtually unanimous support from the economists, and defeat by the Lords, where the Bishop of Llandaff was the only economist to oppose full civil rights for Jews. Not until 1858, after Rothschild had been five times elected, and four times refused a seat when he refused to take the Christian oath, were the Jewish disabilities removed. It was the old story in the Commons—no economist was opposed. Time was catching up with the House of Lords, where on second reading the measure was approved, 143–97, with Brougham, Grey, Lansdowne, Monteagle, and Overstone in the majority and, with the bishop of Llandaff now dead, no economist in the minority.[49]

---

45. 3 H, 18: 59, 22 May 1833.
46. 3 H, 20: 249, 1 Aug. 1833.
47. 3 H, 33: 1232, 31 May 1836.
48. 3 H, 33: 1233–34, 31 May 1836.
49. 3 H, 151: 727, 1 July 1858.

Chapter 12

The Humanitarian Movement
and Human Rights

Closely allied to the question of civil rights and removal of religious disabilities were a number of philosophical and political issues, only tangentially economic, as to the relation of authority to individuals. They covered a wide spectrum of issues related to each other by a humanitarian connection of being the outgrowth of the Enlightenment.

Abolition of Slave Trade and of Slavery

The most important of these humanitarian issues was the abolition of the slave trade and of slavery. In 1792 Thornton, a great economic analyst and a successful banker who also had strong feelings on moral issues, attacked the slave trade: " . . . he called upon all those to whom the character of a British merchant was dear, to come forward, and rescue that respectable name from disgrace, by putting an end to a system of barbarity, rapine, and murder."[1] But for the next decade the little that other economists had to say on the slave trade showed no enthusiasm for its abolition. Lord Hawkesbury, apparently with concern for the protection of property rights, opposed abolition;[2] Lauderdale, the unpredictable, in opposing ending the slave trade, spoke of the "impropriety of abolishing a trade in which the property of so many was engaged to such an extent, legally and with the sanction of parliament for so long a period."[3]

A decade later Petty spoke of the slave trade as "this abominable traffic";[4] King opposed the slave trade;[5] and Lauderdale reversed his

1. P.H., 29: 1088, 2 Apr. 1792.
2. P.H., 29: 1353–54, 8 May 1792.
3. P.H., 31: 470, 2 May 1794.
4. 1 H, 7: 596–98, 10 June 1806.
5. 1 H, 8: 669, 5 Feb. 1807.

earlier opposition on the ground that "the persons engaged in the trade had had amply sufficient notice of the intention of the legislature to abolish it, and, therefore, ought not now to complain of injustice."[6] Rose, although in principle not opposed to abolition of the slave trade, in practice found reasons for not doing so, including the idea that "on the score of humanity, it was much better it should be carried on by this country, on account of the superior good treatment which slaves met with in British ships."[7]

The slave trade was abolished in 1807,[8] but parliamentary debate over slavery, and over the suppression of the slave trade by other countries, continued for nearly half a century. The issue continued to divide economists, often along lines that put on opposite sides those who were allies on other issues. A plausible hypothesis for this split of opinion is found in two ideas, sometimes in agreement, sometimes in conflict, that permeated economics from Adam Smith to John Stuart Mill: the humanitarian and freedom-of-choice ideas associated with the Enlightenment, and the materialistic idea of maximizing economic output.

Horner on several occasions discussed the continuing slave trade and pressed for stronger measures against it,[9] but made no outright attack on slavery. Beginning in 1814 Lansdowne repeatedly urged more vigorous action to stop the slave trade. No economist defended the trade, but Alexander Baring laid stress on the difficulties of forbidding credits to those engaged in it,[10] and Huskisson spoke of the cost in lives and treasure of trying to suppress the slave trade.[11] Hume urged diplomatic pressure on Spain to stop that country's slave trade,[12] but regularly opposed the continuing expense of the African slave-trade squadron on what was basically a cost-benefit analysis: the heavy toll in British money and lives was too high a price to pay for the reduction in the number of slaves taken across the Atlantic. His solution was also phrased in economic terms: by introducing free labor into the British colonies slave labor would become unprofitable elsewhere: "If half the time, trouble, and ex-

6. 1 H, 7: 1144, 15 July 1806.
7. 1 H, 6: 839, 21 Apr. 1806. Rose said much the same thing four days later, 6: 917, 918.
8. 47 Geo. III, c. 36.
9. 1 H, 28: 384–90, 413, 28 June 1814; 29: 511–12, 24 Nov. 1814; 29, 1005, 1006, 23 Feb. 1815; 30: 609, 14 Apr. 1815.
10. 1 H, 31: 170–71, 174, 5 May 1815.
11. 2 H, 18: 977–79, 5 March 1828.
12. 3 H, 135: 1483–86, 9 Aug. 1854.

pense had been devoted to the increase of free labour in our own Colonies, we should have done much more in effecting the suppression of the Slave Trade, than we can now console ourselves with having done."[13]

Some who were revolted at the well-publicized barbarities of the slave trade stopped short of favoring the abolition of slavery. Petty, strong opponent of the slave trade, in 1807 opposed even considering a bill for the abolition of slavery: "To emancipate the negroes, would not be to add to their happiness, even if the legislature had a right to interfere with the property of the colonies."[14] Brougham, from his first entrance into Parliament in 1810, wanted to abolish slavery in the British colonies, and to stop the continuing slave trade by other countries, and after the death of Henry Thornton in 1815 and Horner in 1817, he was for years almost the only economist to play an active role in these matters. And his ability to think in economic terms is shown in his analysis of the improvement that had resulted from the legislation of 1807: " . . . the reduced prices of slaves on the coast since the acts passed; instead of 100 dollars, they now sold for 20; a reduction wholly owing to the lessened demand, for no man could pretend that the supply had been increased."[15]

In 1826 for the first time did parliamentary economists have much to say about the abolition of slavery. No economist defended slavery as an institution, but a number saw so many difficulties, either administratively or as a result of political disorder, in abolition, that in the immediate setting they were in effect political allies of the defenders of slavery. Horton looked forward to "the final extinction of slavery itself," but wanted no hasty action.[16] Hume wanted emancipation in time, but put in the qualification: "Ministers had established certain regulations for the amelioration of the slave population, and he thought that ought for the present to satisfy the advocates of emancipation."[17] Alexander Baring spoke of the need to preserve property.[18] And Lansdowne said: "With regard to the measures for emancipation, there could be but one sentiment, which was, that they ought to be gradual, and of a nature calculated

13. 3 H, 80: 214, 5 May 1845. Hume expressed the same idea on several other occasions.
14. 1 H, 9: 142–43, 17 March 1807.
15. 1 H, 27: 658–75, 688–89, 15 June 1810.
16. 2 H, 14: 989–92, 1022–32, 1 March 1826.
17. 2 H, 14: 993–94, 1 March 1826.
18. 2 H, 15: 489–90, 20 Apr. 1826.

to ensure that moral improvement, by which alone the negroes could be fitted for the enjoyment of freedom."[19]

In the face of the pressing domestic problems convulsing the country in the late 1820s, the slavery issue went into political retirement for a few years. It emerged again in 1830, with Brougham again in the forefront.[20] Althorp added his voice to the criticism of slavery, but like Lansdowne a few years earlier felt that no precipitous action should be taken.[21] Peel cast the cloak of national policy and of humanity over the maintenance of slavery abuses: " . . . he hoped that no feeling of compassion for the slaves would be suffered to pervert the cool and deliberate judgment of the House, and hurry it into actions that might be equally injurious to the interests of the slaves, the interests of humanity, and the interests of the planters."[22] Howick, a supporter of emancipation, said of Peel's attitude: "The right hon. Baronet had pursued the same course with regard to Slavery that he had pursued with regard to Reform and the Catholic question. The right hon. Baronet was a waiter upon time, and he left others to clear the road of all the difficulties that might beset it."[23] Cobbett, whose focus of concern was the agricultural worker of England, was not opposed to emancipation, but felt that slaves were "both fed and clothed a good deal better than the working people in England, Ireland, and Scotland,"[24] and with characteristic bluntness he opposed a farthing of compensation to planters: "Either these slaves were property, or they were not. If they were we had no right to meddle with that property; if they were not property, we were not bound to give compensation for them."[25]

After 1832, with Catholic rights and Parliamentary Reform out of the way, at least for that generation, and the Whigs in power, it was clear that slavery would soon end. The only question was when, and on what terms. The votes were not for or against slavery, but on such details as the amount of compensation for slave owners, and the conditions of apprenticeship, which was to be a half-way stage to complete emancipation. The bill for emancipation was passed in

19. 2 H, 15: 396, 19 Apr. 1826.
20. 2 H, 25: 1171–92, 1210–14, 13 July 1830.
21. 3 H, 1423–28, 15 Apr. 1831.
22. 3 H, 3: 1458, 15 Apr. 1831.
23. 3 H, 13: 63, 24 May 1832.
24. 3 H, 15: 1179–80, 27 Feb. 1833; 16: 729–30, 18 March 1833.
25. 3 H, 20: 204–5, 31 July 1833.

both houses without a recorded vote and became law on 23 August 1833.[26]

The majority of parliamentary economists took a stronger position against the slave trade and slavery than did their noneconomist colleagues, but except for those who had some association with the Clapham Sect—Thornton and Horner, and in a minor degree Brougham—the ending of slavery, or even the ending of the slave trade, was not at the center of their reform interests. There were so many things right at home calling for change, and the enthusiasm and energy for reform were in limited supply.

Criminal Laws and the Death Penalty

The criminal laws of England, at the close of the eighteenth century, were ripe for reform. Particularly shocking were the crimes—said to be around two thousand and including stealing property worth one shilling or more—to which the death penalty applied. The law was so severe that in practice juries and judges saw to it that there were no executions for most of the crimes punishable by death. Particularly acute, however, were the many executions for forgery, and the public revulsion against executions for forgery of Bank of England notes was an influence that helped to bring about the resumption legislation of 1819.[27] In 1821 a motion to go into committee on the Forgery Punishment Mitigation bill was approved 118 to 74, with eleven economists, including David Ricardo, in the majority, and only Gilbert and Huskisson in the minority.[28] In 1830 a move to drop the death penalty in most cases of forgery was approved in the Commons 151–138, with twelve economists in the majority, and only Gilbert and Parnell in opposition.[29] The bill[30] passed the Lords without recorded vote. Seven years later a motion to abolish the death penalty in all cases except murder was defeated 73–72, with four economists—Graham, Howick, Parnell, and Peel—in the majority, and five—Cayley, Grote, Hume, Molesworth, and

---

26. 3 & 4 Will. IV, c. 73.
27. For a discussion of this point see my *The Development of British Monetary Orthodoxy*, pp. 71–73.
28. 2 H 5: 971–73, 23 May 1821.
29. 2 H, 25: 77–78, 7 June 1830.
30. 11 Geo. IV & 1 Will. IV, c. 66.

Perronet Thompson—in the minority.[31] This motion represented, for the period of this study, the strongest of the parliamentary attempts to abolish the death penalty. The high tide of humanitarianism, which had been strong in the 1830s, was waning, and in 1856 a motion for select committee on the death penalty was defeated 158–64, with six economists in the majority, and only Muntz favoring the committee.[32]

Transportation of Convicts

Closely allied to the question of the death penalty was prison policy and the transportation of convicts. When in 1824 the amendment of the transportation act came up in the Commons, Peel supported it in a way that just assumed that transportation was right;[33] and Horton spoke approvingly: "He wished to have it generally understood, that transportation would now become a severe and real punishment."[34] Four years later Rice criticized transportation on the ground that it was an inducement to crime, and said that letters from Australia told how well off convicts were.[35] Hume, as so often thinking in terms of cost-benefit analysis, favored transportation as compared with expenditures on a home penitentiary, partly on cost grounds, partly on grounds that have a modern ring, i.e., that in prison convicts learn about crime.[36] Torrens never faced the transportation question head on, but as one interested in Australian colonization, and who looked forward to the development of self-governing colonies, his remarks showed no enthusiasm for convict settlement of Australia.[37]

Like slavery, transportation was not an issue in which many economists were deeply involved. In this lack of concern the economists reflected a general parliamentary attitude. Australia was a long way off, and the continuance of transportation meant that Parliament could evade hard thinking about domestic penal reform, or

31. 3 H, 38: 922–23, 19 May 1837.
32. 3 H, 142: 1261–63 10 June 1856.
33. 2 H, 11: 1001–2, 1 June 1824.
34. 2 H, 11: 1092–93, 4 June 1824.
35. 2 H, 18: 799–804, 28 Feb. 1828.
36. 2 H, 24: 938–41, 21 May 1830.
37. 3 H, 4: 1443–44, 18 July 1831; 10: 505, 508, 17 Feb. 1832.

about the political and economic conditions in Britain and Ireland that helped to produce the criminals. The two economists most actively opposed to transportation—Molesworth and Archbishop Whately—concentrated primarily on the relation of transportation to colonial policy and social reform. Molesworth, who had a vision of self-governing British colonies, objected to an Australian transportation policy that made less likely the early realization of his dream. This opposition is suggested by his remark that the Australian colonies were inhabited "by the ruffians, felons, prostitutes, and outcasts of England."[38] In 1837 the Commons, on urging by Molesworth, appointed a Select Committee on Transportation, with Howick, Molesworth, and Peel as members; and later that year, after Victoria's accession to the throne, the committee was reappointed with the same economist members. Lansdowne, speaking for the government, favored limitation but not the complete ending of transportation;[39] and several other economists, including Brougham,[40] Hume,[41] and Howick (Lord Grey in 1845),[42] took essentially the same equivocal view of supporting transportation if properly administered. The Act of 1824[43] had in effect given to the king—which meant the government of the day—virtually complete authority over transportation, stating in particular to which colonies convicts should be sent, and how many to each. Hence the working decisions on transportation were not made by Parliament, but by administrative officials, who in turn appear to have been influenced more by protests and petitions from Australia than by parliamentary action. Transportation to New South Wales was stopped in 1848 by administrative action, but continued to other colonies, although against protest from local inhabitants. Hume, who came to the conclusion that there should be no transportation in defiance of the wishes of colonists,[44] supported Molesworth's motion for ending transportation to Van Dieman's Land.[45] Indicative of the parliamentary apathy is the fact that debate on Molesworth's motion stopped when a point of

38. 3 H, 34 1463, 22 Dec. 1837.
39. 3 H, 54: 311–14, 19 May 1840.
40. 3 H, 90: 921–26, 5 March 1847.
41. 3 H, 93: 164–68, 4 June 1847.
42. 3 H, 109: 852–80, 14 March 1850.
43. 5 Geo. IV, c. 84.
44. 3 H, 108: 799–800, 14 Feb. 1850.
45. 3 H, 116: 1191, 20 May 1851.

order was made that less than forty members were present. Two years later in the Lords, Grey's motion to retain transportation was defeated 54–37, with no other economist voting with Grey, and Lansdowne and Overstone opposing the continuance of transportation.[46] Transportation was gradually phased out by administrative action, and ended in 1868.

A suggestive theoretical point on the benefits of transportation in providing the infrastructure for economic development came from Grey and Monteagle in the debate of 1850. They argued that but for transportation economic development in Australia would have been impossible, or greatly delayed. Monteagle spoke of convicts as "the pioneers of civilization";[47] and Grey combined economic development analysis with prophecy: "It must also be remembered, that the flourishing communities now spreading over Australia, and which promise, at no distant date, to become a great nation, are in fact the creation of the system of transportation. I believe that but for transportation, communities of this magnitude and wealth would never have been created in Australia."[48] The idea warrants further study by students of economic development.

Military Recruiting and Discipline

In the early years of this study the recruiting and discipline in the armed forces were marked by an inhumanity that today is almost unbelievable. Recruitment in the army was for life. Press gangs forcibly supplied sailors who were not tempted by the low pay and brutal discipline of the royal navy. Men were flogged for what were sometimes trivial offenses, and even for political statements. The army and navy in their administration were independent fiefdoms, which on grounds of national security resisted any parliamentary interference with their internal affairs. This independence made the armed services the target of economists' attack on several grounds. First was the expense, on which those prone to cost-benefit analysis, such as Hume and Parnell, hammered. Humanitarians such as King and Perronet Thompson frequently challenged the

46. 3 H, 127: 78, 10 May 1853.
47. 3 H, 110: 204, 12 Apr. 1850.
48. 3 H, 110: 206, 12 Apr. 1850.

draconian nature of military and naval discipline. And, in some degree drawing on these two types of criticism, there was a more general criticism, mounting in intensity after the Reform Act of 1832, of the armed forces as a stronghold of privilege and patronage. In contrast with the apathy of a large proportion of the parliamentary economists on slavery and transportation of convicts, it was rare to find an economist, other than the Tory politician-economists, who did not have some ground for criticism of the armed services. In 1797, at the time of the naval mutinies Sinclair opposed the tough official policy toward the mutineers.[49] King favored a limited army enlistment,[50] as did Lauderdale[51] and Thornton.[52]

Against flogging came continuous parliamentary criticism. On this issue economists were divided, but their general attitude was more critical than that of their noneconomist colleagues. Francis Burdett's motion for an appeal to the Prince Regent to abolish flogging in the army was defeated 94–10, but Brougham gave a powerful speech in favor of the motion, and he and Parnell supported it.[53] The next year Brougham attacked the idea that Parliament had no right to interfere with management of the army, and the mild proposal that the army furnish to Parliament information on floggings was defeated 49–17.[54] Thornton's opposition to corporal punishment in the militia received no support.[55]

In 1824 a motion to forbid corporal punishment in the army was defeated 127–47, with the economists providing eight of the minority—Althorp, Alexander Baring, Grenfell, Hume, Loyd, Parnell, Rice, and Western.[56] Shortly afterward Hume criticized both flogging and impressment for the navy, and said that impressment would not be needed if pay and conditions in the navy were improved. His motion that the House consider impressment was defeated 108–38 with Brougham and Rice also supporting the motion.[57] In 1833 a motion that flogging be inflicted only in case of

49. P.H., 33: 814–15, 5 June 1797.
50. 1 H, 7: 654, 13 June 1806.
51. 1 H, 7: 683–84, 17 June 1806.
52. 1 H, 8: 547, 23 Jan. 1807.
53. 1 H, 20: 710, 18 June 1811.
54. 1 H, 22: 393, 15 Apr. 1812.
55. 1 H, 21: 1315, 16 March 1812.
56. 2 H, 10: 1039, 15 March 1824.
57. 2 H, 11: 1197, 10 June 1824.

mutiny or drunkenness lost 151–140, with seven economists, including Torrens, the colonel of Marines, supporting the motion, and five opposing it.[58] Several further attempts to abolish flogging were defeated, and the debates were marked by the strong criticism of flogging by Perronet Thompson, a military officer,[59] and its defense by Howick, ordinarily a defender of humanitarian moves, who as secretary of war came to take the military establishment position on flogging.[60] In 1836 an amendment for its abolition was defeated 212–95, with seven economists—Thomas Attwood, Clay, Grote, Hume, Molesworth, Morrison, and Perronet Thompson—supporting it, and seven—Graham, Howick, Parnell, Peel, Rice, Scrope, and Poulett Thomson—opposing it.[61] Criticism of flogging continued for the next three decades with the results essentially the same: overwhelming defeat of measures to abolish or limit flogging, or even to get details about flogging cases, but with economists taking a more critical attitude than did their noneconomist colleagues.

Despite the failure of those opposed to flogging to win any legislative successes, it is probable that its critics, by their constant airing of abuses, achieved something by reducing the armed services' use of flogging, especially for minor offenses. In 1867 the Commons, by a vote of 108–107, passed a resolution against flogging in the army in peace time. No economist opposed the resolution, and three—Fawcett, Hankey, and John Stuart Mill—supported it.[62] No legislation resulted, but changing public opinion had its effect, and in 1868 the Articles of War severely limited the use of corporal punishment.

Libel Laws

A problem with some humanitarian aspects was the state of the libel laws, which with their severity all too often were used against publications advocating reform. Here again the weight of economist opinion was for reform. In 1827 Hume's motion for repeal of the libel provisions of the Six Acts was defeated 120–10, with Howick

---

58. 3 H, 17: 68–70, 3 Apr. 1833.
59. 3 H, 31: 893–94, 25 Feb. 1836; 3 H, 32: 967–69, 13 Apr. 1836.
60. 3 H, 32: 982–97, 13 Apr. 1836.
61. 3 H, 32: 1009–12, 13 Apr. 1836.
62. 3 H, 185: 1989–91, 15 March 1867.

and Hume in the minority.[63] Three years later an amendment to make even more severe the libel laws against newspapers was, with less than one-sixth of the Commons voting, carried 68–47, with seven economists—Matthias Attwood, Davenport, Howick, Hume, Rice, Poulett Thomson, and Western—in the minority.[64]

Legislation Affecting Women

In the years of this study there was nothing that could have been called a "woman's movement," but a number of isolated incidents throw sidelights on the social and legal attitudes of economists toward women. The trial of Queen Caroline for adultery, in 1820, strictly speaking did not involve the rights of women, but was basically a political issue, in which the defenders of the queen were motivated by distaste for the Tory government of the day. But at least in retrospect it would appear that the defenders of Queen Caroline, even if they believed that she was guilty as charged, in some degree came to her defense because of the feeling that she was to be publicly disgraced for extramarital improprieties that for generations had been regarded as appropriate activities for male members of the royal family. A motion to postpone debate on a secret committee to inquire into the conduct of the queen was defeated 195–100, with seven economists—Althorp, Graham, Grenfell, Hume, Parnell, David Ricardo, and Western—on the losing side.[65] Brougham, as attorney for the queen, put up a magnificent defense, combining virtuosity on legal details, devastating cross examination of witnesses against the queen, and dramatic oratory of a high order.[66] The Lords voted 108–99 for a third reading of the Bill of Pains and Penalties against Her Majesty, with Lansdowne and King in the minority.[67] The Liverpool government, for reasons still not completely clear, withdrew the bill.

63. 2 H, 17: 1083, 31 May 1827.
64. 2 H, 25: 1138–39, 9 July 1830. On another vote July 6 on essentially the same issue, Althorp, Brougham, and Graham also voted against making the libel laws more severe (2 H, 25: 1071).
65. 2 H, 1: 1398–1400, 26 June 1820.
66. Brougham's cross examination and speeches take up a large part of 2 H, 2 and 3.
67. 2 H, 3: 1744–46, 10 Nov. 1820. The names of the majority are not listed, but Lauderdale, in several speeches and other votes, had taken a position critical of the Queen, and this was the first break on an important issue of the Whig economist phalanx of King, Lansdowne, and Lauderdale.

This did not end the matter, however, nor stop the economists' criticism of the government's policy toward the queen. A motion critical of the action of the government in the Queen Caroline case was defeated 324–178, with eleven economists in the minority, and six—Gilbert, Loyd, Huskisson, Peel, Vansittart, and Wilmot—in the majority.[68] Similarly a motion whose effect was to omit the queen's name from the litany, was carried 310–209, with the same eleven economists supporting the queen's cause.[69]

The first question directly involving sexual discrimination in which economists were involved was on a proposal to admit ladies to the House of Lords gallery. It is difficult to tell how much tongue in cheek there was in Brougham's opposition: " . . . he thought that the Ladies would be infinitely better employed in almost any other way than in attending the Debates of that House . . . not even his noble Friend [Lord Wharncliffe] felt a more absolute and entire devotion to the sex than he did; but he wished also always to see them in their proper places."[70] The same year the Commons approved a motion, 153–104, to admit ladies to their gallery, with Cayley, Fielden, Gisborne, Molesworth, and Pryme supporting the motion;[71] and shortly afterward Grote, Hume, Perronet Thompson, Poulett Thomson, and Scrope also voted favorably on the admission of women.[72]

In the 1850s more substantive issues involving the legal position of women and marriage laws that affected both men and women came up a number of times. A long-standing provision of English ecclesiastical law, introduced into the civil law in 1835, forbade the marriage of a man to his deceased wife's sister. Irrational as this provision may seem from today's vantage point, it was stoutly defended by many spokesmen for the Established Church and by emotional conservatives. In 1850 the Commons, by a vote of 182–130, approved an amendment that would have dropped the prohibition.[73] Supporting the amendment were eight economists—Clay, Cobden, Hume, Lewis, Molesworth, J. L. Ricardo, Scrope, and Perronet Thompson; Cayley, Graham, and Peel opposed it. The bill

68. 2 H, 4: 507, 6 Feb. 1821. Every economist but Matthias Attwood voted.
69. 2 H, 4: 219, 26 Jan. 1821.
70. 3 H, 29: 679–80, 17 July 1835.
71. 3 H, 29: 640–41, 16 July 1835.
72. 3 H, 30: 49, 4 Aug. 1835.
73. 3 H, 109: 455–57, 6 March 1850.

died, as did subsequent bills to the same effect, and it was not until 1907 that the ban on marrying a deceased wife's sister was lifted.

The right of a married woman to her own earnings became a subject of parliamentary debate in the middle 1850s. Brougham, with a sharp criticism of existing law, presented and approved of a petition to give women this right.[74] Lansdowne supported Brougham's position,[75] as did Muntz[76] in the Commons, but no measure came to a vote. In 1868 the Commons approved the second reading of a Married Women's Property bill, in a tie vote of 123–123, with the Speaker casting the deciding favorable vote. Four economists supported the bill—Fawcett, Hankey, Lowe, and John Stuart Mill—and no economist opposed it.[77] No further action was taken on the bill in this session.

In 1867, in the closing days of debate on the Second Reform Act, John Stuart Mill introduced an amendment extending the vote to unmarried women and widows on the same terms as men, and spoke at length in support thereof. He made clear that his eventual objective was equal rights for all women, but at the time was making a more limited proposal. His words rank high as prophecy:

I certainly do think that when we come to universal suffrage, as some time or other we probably shall come—if we extend the vote to all men, we should extend it to all women. . . . If we should in the progress of experience . . . come to the decision that married women ought to have the suffrage, or that women should be admitted to any employment or occupation which they are not now admitted to—if it should become the general opinion that they ought to have it, they will have it.[78]

Mill's motion was defeated 196–73, with no economist opposing it, and Fawcett and Mill supporting it.[79]

74. 3 H, 141: 120–21, 14 March 1856; he developed his argument in more detail in 3 H, 144: 605–17, 13 Feb. 1857.
75. 3 H, 142: 1972–75, 26 June 1856.
76. 3 H, 142: 1279, 10 June 1856.
77. 3 H, 142: 1376–78, 10 June 1868.
78. 3 H, 187: 843, 20 May 1867.
79. 3 H, 187: 843–45, 20 May 1867.

Chapter 13

Imperial Britain: Ireland, the Colonies, and the World

Common to the thinking of most parliamentary economists was the emphasis on economic considerations in judging national policy. It was not that economists ignored other tests of policy, such as military and naval might, the prestige that came from governing other lands, and even in some cases the power and prestige of the Established Church, or the maintenance of an aristocracy. But in general they placed less emphasis on such considerations than did their noneconomist colleagues. There was a typical economist's, as opposed to a noneconomist's, approach to a series of problems associated with the political power of Britain. Whereas the noneconomist was prone to ask whether a policy was likely to strengthen the political power and prestige of Britain, the economist was more likely to look at the problem through the glasses of national wealth or individual material well-being. A subtle but nevertheless very real difference between the approach of the noneconomists and economists was that economists generally took a more tolerant view toward the economic interest of non-British peoples and had greater respect for their native intelligence. The economists were more willing to solve difficult problems by compromise and concession; the noneconomists were more likely to see the solution in a display of military or naval power. To say that economists were less nationalistic, less racist minded, less prone to find in power the solution to a problem would oversimplify a complex pattern of attitudes, yet this idea has a core of truth.

Irish Problems

In varying forms these attitudes are illustrated by the controversies over Ireland, the colonies, and foreign relations. A review of what the economists had to say about Ireland underscores the role that Irish problems played in British politics. Many of these problems were prevalent in England, but existed in a more acute form in the Irish setting: the relation of church and state when the great majority were not adherents of the Established Church, discrimination against those not adherents of the Established Church, poverty, suspension of civil rights in time of political unrest.

Before the Union of 1800 economists made few comments on Irish affairs, and no economist said anything important in the debate on the Irish trade proposals of 1789 or on the Act of Union. The Act of Union (39 & 40 Geo. III, c. 67) was adopted without recorded vote in either House, amidst Whig charges that political corruption and bribery were used to secure passage. Nevertheless, sympathetic as were a large percentage of the economists to the claims of Ireland, no economist openly supported repeal of the Union, and both Parnell and Rice in 1832 lost their Irish seats because of Daniel O'Connell's wrath at their refusal to support repeal.

With continuing political unrest in Ireland, sometimes breaking out in waves of terrorism against landlords, the question arose regularly as to whether the more important action was to relieve economic distress and remove political and religious discrimination, or to take a firm stand in repressing disorders. This trade-off problem between reform and law-and-order measures involved in many marginal cases judgment of a subjective type rather than a clear-cut issue of principle. This explains why on occasion even some strong champions of Ireland's claims nevertheless lined up with Peel in voting for repressive measures. Yet the overall picture is clear: economists as a group were much more inclined to the reform than to the hard-line, law-and-order view.

In 1801 the Irish Martial Law bill passed the Lords 90–7, with King one of the seven Lords filing a protest against it.[1] In 1805 Petty[2] in the Commons and King[3] in the Lords opposed continued suspension of habeas corpus in Ireland, setting a pattern for their long support of reform, rather than repression, as the solution to Irish unrest. And in 1808 Parnell wanted to hold up a parliamentary grant to an Irish Protestant school on the ground that its catechism encouraged religious animosity. To the question, "What religion are

1. 1 H, 1: 1213–16, 23 March 1801.
2. 1 H, 3: 522–23, 15 Feb. 1805; 3: 560–61, 19 Feb. 1805.
3. 1 H, 3: 541, 18 Feb. 1805; 3: 719–20, 6 March 1805.

you of?" he said that the children were taught to reply: "I am, thank God! a Protestant."[4]

Horner, Parnell, and Lansdowne were on the alert for abuses in government policy toward Ireland, and particularly in patronage. Parnell opposed an appropriation for the publication of notices in the Dublin *Gazette*, as "only giving to the Irish government the means of corrupting a part of the Irish press."[5] And speaking of the activities of the Orangemen, he called them "an association which renders the North of Ireland less civilized, and less secure than the savannahs of the savage Americans."[6] Grenfell, Peel, and Vansittart took a hard line on Ireland, and a remark of Peel's is revealing as to his general view of the social order: "the returning habits of subordination among the lower orders of the peasants."[7] In 1814 Alexander Baring supported an Irish Preservation of the Peace bill, but blamed the government for an Irish policy that had made such a bill necessary: " . . . there was nothing in the nature of Irishmen, any more than of Welshmen or Scotchmen, disposing them to turbulence or anarchy; but the people were everywhere what their laws and institutions made them."[8] An indication of economists' sentiment came in a vote in 1819, on a motion to exclude Ireland from the operations of the Seditious Meetings Prevention bill. The motion was defeated, 265–69, with Althorp, Brougham, Graham, Hume, Parnell, and David Ricardo in the minority.[9]

The uneasy equilibrium between the hard-line and the reform approach to peace in Ireland was revealed in 1822, when the Tory government proposed repressive measures. Parnell then felt that conditions in Ireland warranted such actions;[10] and Lansdowne said that he would regretfully vote for the bill, but hoped the ministers would deal with the root of the troubles in Ireland.[11] The bill was approved in the Commons, 109–28, with Brougham, Hume, David Ricardo, and Rice in the minority,[12] and five months later, in an unsuccessful motion to shorten the duration of the Irish Insurrection

4. 1 H, 11: 9, 11 Apr. 1808.
5. 1 H, 25: 792, 12 Apr. 1813.
6. 1 H, 28: 35, 20 June 1814.
7. 1 H, 29: 336, 18 Nov. 1814.
8. 1 H, 28: 807, 20 July 1814.
9. 1 H, 41: 1090–91, 13 Dec. 1819.
10. 2 H, 6: 130, 7 Feb. 1822.
11. 2 H, 6: 210–17, 9 Feb. 1822.
12. 2 H, 6: 185, 8 Feb. 1822.

bill, Parnell joined the other four economists in the minority of 37.[13] Althorp, Brougham, Hume, Parnell, and Rice, and King and Lansdowne in the Lords, repeatedly criticized government policy in Ireland. Although David Ricardo never spoke on the Irish question, his votes were invariably in support of measures pointing toward reform. King said: "Those who had anything to do with its government, should hide their heads for shame, at the mention of such a disgrace to the civilized world."[14]

In 1825, when Ireland was again in a state of disorder and the Catholic Association was pressing the cause of Catholic emancipation, the government moved to suppress the association. The old arguments pro and con were repeated and the familiar voting pattern reappeared—the government measures winning overwhelmingly but the economists providing an opposition far out of proportion to their numbers. The third reading of the bill was approved 226–96, with Althorp, Brougham, Hume, Parnell, and Rice in the minority;[15] and on other votes Alexander Baring and Grenfell also opposed the hard line government measure. In the Lords both King and Lansdowne opposed suppressing the Catholic Association. In 1830 Parnell denounced the office of Lord Lieutenant "as a positive evil" and moved for its abolition. His motion was defeated, 178–106, with ten economists in the minority, including Davenport, Graham, Poulett Thomson, and Whitmore, in addition to the regular critics of Irish policy.[16]

Seven new members of the Reform Parliament—Thomas Attwood, Clay, Cobbett, Fielden, Grote, Molesworth, and Pryme—joined the economist critics of the "get-tough" approach to Irish unrest. The Coercion Bill of 1833, supported by the Whig government, was approved 345–86, with eight economists in opposition: Thomas Attwood, Clay, Cobbett, Fielden, Grote, Hume, Molesworth, and Torrens.[17] In the debate Torrens well summarized the philosophy of the reform approach: " . . . he believed that when full and complete justice should be done, political discontent and agitation would expire with their cause."[18]

13. 3 H, 7: 1547, 8 July 1822.
14. 2 H, 9: 1063, 19 June 1823.
15. 2 H, 12: 710, 25 Feb. 1825.
16. 2 H, 24: 526–27, 10 May 1830.
17. 3 H, 16: 1283–84, 29 March 1833.
18. 3 H, 16: 684, 15 March 1833.

Rice, although opposing repeal of the Union and occasionally willing to go part way on get-tough measures, nevertheless felt that the
basic trouble in Ireland sprang from the bigotry of the Protestant
Scotch-Irish. As he put it in a moment of exasperation:

Admiring, as he did, the country [Scotland], to which the hon. Member
belonged, admiring it for its eminence in the arts of industry and peace, he
must say, that they owed the greatest part of the religious heartburnings
and animosities which now distracted Ireland to the mischief-making
Scotchmen who had come amongst them, Scotchmen, who judging from
their own narrow minds and illiberal feelings, had sought to impart to that
country not what was generous and enlightened in their own, but that
which was peculiar, and had done more mischief to the cause of religious
truth in Ireland than all the exertions of the hon. Gentleman himself ever
could remedy.[19]

Although Muntz did not favor repeal of the Union, he saw no
reason why Irish meetings in favor of repeal should be forbidden,
and his general attitude toward the Irish situation is revealed in his
remark: "He believed that if Irishmen were treated as Englishmen
they would be very different people from what they were now."[20] In
1846, when Ireland again was seething with revolt, the delicate balance between reform and get-tough as the means of pacifying the
country is brought out by the views of the economists in the Lords
on the repressive Protection of Life (Ireland) bill. Both Brougham
and Lansdowne favored the bill, on the ground that no measures
would be successful in Ireland unless life and property were protected;[21] Monteagle regretfully supported it because the situation in
Ireland called for it;[22] but Grey protested against its extreme provisions.[23] In the Commons the economists were overwhelmingly against
the bill, which was killed 292–219, with nine economists—Cayley,
Clay, Cobden, Gisborne, Hume, Molesworth, Muntz, J. L. Ricardo,
and Scrope—voting against it, and only the two economists in government, Peel and Graham, supporting it.[24] This vote brought down
the Peel government.

In later debates over Irish disturbances there was little change in

19. 3 H, 42: 788, 5 May 1838.
20. 3 H, 70: 139–41, 19 June 1843.
21. 3 H, 83: 1367–76, 23 Feb. 1846.
22. 3 H, 84: 710–13, 6 March 1846.
23. 3 H, 84: 696–702, 6 March 1846.
24. 3 H, 87: 1027–31, 25 June 1846.

the economists' position—in the Lords Brougham, Lansdowne, and Monteagle continuing to hold the view that repression of outrages was the essential first step, but in the Commons the great majority of economists feeling that reform was a prerequisite to peace in Ireland. As Hume put the case: "The people of Ireland had not been treated as men, they had not been treated as freemen; they had been dealt with as slaves. They had been treated doubly ill: they had been crushed by the proprietors of the soil, and neglected by the Legislature."[25] Two years later, in a plea for extending the franchise in Ireland, he said that the Irish had fewer rights than Hottentots, and added that "he hoped the Government would take a Liberal view of the matter, let them treat the Irish as they treated Hottentots."[26]

In Mill's short career in Parliament he spoke on several aspects of the Irish situation: praise for the government's plan to give greater fixity of tenure to small tenants;[27] support of the petition to spare the lives of men who had been sentenced to death for participation in rebellion in Ireland;[28] and disestablishment of the Church of Ireland, of which he said: "If there ever was a question on which I might say the whole human race had made up its mind, it is this."[29] But it is doubtful whether Mill's voice or vote in Parliament had any appreciable influence on policy. What he had said and written before entering Parliament undoubtedly had played a role in shaping support for reforms in government policy toward Ireland, but he was not a parliamentary leader in putting through these reforms, which were well on the road to acceptance before he took his seat at Westminster.

Colonial Policy

In many ways the problems of the colonies were those of Ireland in a lower key: local self-government, patronage administered by and for the benefit of the Westminster establishment, the nature of the political tie to Britain, even the extent to which the Established Church was to have a privileged position. On these issues economists lined up much as they did on Irish problems: more self-gov-

25. 3 H, 97: 872, 22 March 1848.
26. 3 H, 108: 1291, 22 Feb. 1850.
27. 3 H, 133: 1087–97, 17 May 1866; 160: 1525–26, 12 March 1868.
28. 3 H, 187: 1894–95, 14 June 1867.
29. 3 H, 190: 1516, 12 March 1868.

ernment and less concern about the imperial tie; more concern for the rights of individuals; opposition to the privileges of the Established Church. On one matter, however, there was a different approach. In much of the economists' discussions of Ireland ran the idea of financial exploitation by England, whereas discussion of the colonies was often colored with the idea that the colonies were a financial burden on England.

Not until after the Napoleonic wars did economists make more than passing remarks on colonial policy. It was Hume who first pressed the criticism, partly on the ground of the arbitrary rule by political appointees of Westminster, but even more because he felt colonial expenditures were a financial burden on the mother country.[30] Speaking of the newly acquired Ionian Islands, he said, "A variety of useless offices had been created, or at least filled, by the friends of ministers."[31] His motion for an investigation was defeated 152–67, with five economists in the minority—Althorp, Brougham, Grenfell, Hume, and David Ricardo.[32] The only economist to challenge Hume was Wilmot, who throughout his twelve-year parliamentary career was a consistent defender of colonial possessions, and of maintaining a strong hand of control from Westminster. The following year Hume stated in strident tones a view that economists were to reecho in the next thirty years: "It would be better for England to be destitute of colonies, than to be subjected to the enormous expense entailed on us by them. They were a mere drain on the country."[33] He told a distressing story of dictatorial rule in Newfoundland, which he said was in the situation of a ship commanded by an admiral.[34] His motion for a committee on the state of the colony was defeated 42–27, with Hume, David Ricardo, and Whitmore in the minority.[35] Seven years later Hume again attacked the Newfoundland situation, and although his motion for an investigation was defeated, 82–29, the minority included seven economists—Althorp, Brougham, Graham, Hume, Rice, Poulett Thomson, and Whitmore.[36] A similar motion for a Select Committee on the administra-

30. 1 H, 40: 268–72, 10 May 1819; 40: 1077–82, 10 June 1819.
31. 2 H, 4: 933–35, 28 Feb. 1821.
32. 2 H, 7: 596–97, 14 May 1822.
33. 2 H, 8: 595, 14 March 1823.
34. 2 H, 9: 245–54, 14 May 1823.
35. 2 H, 9: 255, 14 May 1823.
36. 2 H, 24: 593, 11 May 1830.

tion of Ceylon met the same fate—defeat 82–38, with six economists in the minority.[37]

Hume and Alexander Baring, in disagreement on many issues, were in general agreement in supporting more self-government for the colonies, and in resisting attempts to give the Church of England a privileged position there. Baring, in opposing the grant of lands in Canada for the Church of England, "was anxious that the House should not sow the seeds of that very dissention which we now so lamentably deplored in Ireland."[38] Three years later Howick objected to an appropriation for the propagation of the gospel in Canada, both on grounds of economy and objection to any action aimed at making one religion dominant there, and said that the privileged position of the church was one of the causes of Canadian discontent.[39] The appropriation was approved, 148–46, but the minority included seven economists—Althorp, Graham, Hume, Rice, Poulett Thomson, and Western.[40] Alexander Baring, despite his growing political conservatism and his pride in the imperial interests of Britain, had a deep sensing, perhaps from his intimate knowledge of the United States, of the urge toward self-government and independence among British peoples overseas. He even suggested that it might be better to abandon the colonies:

Now, he would contend, that Canada could not be kept as a colony of this country for a permanency, even if there were no hostile nation near it. It might be retained for thirty, forty, or fifty, years; but he repeated, that Canada was a country which could not be permanently attached to a European state.[41]

A decade later, when in the Lords as Lord Ashburton, with an anticipation of de Gaulle's suggestion of over a century later, Baring spoke of danger "if Lower Canada were established as a republic under the protection of France," and at the same time questioned the value of the colonies.[42]

Economists continued to press for greater self-government in Canada. When rebellion broke out in 1837, Grote said: "He, for

37. 2 H, 24: 1171, 27 May 1830.
38. 2 H, 16: 587, 20 Feb. 1827.
39. 2 H, 25: 341, 14 June 1830.
40. 2 H, 25: 346, 15 June 1830.
41. 2 H, 19: 1632, 4 July 1828.
42. 3 H, 40: 847–53, 8 Feb. 1838.

one would never consent to the employment of force to maintain the connexion between the mother country and the colony, whenever that connexion became onerous to the latter."[43] Further evidence of the divergence between the views of Parliament and the views of its economist members—and also the divergence of views among economists—came on a resolution, backed by the Whig government, for a hard-line policy toward Canada. The resolution was carried 269–46, with Graham, Howick, Parnell, Peel, Rice, and Poulett Thomson in the majority, and Clay, Grote, Hume, Molesworth, and Perronet Thompson in the minority.[44] Molesworth hoped for a peaceful separation of Canada from Britain,[45] as did Grote.[46] A compromise finally worked out by administrative action in 1848 gave Canada more self-government, and eventually led to complete self-government.

The economists' attitude toward Cape Colony and Australia closely followed the Canadian pattern. In the case of Cape Colony Alexander Baring in particular urged the need for more self-government.[47] In Australia Huskisson[48] and Gilbert[49] opposed the introduction of trial by jury and self-government, but Hume[50] and Rice[51] were favorable toward a greater degree of self-government. A split among the economists came over the question of the meeting of jail and police costs in New South Wales. Grote,[52] with the support of Molesworth,[53] felt that part of the cost of jails and police should be met by the mother country. Opposed was the unusual alliance of Peel and Hume, each one inspired by his particular economic crotchet—Peel by the feeling that such an expense might endanger the financial stability of England,[54] and Hume by his insistence that no colony should be a financial burden on England.[55] In the Lords both Mont-

43. 3 H, 39: 1456–67, 22 Dec. 1837.
44. 3 H, 37: 1290–93, 14 Apr. 1837.
45. 3 H, 39: 1456–67, 22 Dec. 1837.
46. 3 H, 40, 59–65, 16 Jan. 1838.
47. 2 H, 13: 1167, 16 June 1825; 17: 1168–70, 8 June 1827; 17: 1437–38, 29 June 1827.
48. 2 H, 18: 1553–55, 1559, 18 Apr. 1828; 19: 1459–62, 20 June 1828.
49. 2 H, 19: 1462, 20 June 1828.
50. 2 H, 19: 1462–63, 20 June 1828.
51. 2 H, 18: 1566, 18 Apr. 1828.
52. 3 H, 57: 598–607, 25 March 1841; 57: 974–79, 22 Apr. 1841.
53. 3 H, 57: 997–98, 22 Apr. 1841.
54. 3 H, 57: 998–1003, 22 Apr. 1841.
55. 3 H, 57: 1006, 22 Apr. 1841.

eagle[56] and Gray[57] urged greater self-government for Australia. In the Commons Molesworth warned that unless reforms were made the colonies would be lost, in the same way that the United States had been lost.[58] By 1850 self-government for the colonies had been settled—the only questions at issue were details, and the Australian Colonies Government bill was passed in both Houses without recorded vote.[59]

Foreign Affairs

On foreign affairs economists were less nationalistic, less eager to fight for the country's honor and glory, less anxious to force other countries to have a government like that of England, more prepared to believe that foreign countries would take a reasonable approach that would permit compromise without the shedding of blood. Although never stated in so many words, implicit in much of the attitude of economists was that carrying on a profitable trade was more important than some nebulous notion of national honor.

This position is revealed in the attitude toward France following the Revolution. Until 1800 the only economist to take a hard line toward France, and to support the war with enthusiasm, was Hawkesbury.[60] On the other hand, Lauderdale[61] and King[62] either criticized the war or were favorable toward peace negotiations; and Lauderdale opposed the idea, then held by many English, that England should try to determine the form of France's government. In the Commons Thornton "trusted that every symptom of a disposition to peace, whether in Great Britain or in France, would tend to encourage the same disposition in the other country,"[63] and supported the resolution of William Wilberforce, his fellow member of the Clapham Sect, that the existence of a particular form of govern-

56. 3 H, 106: 1115–19, 2 July 1849.
57. 3 H, 106: 1120–26, 1130–31, 2 July 1849.
58. 3 H, 108: 567–79, 8 Feb. 1850.
59. 13 & 14 Vict., c. 59.
60. P.H., 30: 421–22, 12 Feb. 1793; 31: 681–83, 30 May 1974; 34: 1062, 28 Jan. 1800.
61. P.H., 31: 1452, 30 March 1795; 31: 1276–77, 27 Jan. 1795.
62. P.H., 36: 1507–9, 25 May 1803.
63. P.H., 31: 1246, 26 Jan. 1795.

ment in France should not preclude peace negotiations. Western[64] and Sinclair[65] both expressed peace sentiments.

After Napoleon's escape from Elba the question arose whether England should at once move against him or wait until Napoleon started a war. A peace amendment was voted down, 220–37, with Althorp and Horner the only economists in the minority.[66] After the war most economists who spoke on the matter were critical of Castlereagh's cynical power politics. Alexander Baring on several occasions criticized British support for the tyranny of Ferdinand in Spain, and the deposing of the king of Ceylon.[67] Horner made a similar criticism,[68] and Brougham "protested against our right to interfere with another nation, by dictating to it the form of government it should adopt or by imposing on a great people any king or family it might be our wish to see reign over them."[69] Brougham's motion, critical of the government policy toward Spain, was defeated 123–42, with Brougham, Grenfell, and Horner in the minority.[70] The economists' criticism was directed not only at the substance of Castlereagh's foreign policy, but also at the secrecy with which it was carried on. With the exception of Vansittart, a member of government, no economist spoke in support of Castlereagh's foreign policy. Alexander Baring was critical of the government for interfering in the Dutch-Belgian and Portugese problems.[71] After the Polish uprising of 1833 Cobbett deplored sending the Poles to Siberia, but said this punishment was not as bad as driving the Scotch from their homes: "He always distrusted those who went to a distance to find objects of compassion, when they might discover them so much nearer home."[72]

There were exceptions to the dominant noninterference attitude of the economists. Thomas Attwood combined a sturdy middle-class patriotism with a particular dislike of Russians. His motion not to

64. P.H., P.H., 33: 427, 10 Apr. 1797.
65. P.H., 33: 1024–25, 10 Nov. 1797.
66. 1 H, 30: 463, 7 Apr. 1815. The names of the majority are not listed, but Alexander Baring, in a speech the following month, urged an immediate attack on France (31: 466–67, 26 May 1815).
67. 1 H, 32: 66–69, 2 Feb. 1816.
68. 1 H, 29: 1158–60, 1 March 1815.
69. 1 H, 32: 578–93, 609–10, 612, 15 Feb. 1816.
70. 1 H, 32: 613, 15 Feb. 1816.
71. 3 H, 16: 907–10, 26 March 1832.
72. 3 H, 16: 19–20, 1 March 1833.

recognize any disposition of Polish territory contrary to the Treaty of Vienna was defeated 177–95, with nine economists—Althorp, Graham, Grote, Howick, Peel, Rice, Scrope, Torrens, and Whitmore—in the majority and five—Thomas Attwood, Cayley, Cobbett, Hume, and Molesworth—in the minority.[73] Attwood's simplistic view was "England could at one blow crush the bully to dust";[74] two years later he was even more belligerent: "Now we must go to war."[75] Muntz, successor to Attwood's Birmingham seat, in 1853 took a similar tough attitude toward Russia.[76]

Relations with Greece involved several considerations that in individual cases pulled at cross-purposes: sentimental attachment to the restored Greek nation; dislike of the German royal family imported to sit on the Hellenic throne; and what were conceived to be Britain's diplomatic interests. In 1850 a motion calling for a more determined stand against Greek actions was carried 310–264. The voting produced another collection of strange bedfellows, with eight economists—Cayley, Clay, Lewis, Muntz, J. L. Ricardo, Scrope, Perronet Thompson, and Wilson—in the majority, and five economists—Cobden, Graham, Hume, Molesworth, and Peel—in the minority.[77] During the Crimean War economists said little, either pro or con, on the prosecution of the war, other than hawkish speeches by Hume,[78] Clay,[79] and Molesworth, in one of which Molesworth said of Cobden: "I have disagreed with him on his extraordinary views with regard to the possibility of universal peace."[80] Brougham, in a criticism of the foreign policy of the Derby government, well summarized a feeling that a large majority of parliamentary economists had held since the early protests of Lauderdale and King against attempts to influence France's government:

. . . he must protest against what appeared to be a too generally prevailing notion, at least out of doors, among those who were rather prone to be led away by their feelings than guided by their judgment, that it was the vocation of this country—or, as it was called in the half-English language of the

73. 3 H, 19: 463, 9 July 1833.
74. 3 H, 22: 659, 25 March 1834.
75. 3 H, 31: 640, 19 Feb. 1836.
76. 3 H, 129: 1794–96, 16 Aug. 1853.
77. 3 H, 112: 739–43, 28 June 1850.
78. 3 H, 135: 1390–91, 7 Aug. 1854.
79. 3 H, 138: 1598–1600, 7 June 1855.
80. 3 H, 134: 1841, 3 Aug. 1855.

day, the mission of the country—to intermeddle in the affairs of foreign nations for the purpose of redressing the grievances of subjects of foreign princes, of restraining the conduct of those princes, and of propagating constitutional government all over the world.[81]

81. 3 H, cxxxxiv, 80, 3 Feb. 1857.

Chapter 14

Reform of Parliament and of Local Government

The great majority of economists in Parliament, aside from the Tory politicians Peel, Rose, and Vansittart, were supporters of electoral reform. Central to this was the widening of the franchise, but what the economists wanted embraced much more, in particular the reduction of parliamentary representation by constituencies of small population and the increase of representation by urban areas, some of which, such as Birmingham, before the Reform Act had sent no members to Parliament. Closely associated with the franchise and the size of constituencies was the campaign for the secret ballot. So the move for election reform moved on many fronts. In its early years the reform movement did not call for anything approaching universal manhood suffrage, and many of the earlier reformers emphasized that they were against anything so radical.

Association of Economic Reforms and Parliamentary Reform

It is understandable that the predominant view of economists was favorable to parliamentary reform, for it was in line with their general view of judging established institutions in light of reason, and of their opposition to monopoly in all fields. But the economists' support of parliamentary reform was more than just a philosophic view of children of the Enlightenment. It was the belief of most economists before 1832 that economic improvement was possible only by legislative action to wipe out ancient citadels of privilege and monopoly, and that such legislative action could come only with a parliamentary reform that would create a House of Commons more responsive to public opinion and public wants. This was said, many times in many settings, by the parliamentary economists, but one of the most succinct statements came from Hume in 1831 in a debate on timber duties, shortly before Commons approved of the

Reform bill: " . . . there was not a man who voted for Reform, who did not regard it as the means of obtaining something better . . . the people must see the inutility of all attempts to carry great measures of national utility through Parliament till the Bill had enabled them to return such a House of Commons as dare not imitate the conduct of the majority on the Timber Duties."[1]

Early Position of Economists on Parliamentary Reform

Before the revolution in France parliamentary reform had support from many political leaders including Burke and Pitt. But the revolution, for the great majority of upper-class British, put under a cloud anything that suggested giving more power to the people. In 1809 a bill was introduced to stop election bribery and the sale of parliamentary seats, but made no change in the franchise or in parliamentary constituencies. It was a mild measure that barely scratched the surface of a deep-seated abuse, but it met strenuous and in some cases almost hysterical opposition from many conservative members. Among economists, however, Giddy was the only one critical of the bill. He made clear his political philosophy: " . . . he thought that property and power should invariably be connected together, for without that connection, no peace could be maintained in society. Corruption, influence, and property, were as closely connected as usury and money."[2] Thornton[3] and Petty[4] supported the bill, but felt it should have been much stronger. The following year Giddy[5] and Jacob[6] spoke against a motion favorable to a reform of Parliament. The motion was defeated 234–115, with six economists—Alexander Baring, Brougham, Horner, Parnell, Thornton, and Western in the minority.[7]

In the years immediately after the close of the Napoleonic wars, when fears of plots against the social order were widespread and the Six Acts were passed, the move for parliamentary reform made little headway. Among economists Brougham was the only one to

---

1. 3 H, 4:523–24, 30 June 1831.
2. 1 H, 14:723, 26 May 1809. Giddy said much the same thing on 6 June 1809, 14:902–3.
3. 1 H, 14:993–94, 12 June 1809.
4. 1 H, 14:902, 6 June 1809.
5. 1 H, 17:133–37, 21 May 1810.
6. 1 H, 17:142, 21 May 1810.
7. 1 H, 17:164–65, 21 May 1810.

push it, and he made it clear that he opposed universal suffrage or annual parliaments.[8] In the minds of many members of Parliament, including some economists, even mild measures of reform were the entering wedge of revolution. Grenfell said of the reform movement: " . . . machinations of those men, some of them deluded, but others wicked and dangerous, who under the name of reform, were endeavouring to effect revolution, and to involve the country in anarchy and confusion."[9] And in Wilmot's view the agitation for reform "coincided so accurately, in point of time, with those meetings throughout the country which he could characterize by no other name than seditious."[10]

In the early 1820s the presence of new economists in Parliament, notably Hume and David Ricardo, the increasing publicity given to the more egregious cases of bribery and representation of rotten boroughs, and some reaction from the high water mark of hysteria about revolution gave impetus to the move for parliamentary reform, with economists playing an important role. Grenfell did an about face, and said that after the recent action of the Commons in supporting the omission of Queen Caroline's name from the Liturgy following the dropping of her trial for adultery, he felt that Parliament did not represent the public's views.[11] Peel, in opposing a motion to disfranchise Grampound, where political corruption had been rife, and transfer its seat to Leeds, laid bare his political philosophy on the proper role of the ordinary man in government: " . . . there were circumstances in the locality of Leeds that made it disadvantageous to give an unlimited right of voting. It was a great manufacturing town, and such an abstraction of the people from their habits of industry would work a great disservice."[12]

Lord John Russell's motion favorable to a reform of Parliament, and calling for a committee of investigation, was defeated, but the vote as compared with earlier votes suggested that parliamentary reform was an idea whose time was coming. The motion lost, 155–124, but only three economists—Gilbert, Huskisson, and Wilmot—opposed it, whereas seven—Althorp, Alexander Baring, Brougham,

---

8. 2 H, 35:155–56, 31 Jan. 1817; and on other occasions.
9. 1 H, 35:222 7 Feb. 1817.
10. 1 H, 40:1478, 1 July 1819.
11. 2 H, 4:223–24, 31 Jan. 1821.
12. 2 H, 4:1073, 2 March 1821.

Hume, David Ricardo, Rice, and Whitmore—supported it.[13] Russell continued to press for parliamentary reform, and in 1823 Ricardo gave a long speech in favor of Russell's motion. On one issue, however, that for the next fifty years was to play a prominent role in the demands for electoral reform, Ricardo differed from Russell. Ricardo felt that without the ballot—that is, secret voting—no electoral change would be effective in making the Commons responsive to public opinion:

The simple question for them to determine was, whether they would not purify the House, when it was notorious that it could not be considered, in the fair sense of the words, to represent the people? . . . The question of reform was naturally divided into three considerations. First, the extension of the suffrage; secondly, the mode of election; and thirdly, the duration of parliaments. As to extension of the suffrage, important as he felt that topic to be, and convinced as he was that it ought to be extended much beyond its present limits, still the other two points appeared to him to be of deeper interest. In the arrangement of the suffrages, the whole of the people might be represented, and yet the House might be composed of persons whose elections had been procured by improper means. It was for this reason that he was compelled to dissent from his noble friend's proposal for transferring a portion of the representatives from close boroughs to extensive counties. He thought the whole system of election which prevailed at present was illegal. Of what use was it that the power of choosing its representatives should be given to the people, unless the free exercise of that right were also secured to them? He contended, that so long as the influence of the aristocracy possessed, as it did now, the means of biassing the votes of the people, this House could not be a fair representation of that people. Let it not be supposed, that he wished to deprive the aristocracy of that just influence which it derived from its wealth and respectability; but he thought that it became most pernicious, when it was exercised for the purpose of influencing elections. Of its practical evil, every person's own knowledge would furnish many and ample proofs. How could it be expected, that a man whose means of procuring a livelihood depended mainly upon the patronage and support of those who were in a more elevated rank—how could it be expected, for instance, that the inferior class of tradesmen—should withstand the threats and terrors which might be put into execution, to prevent them from voting according to their conscience? To look for this would be to call upon small freeholders for a degree of severe virtue which had no corresponding example in the higher ranks of society. There was but one method of obviating these difficulties; which was by altering the mode of election, and adopting the ballot instead of open votes. If this were done, they would have a house of commons

13. 2 H, 5:624–26, 9 May 1821.

which would fairly represent the people. . . . The demands of the people might be easily satisfied. They asked only for that which was perfectly reasonable—that they might have a voice in the public councils, and the power of restraining the expenditure of their own money.[14]

The motion was defeated, 280–169, with the same seven economists in the minority as on the motion of 9 May 1821.[15] For the next six years the issue of parliamentary reform was quiescent, overshadowed by the financial problems of 1825 and 1826, the Irish situation, and in particular the controversy over Catholic emancipation.

The Reform Act of 1832

As debate on parliamentary reform revived in 1830, economists emphasized the connection between reform of Parliament and economic reform. Lord King, speaking of the many petitions that had come to him, said "They all concurred in demanding cheap government, cheap law, cheap corn, cheap coals, a free trade, and a reform in Parliament."[16] In 1826 Lord Howick, fresh from taking private lessons in political economy from McCulloch, was elected to the Commons, bringing with him a concern for economic principles and an urge for reform on all fronts. He soon stressed the association of "profligacy and extravagance" and the unreformed Commons: "To him it appeared that nothing could essentially serve the country but a perfect and complete reform of the house."[17] Hume linked together parliamentary reform, abolition of the Corn Laws and reduction in expenditures;[18] Parnell gave as one reason for reform the need to have in Parliament more men who understood political economy;[19] and Gisborne said that the unreformed Parliament had not handled finances in the public interest, and cited high salaries and pensions.[20] Several motions favorable to reform were defeated, but the economists' votes were overwhelmingly for reform. A bill to give representation to the burgeoning cities of Birmingham, Leeds, and Manchester was defeated 188–140, with twelve

14. 2 H, 8:1280–81, 1283, 24 Apr. 1823. The speech is in Ricardo, *Works*, 5:283–89.
15. 2 H, 8:1287–89, 24 Apr. 1823.
16. 3 H, 1:1290, 17 Dec. 1830.
17. 2 H, 22:717–18, 13 Feb. 1830.
18. 3 H, 2:6–7, 21 Dec. 1830.
19. 3 H, 3:360–61, 11 March 1831.
20. 3 H, 3:20–27, 4 March 1831.

economists—including Alexander Baring and Huskisson, who were both opposed to any sweeping reform—in the minority, and only Gilbert and Peel against this limited move.[21] Peel, in opposing this measure, which he feared was a step toward universal manhood suffrage, criticized the oppressive legislation of the American state of Georgia under universal white manhood suffrage.[22] With the perspective of history the views of some of the economists in the forefront of supporters of reform were extremely mild, and would today be considered archreactionary. For example, Brougham objected both to the ballot and to universal suffrage;[23] Althorp, although favorable to the ballot, opposed universal suffrage,[24] and Western was "decidedly opposed to the principle of election by ballot. It would banish every species of confidence, and communication, and interchange of opinion between the elected and the electors, and would be productive of eternal suspicion of hypocrisy. It was an un-English, an un-Irish principle. The adoption of such a principle, he considered, would be destructive of the spirit of our Constitution."[25]

The Reform Bill, after many amendments, passed the Commons on the second reading, 302–301, with eleven economists in the majority, and four—Matthias Attwood, Alexander Baring, Gilbert, and Peel—in the minority.[26] Subsequent votes, after dissolution and the meeting of the new Parliament in June 1831, showed essentially the same picture, with Torrens, newly elected, adding to the reform cause his vote and his philosophy: "A temporary excitement might with safety be resisted, but the present demand for Reform sprung from the principles of human nature, and could not be successfully opposed."[27]

Following the passage of the Reform Bill by the Commons on 21 September 1831, the Lords defeated it, 199–158, with Brougham, King, and Lansdowne voting for the bill, and Bexley, Lauderdale, and the bishop of Llandaff opposing it.[28] After the constitutional crisis created by the Lords' rejection of the bill, in 1832 the Commons

21. 2 H, 22:915, 23 Feb. 1830.
22. 2 H, 22:902–9, 23 Feb. 1830.
23. 2 H, 24:1244–53, 28 May 1830.
24. 2 H, 24:1230–34, 28 May 1830.
25. 2 H, 22:1337, 5 March 1830.
26. 3 H, 3:806–18, 22 March 1831.
27. 3 H, 4:771, 4 July 1831.
28. 3 H, 8:339–44, 7 Oct. 1831.

supported the bill in second reading, 355–239, with twelve economists in favor, and Matthias Attwood, Alexander Baring and Peel opposed.[29]

As emotions intensified, economists repeated their arguments that parliamentary reform was necessary to bring about economic reform. Torrens, challenging the Tory claim that the present system of representation had worked well, asked rhetorically: "Was it in the amount of the debt, of the taxes, or the poor rates? Was it in the agricultural districts, where the rural population were serfs and helots of the soil? Was it in the manufacturing towns, where the system of infant slavery prevailed?" He then continued in the best Torrensian style, with words that rank high as political philosophy: "Society was essentially progressive. . . . The resistance of the Tory party to the rising spirit of liberty in North America occasioned the most calamitous war in which this country ever was engaged. . . . Time, the despotic innovator."[30] And Parnell, in the full flush of enthusiasm just after the passage of the Reform Act, said that the Chancellor of the Exchequer "would be impelled to be economical by the new influence which would grow out of Reform in Parliament, by a different description of members being chosen by the new electors of the United Kingdom. In this way he looked forward to seeing that the first great practical benefit the public would derive from the Reform of Parliament would be an efficient financial reform."[31] The Lords, under the threat of the creation of more Lords, passed the bill on second reading, 184–175, with Brougham, Lansdowne, and the bishop of Llandaff supporting the bill, leaving Bexley, the Tory politician, and Lauderdale, the reformer of earlier years who had repudiated the ideas of his youth, as the only economist Lords in opposition.[32] The English Reform Act became law on June 7, 1832.[33]

---

29. 3 H, 11:780, 22 March 1832. Every economist voted except Gilbert, who had voted against the Reform bill the previous year. It is not clear whether Gilbert was unavoidably absent, or whether he deliberately abstained from voting on a bill about which he had mixed feelings—he felt that some reform was necessary but that the bill went too far. He wished the bill amended, and said: "It appeared to him that the great object of the Bill should be to extend the franchise, as far as possible, to all persons of intelligence and property, so as to combine them against the friends of anarchy and confusion" (9:1100, 1 Feb. 1832). In May, when it was evident that the bill would pass, Gilbert urged all independent members to support it (12:975–76, 14 May 1832). There was no recording of individual votes on the third reading.
30. 3 H, 11:514–16, 20 March 1832.
31. 3 H, 14:866–67, 27 July 1832.
32. 3 H, 12:454, 13 Apr. 1832.
33. 2 & 3 Will. IV, c. 45.

Reform of English Municipal Corporations

The Reform Act did not settle the electoral problem; it only averted a civil war and provided a beachhead from which those who wished more thoroughgoing reforms could move. The ink was hardly dry on the king's signature before they mounted their drive. Radical as the measure may have seemed to many at the time, by the standards of modern democracy the election situation was still in an archaic state of aristocratic domination. The total electorate was barely 14 percent of the adult male population. Public polling enabled landlords, employers, and patrons of local tradesmen to put pressure on voters. The electoral monstrosity of Old Sarum was ended, but boroughs with only a few thousand residents, and in some cases with less than two hundred voters, continued to return two members.[34] The municipal corporations presented a picture of corruption, inequitable taxation, and exclusion of many freeholders from any share in local government, and any voice in the election of members of Parliament.

Graham regarded the Reform Act of 1832 as final, and resisted any moves for more electoral reform, but all of the other parliamentary economists who had supported the Reform Act wanted further reform, although they were not agreed as to just what it should be. The Reform Act was followed by a substantial increase in the parliamentary representation of economists, and particularly men of more radical, or at least politically liberal, views. Eight new economists were elected in 1832 to the first Reform Parliament—Thomas Attwood, Cayley, Clay, Cobbett, Fielden, Grote, Molesworth, and Pryme—equal in number to those elected for the first time in the four previous elections. Early in 1833 Scrope was winner in a by-election for Stroud, following the resignation of David Ricardo, son of the economist, who had defeated Scrope in 1832.

Althorp, shortly after the first meeting of the Reform Parliament, said that "the complaints of the malversations of Corporations were constantly and universally heard," and moved for select committees on the municipal corporations of England, Wales, and Ireland.[35] Althorp, Clay, Peel, Pryme, and Poulett Thomson were members. No legislative action followed, but Althorp's remark was a warning of

34. Derek Beales, *From Castlereagh to Gladstone* (London: Belson, 1969), p. 86.
35. 3 H, 15:646–47, 14 Feb. 1833.

what was to come: "No man could be more convinced than he was of the necessity of making a Reform in Corporations, and he should be sorry to remain a member of any Government who would not attempt it."[36]

On 5 June 1835 Lord John Russell presented for the government a bill for the reform of the municipal corporations of England and Wales. The story of the Reform Act of 1832—an attempt by the archconservatives in Parliament to block any effective reform—was repeated. Peel restated a view that he had expressed many times before:

Of this I am satisfied, that no system of Municipal Government, however specious in its theory, will promote the object for which alone it ought to be designed, will ensure the maintenance of public order, the pure administration of justice, or the harmony and happiness of the societies to which it is to be applied, unless its direct tendency be to commit the management of Municipal affairs to the hands of those who from the possession of property have the strongest interest in good government, and, from the qualification of high character and intelligence, are most likely to conciliate the respect and confidence of their fellow citizens.[37]

Economists did not play a prominent part in debate in supporting the corporation reform bill, but their votes left no doubt of their position. A crucial clause in the bill was carried 278–232, with fourteen economists in the majority, and only Graham and Peel in opposition.[38] The bill was drastically amended in the Lords. Ashburton expressed his fear of universal suffrage: "He could not conceive how malevolence itself could introduce into any place which was the resort of manufacturing industry a greater curse than the Corporation Reform Bill must inevitably prove."[39] The Lords rejected, 144–82, the Commons provision, with Brougham, Lansdowne, Spencer (formerly Lord Althorp, who had moved to the Lords in 1834, on the death of his father), and Western supporting the Commons version.[40] A compromise between the Commons and Lords bills that still narrowly restricted the franchise was finally passed without recorded vote.[41]

---

36. 3 H, 20:263, 1 Aug. 1833.
37. 3 H, 28:571, 5 June 1835.
38. 3 H, 28:1112–16, 23 June 1835.
39. 3 H, 30:192, 10 Aug. 1835.
40. 3 H, 30:1372–73, 4 Sept. 1835.
41. 5 & 6 Will. IV, c. 76.

Reform of Irish Municipal Corporations

A more intense conflict, with even sharper difference of opinion, arose the following year over the move from Melbourne's Whig government to reform the Irish municipal corporations. In addition to the issue, in the English situation, of abolishing the ancient privileges of a small group and granting some approach to representative democracy, at the heart of the bitterness over the Irish situation was the dominance by a small minority of Protestants of municipal corporations of which an overwhelming percentage of the residents were Catholics. The issue was epitomized by the remarks of Gisborne and Peel. Gisborne said: " . . . notwithstanding all the declarations of the Gentlemen opposite, in favour of Reform, the real principle upon which they had always acted, and upon which they were always prepared to act, was this, that any abuse or corruption had better be preserved, than by its removal to give an increased popular power."[42] Peel's answer in effect admitted the thrust of Gisborne's attack: "I do feel justified, therefore, in withholding my assent to a measure which will be the signal for fresh animosities, and which will endanger the security of the Protestant Church and Protestant Establishment of Ireland."[43] A motion in the Commons to weaken the bill was defeated 307–243. Fifteen economists voted in the majority, and only three—Matthias Attwood, Graham, and Peel—tried to stem the flood waters of change.[44] The Lords, by a vote of 220–123, killed the Commons bill, with Ashburton and Bexley holding out against the Commons.[45] The story was repeated in session after session—the Commons voting for reform of the Irish municipal corporations, the Lords amending the heart out of proposals; the economists in the Commons overwhelmingly for reform, the economists in the Lords also favoring reform, but by a smaller margin. Finally, in 1840, in the fifth session in which a bill for Irish corporation reform was introduced, a law was passed providing most, but not all, of the reforms that the Commons wished. By then the supporters and opponents of Irish corporation reform had fought themselves to a standstill—supporters realized that they could

42. 3 H, 32:725, 28 March 1836.
43. 3 H, 32:741, 28 March 1836.
44. 3 H, 32:119, 8 March 1836.
45. 3 H, 34:963–67, 27 June 1836.

not get all they wished, and all but the last-ditch reactionaries knew that something must be conceded to avoid another Irish crisis. The bill passed the Commons 182–34, with Graham and Peel joining five other economists in voting for the bill, and no economist opposing it.[46] The bill passed the Lords without recorded vote, and became law on 10 August 1840.[47]

Moves for Further Parliamentary Reform

The gradation of opinion among economists as to just how far electoral reform should go is shown by a motion to shorten the duration of Parliament—a move supported by many as a means of making Parliament more responsive to public opinion. The motion was defeated 213–164, with eleven economists in the minority, and eight—Althorp, Gisborne, Graham, Howick, Peel, Rice, Poulett Thomson, and Whitmore—opposing the motion.[48] Aside from the reform of municipal corporations, for many years the chief objective of reform was not the extension of the franchise, or even the giving of greater representation to more populous areas, but the adoption of the secret ballot. When the Reform Parliaments did not move fast enough or far enough to satisfy many, including economists, who were pressing for change on many fronts, the situation was blamed on the open polls, which, it was felt, prevented many tenants, employees, and small shopkeepers from voting for the candidates they preferred.

Grote, first elected in 1832 to the Reform Parliament, quickly became the leading parliamentary spokesman for the ballot. His motion for vote by ballot was defeated, 211–106, with ten economists favoring the ballot, and eight opposed, with several who had given strong support to the Reform Act of 1832 indicating that the ballot was going too far. The division is broadly indicative of a split that took place a number of times in the 1830s and 1840s between economists who wanted to press ahead with more radical reform, and those who favored reform but on a more limited scale:[49]

46. 3 H, 52:1068–70, 9 March 1840.
47. 3 & 4 Vict., c. 108.
48. 3 H, 19:1150, 23 July 1833.
49. 3 H, 17:667–70, 25 Apr. 1833.

In favor of ballot	Against ballot
Thomas Attwood	Althorp
Clay	Cayley
Cobbett	Graham
Fielden	Howick
Grote	Peel
Hume	Pryme
Molesworth	Rice
Morrison	Whitmore
Parnell	
Torrens	

Grote continued to press for the ballot, and votes each year from 1834 to 1839 showed the same pattern—defeat by a margin of about two to one, but with the majority of economists supporting the ballot. Muntz, elected in 1840 to replace Thomas Attwood after the latter's resignation, and Cobden and John Lewis Ricardo, elected in 1841, were economists who also favored the ballot and widening the franchise.[50] Fielden said that a remedy to the country's abuses could "not be expected till Parliament was more opened to the influence of the working classes."[51]

In 1839 Thomas Attwood presented to the Commons the Chartist petition calling for far-reaching electoral reforms, and moved its consideration,[52] and Fielden seconded the motion. It was defeated 235–46, with five economists—Thomas Attwood, Fielden, Grote, Hume, and Molesworth—supporting it, and eight economists—Clay, Graham, Howick, Parnell, Pryme, Rice, Scrope, and Poulett Thomson voting against the motion.[53] In 1849 another Chartist petition was presented, and the Commons, by a vote of 222–13, refused to endorse it.[54] The only economists to support the petition were Hume and Perronet Thompson, and Peel, Muntz, and James Wilson opposed it. Muntz, in explaining his vote, stated an opinion that may have been shared by other economists favorable to some electoral reform who simply refrained from voting. Muntz said that he agreed

50. 3 H, 62:967–70, 21 Apr. 1842.
51. 3 H, 69:511, 18 May 1843.
52. 3 H, 49:220–35, 12 July 1839.
53. 3 H, 49:274–77, 12 July 1839.
54. 3 H, 106:1304–6, 3 July 1849.

with a large part of the petition, but that he could not support the idea of annual parliaments, and he felt that the opening statements of the petition "that the labourer should be the first partaker of the fruits of his industry was very ambiguous."[55] Immediately after the rejection of the second Chartist petition a motion by Hume for a sweeping electoral change—ballot, vote to all householders, three-year parliaments, apportionment of members with more regard to population—was also too strong a diet for Parliament and was overwhelmingly defeated, 351–84. Six economists supported the motion and five opposed it—the trio that had been steadfast against further reform, Cayley, Graham, and Peel, plus two new members, Lewis and Wilson, who were ardent free traders but lukewarm about political innovations.[56]

Hume, Muntz, and Perronet Thompson continued to press, in the late 1840s and 1850s, for the ballot and widening the franchise. The same voting pattern was repeated a dozen times or more— defeat of reform proposals, but by narrower margins as the years moved on, and with the economists giving a substantial majority for further reform. The death of Peel removed the most determined and politically influential opponent among economists; but among the new economists in Commons Butt, in the conservative mood of his early parliamentary years, opposed the ballot as "an un-English mode of voting."[57]

As events were to prove, the opinion of parliamentary economists on electoral reform was at least fifteen years ahead of political leadership in both parties, and of general parliamentary opinion. Wilson, whose remarks were usually confined to banking and fiscal questions, in supporting electoral reform, remarked that this was "a question of a class with which he very seldom meddled;"[58] Lewis, who earlier had opposed the ballot, by 1860 supported reform legislation;[59] and Northcote, a political conservative who had entered Parliament in 1855, in 1859 was speaking favorably of limited reform.[60]

---

55. 3 H, 106:1302–3, 3 July 1849.
56. 3 H, c, 226–29, 6 July 1848.
57. 3 H, 134:110, 13 June 1854.
58. 3 H, 153:531–42, 22 March 1859.
59. 3 H, 157:2172–87, 23 Apr. 1860.
60. 3 H, 153:826–39, 25 March 1859.

Second Reform Act of 1867

By 1860 it was clear that substantial parliamentary reform was coming—the only question was when, the exact form, and whether under a Conservative or a Liberal government. In 1866 the Russell Liberal ministry sponsored a reform bill that was approved, 318–313, on second reading, with five economists— Fawcett, Goschen, Hankey, John Stuart Mill, and Scrope, favoring it; and Hubbard, Lowe, and Northcote opposing it.[61] The bill, however, after several amendments, was withdrawn and the Russell ministry resigned. Lord Derby's new ministry then brought in a reform bill which, after many amendments and much argument over technical details, was finally passed without recorded vote. Probably the best indication of the opinion of parliamentary economists at this time was the vote on an amendment proposed by Gladstone to extend the franchise even further. The amendment lost, 310–289, but seven of the eight economists voted for the amendment, including Hubbard and Lowe, who heretofore had been lukewarm toward further parliamentary reform; and only Northcote opposed the amendment.[62] The bill was finally approved in both houses without recorded vote and became law on 15 August 1867.[63] The ballot was not mentioned in the act and its adoption five years later[64] was an anticlimax to a reform movement in which economists had in vain broken so many lances for nearly forty years.

61. 3 H, 183:152–56, 27 Apr. 1866.
62. 3 H, 156:1699–1703, 12 Apr. 1867.
63. 30 & 31 Vict., c. 102.
64. 35 & 36 Vict., c. 33, 18 July 1872.

Chapter 15

The Economists' Influence in Parliament

To tell how economists got into Parliament, to survey the campaign issues, to indicate how they voted and what they said, to list their committee memberships is relatively easy. To tell how effective an economist, as a member of Parliament, was in shaping legislation is more difficult. To be specific, how did national policy differ from what it would have been had John Stuart Mill, David Ricardo, Thornton, and Torrens simply written about economic problems; had Parnell, Rice, and Scrope remained country gentlemen who wrote books and articles for the *Edinburgh Review* and *Quarterly Review*; or had Brougham, Hume, and Perronet Thompson been repulsed in their political ambitions and devoted to writing and speaking their amazing energy and urge to change the old order?

Measures of Economists' Influence

There were five principal ways in which an economist, as a member of Parliament, could influence legislation: (1) voting, (2) speaking, (3) sponsoring legislation as a private member, (4) being a member and in particular chairman of a select committee, and (5) being a member of government. To generalize as to what some sixty men said or how they voted over nearly ninety years is difficult, particularly when a number—notable examples are the Earl of Lauderdale, Alexander Baring, Butt, Gilbert, Graham, and Peel—changed their views as they grew older, or under the pressure of politics. Furthermore, as so large a proportion of the economists had Whig sympathies, there is always the question whether their votes and their speeches represented their views as economists or their views as politicians. But it is easy to overplay this question. The same intellectual and ideological interests that led men to become economists in the years from Adam Smith to John Stuart Mill usually also gave them a Whig or Radical political orientation. The parliamentary activities of economists have repeatedly underscored that for a large part of the economists of the period—excluding politicians like Peel who were forced to become economists—economics and a liberal political philosophy were two sides of the same coin: a belief in change, a playing down of status, skepticism about the dead hand of tradition, a willingness to let the choices of individuals determine economic processes, political action, and even religious belief.

Much of the economists' attention in Parliament was given to political issues. As indicated earlier (pp. 213–14), this was in considerable part because a great majority of economists, at least until the 1850s, apparently felt that political change was a prerequisite to accomplishing their economic aims. Furthermore, the economists' support of many social and political changes sprang from the same intellectual ideals that led them to challenge traditional practices or ancient legislation that governed the production of goods and services. Diverse as were the paths by which economists traveled to Westminster, there was an approach to a uniform pattern in their political and social philosophy, both in their election campaigns and in their parliamentary careers; and this pattern was almost unanimous if we exclude the Tory politicians who became economists from on-the-job training. Reform of Parliament, the ballot, cutting down the privileged position of the Church of England, disestablishing the Church of Ireland, granting full civil rights to Catholics, Dissenters, and Jews, removing the political and economic privileges of the landed aristocracy, ending abuses in the army and navy showed a high percentage of economist support, frequently when Parliament as a whole overwhelmingly took the opposite view.

There is no hard statistical evidence on the point, but there were many indications that economists were more regular in attendance than were the great majority of their colleagues. What is certain, however, is their participation in roll calls. Judged by modern legislative practices, many members of both houses took their public duties lightly. The characterization by John Stuart Mill in 1868 about the Commons' membership was even more pertinent before 1832: "They desired to diminish the number of men in this House, who came in, not for the purpose of maintaining any political opinions whatever, but solely for the purpose, by a lavish expenditure, of acquiring the social position which attended a seat in the House, and which, perhaps, was not otherwise to be obtained by them."[1] Beginning in 1805 when roll calls became more frequent,[2] in more than 75 percent of the recorded votes less than one half of the members of the Commons and less than one third of the Lords voted. Frequently less than 25 percent of the Commons voted, and in 1844 and 1845 in twenty-five roll calls less than fifty members voted. In less than 5 percent of roll calls between 1805 and 1868 did over 500 members—out of a total membership of 658—vote.

In contrast, most economist members of Parliament had a sense of mission. It was not to acquire the social prestige of being addressed as "Honourable Member," to have political power for its own sake, or to sponsor legislation for their private benefit, but to further ideas in which they believed that a large majority of the economists had sought seats in Parliament. This was particularly true of David Ricardo and John Stuart Mill; only to a slightly less degree could it be said of many others, notably Thomas Attwood, Cobbett, Cobden, Fawcett, Grote, Horner, Hume, Muntz, Pryme, Scrope, Perronet Thompson, Thornton, Torrens, and Wilson. In 278 important divisions in the Commons in which majority and minority are listed, the economist showed a substantially higher percentage of voting than did the entire Commons—66 percent as compared with 54 percent. Before the Reform Act the higher voting record of economists was even more striking; in only one case in thirty-six important divisions was the percentage of the whole Commons voting higher. A man's vote in the Commons was after 1800 but a 658th part of the collective voice of the Commons, but because so many individual voices were silent, economists' influence in voting was certainly much greater than their proportion of total membership. The voting situation in the Lords was similar.

Economists were overwhelmingly against monopoly in its manifold forms, and in favor of free trade in the broadest sense of the term. The vote of economists was almost solidly in favor of lower taxes and reduced government spending. One is hard put to find

1. 3 H, 192:685, 21 May 1868.
2. In 1780–91 there were only 7 roll calls in the Commons, and only one in the Lords; in 1792–1804, 43 in the Commons and 17 in the Lords; but in 1805–1825, 484 in the Commons and 58 in the Lords. From then until 1868 the number of roll calls, although varying sharply from year to year, ran over 50 in the Commons in half the years, and over 15 in the Lords in half the years.

the slightest trace of Keynesian fiscal ideas in the views or votes of parliamentary economists. For this the major explanation lies not in the shortcomings of economists' analysis, but in the facts of political life and establishment practices during much of the period. Most economists believed that taxes were inequitable, both that they weighed too heavily on the poor, and that the rich who paid taxes were the economically productive businessmen rather than the landowners or recipients of funded income. On the other side of the coin they looked at much government outlay as wasteful: military and naval expenditures for display and to provide employment for sons of the aristocracy rather than for national defense; support of the establishment by sinecures and pensions for political services; and grants to unpopular members of the royal family.

Votes are an objective test, and can be quantified, but influence is more difficult to measure. To some degree the speeches of economists and their votes are but two sides of the same coin, but the influence of speeches often goes beyond the influence of votes. A speech, although it reflected the same idea as a vote, may well have influenced the votes of others, either directly or by contributing to a groundswell of public opinion. It is almost certain that the unrelenting attacks of so many parliamentary economists on the Corn Laws, on the Navigation Acts, the inequities of taxation, government extravagance for the benefit of an established order, the privileges of the Church of England, the anomaly of an established Protestant Church of Ireland in an overwhelmingly Catholic country, and the inequities of parliamentary representation had an influence that far exceeded their votes. This was particularly true where the economists, as backbenchers, introduced legislation or motions that became a rallying point for others. The number of economic, political, and social reforms that were sponsored by economists, repeatedly turned down by Parliament, but finally adopted, often after their sponsors had passed from the legislative scene, is impressive. Parnell had moved for the relief of Catholic disabilities, reform of tithes, and the ending of the abuses of the Church of Ireland; Hume had exposed the cost of sinecures and government extravagances; Brougham, Parnell, Rice, and Lansdowne had pressed for government support of education; Scrope had been a pioneer in supporting a poor law for Ireland. Morrison, Clay, and Brougham had urged the need for railroad legislation; Grote had repeatedly moved for the secret ballot; Hume, Hubbard, and Northcote had sponsored income-tax reform. David Ricardo never played a crusading role in Parliament, but his restrained criticism of the Corn Laws, his pleas for parliamentary reform and for religious toleration, his defense of specie payments gave him an influence much greater than that of a man with a single vote. Brougham's comment on Ricardo's influence applies only in less degree to other economists' support of reforms whose political time had not yet come:

... even his extreme opinions upon questions connected with the reform of the constitution in Church and State gave no offence; for he appeared not to court the opportunity of delivering them, but as if compelled by a sense of duty to declare his mind, careless or indisposed otherwise to make a speech. Few men have, accordingly, had more weight in Parliament; certainly none who, finding but a very small body of his fellow-members to agree with his leading opinions, might be said generally to speak against the sense of his audience, ever commanded a more patient or even favourable hearing.[3]

Particularly difficult to measure is the influence of economists as members of committees. But from the extensive membership of economists on committees, their attitude toward their legislative role, and what is known of the activity of members on committees and the authorship of committee reports, it is safe to say that economists played a relatively greater role as committeemen than their numerical representation in Parliament. In all, economists provided nearly four thousand members of parliamentary committees (other than standing committees) in the years 1780–1868, and appeared as witnesses 164 times before parliamentary committees.[4]

Economists as Members of Government

A final consideration bearing on the influence of economists in Parliament was their role as members of government. As might be expected, men who were basically politicians, and became economists only when necessary to carry on their political functions, were the more likely candidates for such political roles. Peel was prime minister after serving as Home Secretary; Rose held several minis-

3. *Historical Sketches of Statesmen who flourished in the Time of George III, Second Series* (London, 1839), p. 191, as quoted in Ricardo, *Works*, 5:xxxiv.
4. Appendix IV gives summary figures for economists' membership on committees, and of their appearances as witnesses before committees.

terial posts, and turned down a Cabinet post; and Vansittart was for eleven years chancellor of the Exchequer. Of the remaining fifty-nine economists, sixteen were at some time in the cabinet; two—Parnell and Wilson—were in the government but not the cabinet; and Horton was undersecretary for war and colonies. The high-water mark of economists' role in government was in the 1830s, when four were in Grey's Cabinet of 1830 and five—all except Brougham members of the Political Economy Club—in Melbourne's first cabinet of 1834, and all but Brougham were again in Melbourne's second cabinet of 1835. It is doubtful if at any time before or since have so many economists in any country been members of government.[5] And from the end of Melbourne's cabinet in 1841 through 1868, except for less than three years at least one economist was always in the government.

Only a limited part of this service of economists in government was in posts where their economic expertise would have been particularly appropriate. This was not an age of specialization, and the man who had the ability and the political standing to be of government stature generally was assumed to be able to fill any post that might be open. The economists who held portfolios of a distinctly economic nature were Lord Henry Petty, chancellor of the Exchequer (1805–7); Huskisson, president of the Board of Trade (1823–27); Poulett Thomson, president of the Board of Trade (1834–39); Rice, chancellor of the Exchequer (1835–39); Lowe, joint secretary of the Board of Control (1852–55) and president of the Board of Control (1855–58); Wilson, joint secretary of the Board of Control (1848–52) and financial secretary to the Treasury (1853–58); Lewis, chancellor of the Exchequer (1855–58); and Northcote, president of the Board of Trade (1866–67). All of these except Huskisson and Wilson were members of the Political Economy Club.

Yet little important legislation other than that sponsored by Peel in his role as political leader and broker in the economic ideas of others can be traced to the role of an economist in government, as distinguished from his influence as a backbencher. The two exceptions were Huskisson and Poulett Thomson, who in their position on the Board of Trade in the 1820s and 1830s did much to liberalize restrictions on foreign trade. Part of the explanation is to be

5. See Appendix V, "Economists in Government, 1783–1868."

sought in the intellectual climate of the day—particularly between the end of the Napoleonic wars and the late 1840s—the economists as a group were well to the left of center on the great issues of the day. Most of the economists—again leaving out the Tory politician economists—wanted in some way to change the world—not only by breaking up economic monopoly and fostering competition but also by reform in politics, in education, and in the relation of church and state. When Tory governments were in power the economists pressed for change and exposed the intellectual weakness of policies inherited from the past. When Whigs were in power the forte of the economists was in urging the more cautious Whigs to move further than they would have otherwise. But the carrying out of the changes, economic, political, and social, for which parliamentary economists argued and battled was largely in the hands of men not ordinarily thought of as economists. This is not surprising. We would hardly expect many men with the interests and analytical abilities of great economists to be political leaders, and insofar as economists become political leaders it usually involves some abandonment of the more analytical and objective approach that we would like to think is the hallmark of an economist. In any case, with the possible exception of Parnell, no original and creative thinker was among the economists who achieved front-bench status. Economists who sat in the front benches believed in and expounded the ideas of political economy, but they did not include such innovative and creative thinkers as John Stuart Mill, Scrope, David Ricardo, Perronet Thompson, Thornton, Torrens, Lord King, Lord Lauderdale, or Lord Overstone.

Influence of Some Individual Economists

It would be tempting, but largely futile, to rate economists as to their parliamentary influence, but a few observations are in order. The special role of Peel, and of Huskisson and Poulett Thomson as members of government in liberalizing international trade has already been mentioned. In some cases—and this is particularly true of David Ricardo and John Stuart Mill—the economists who sat at Westminster were national figures before their parliamentary careers, and their votes and speeches in Parliament may have been but a minor influence on legislation as compared with the influence of their extraparliamentary activities. Others might appear at the end of their years in Parliament to have done little but to battle in vain for causes which their parliamentary colleagues rejected, but causes which were finally victorious after their unsuccessful sponsors had passed from the legislative scene. Situations of this nature were David Ricardo's support of parliamentary reform, religious tolerance, and amendment of the Corn Laws; Grote's annual motion in favor of the ballot; Parnell's attacks on the Corn Laws; Torrens's criticism of tithes; Clay's campaign against church rates; Hume's, Hubbard's, and Northcote's moves for tax reform; Clay's and Morrison's insistence that the rules of competition did not apply to water and gas companies, and to railroads; Lord King's denunciation of the Corn Laws and of the established Church of Ireland. Their efforts did not produce specific legislation with which their names are associated, yet almost certainly these men were a potent contributing force to the legislation that followed. Lord Lansdowne, in an undramatic way, was ahead of his time on a wide range of economic and political issues. Thomas Attwood and Cobbett were by conventional standards failures as members of the Commons in their short parliamentary careers, great as were Attwood's achievements in political agitation, and Cobbett's in popular journalism. Their forte was not as legislators. Yet it would be a mistake to dismiss them out of hand as men who left no impact on parliamentary actions. Attwood's attacks on the gold standard, even at their economic worst, forced more conventional minds to consider how the gold standard could be protected from the Birmingham heretics. It is a plausible hypothesis, but impossible to prove, that the Attwood attacks on the gold standard, defeated and often ridiculed in Parliament, may have influenced Peel in sponsoring the rigid provisions of the Bank Act of 1844, in the thought that this would strengthen the defenses of the gold standard. Attwood's and Cobbett's opposition to the rigor of the new Poor Law of 1834 found little support in their generation, but does not read badly by the standards of the British welfare state of today. Cobbett's attacks on the inequities of taxation, the abuses of the Established Church, and the oppression of child labor won parliamentary approval long after his voice was stilled.

In terms of legislative achievements, Hume's thirty-eight years in Parliament topped those of any other economist. He contributed little to the literature of economics outside of his speeches, but he believed in political economy and understood its broad concepts. He was a forceful, determined, and often abrasive spokesman for ideas that David Ricardo expressed in more restrained language. James Mill wrote to Ricardo on 18 December 1818, just after Hume had taken his seat for Montrose: "I have been able to work him into an approximation to a knowledge of your book—he is a convert to all the doctrines; but he does not yet always apply them correctly— however he is always open to instruction."[6] Four days later Ricardo replied to Mill: "I am glad that you are making such progress with Mr. Hume, I hope that you may succeed in making him a good political economist."[7] And Hume's tribute after Ricardo's death is evidence of his admiration for Ricardo: "With regard to the principles which Mr. Ricardo was so capable of expounding, now that time had worn away many of the ruder prejudices against them, he might say, that not a few of those opponents, who had long theoretically resisted his doctrines, would at this time, though perhaps somewhat unwillingly, allow, that many of his predictions had been fulfilled."[8] After Hume's death Lord Palmerston, who on many issues had disagreed with Hume, paid this tribute:[9]

Sir, he was a man of whom it has been said that he took the lead in almost every branch of improvement, and in every measure of improvement which has of late years been carried into practical operation. . . . Sir, a man of greater industry, a man who devoted the whole labours of his life more entirely to what he considered good and serviceable to his country, never sat within these walls.

And of Hume's speeches the *Dictionary of National Biography* says: "He spoke longer and oftener and probably worse than any other private member, but he saw most of the causes which he advocated succeed in the end."

To evaluate David Ricardo's influence involves more subtle considerations. When Hume fought doggedly for measures that were eventually adopted it is reasonable to believe that he had influence. Ricardo's influence was that of ideas, many from a forum other than Parliament, expressed at a much lower level of intensity than were

6. Ricardo, *Works*, 7, p. 365.
7. Ricardo, *Works*, 7, p. 373.
8. 2 H, 10: 141–42, 12 Feb. 1824. In Ricardo, *Works*, 5:332.
9. 3 H, 136:1881–82, 26 Feb. 1855.

Hume's, and his parliamentary career was only a little over four years. How many votes may have been influenced, even after his death, by his ideas is conjecture, but it is plausible that he did much to strengthen parliamentary criticism of the Corn Laws and support of the gold standard. The experience of Graham may have been unique, but possibly others had the same experience. In 1830, in apologizing for his support of the resumption legislation of 1819, Graham said: "He was then a very young Member, governed by authorities, and overbourne by his friend, Mr. Ricardo, upon whose faith he pinned his own."[10]

John Stuart Mill's parliamentary career lasted only three years and began when he was nearly sixty—the greatest age at which any of the sixty-two economists, with the exception of Cobbett and Samson Ricardo, entered Parliament. Virtually all of his writing had been done before he entered Parliament, and undoubtedly had influenced the thinking of some of the economists who had preceded him in Parliament. But there is no evidence that Mill in his short parliamentary career had any appreciable impact on legislation. His position was that of a tired Olympian, ready to express ideas long associated with his name, but unable to do much in the rough and tumble of parliamentary argument and action.

Parnell, with nearly forty years in Parliament, combined both high intellectual powers and some qualities of political leadership, and to many reforms, both economic and political, he contributed far more than his vote: tax reform, repeal of the Corn Laws, Catholic emancipation, granting of civil rights to Jews, and electoral reform were all advanced by his sponsorship and lucid defense. Thornton's influence is harder to evaluate. As in the case of David Ricardo, it is difficult to separate his influence in Parliament from the influence of his writings. He served thirty-three years, as compared with Ricardo's four, but there was the same low-key approach, the same appeal to reason. He did much to lay the groundwork of the policy of the metallic standard and exchange stability; he was a consistent and respected voice for tax reform, for parliamentary reform, for reductions of sinecures, and for the public's right to know how their money was spent.

Cobden's fame in British history is generally linked with the anti-

10. 2 H, 22:441, 12 Feb. 1830.

Corn Law League, in which he was a prime mover. But it may be that his greatest contribution in this field was as a member of Parliament, of relentlessly pressing on a reluctant Peel the case for free trade in corn. In 1844 he made a masterful speech, which he regarded as his best, against the Corn Laws. Peel, who had sat listening, planning to reply, crumpled his notes, and, turning to Sidney Herbert, said: "*You* must answer this, for *I* cannot."[11] In any case it was the personal conversion of Peel, and not a decision at the polls, that toppled the Corn Laws.

Few members of Parliament, other than Mill, saw more clearly the economic problems of Ireland than did Scrope: a recognition that distress was not the result of inherent Irish laziness but of economic conditions that called for relief even to the able-bodied; and the even more important recognition that the basic economic problem of Ireland was not the relief of unemployment but the provision of productive employment. Scrope, however, was not a parliamentary leader, and no particular legislation, with the possible exception of a Poor Law for Ireland, can be pointed to as stemming from his proposals, although his words were a force for clear thinking in debates too often dominated by emotion.

The brilliant, politically intemperate, and often unpredictable Brougham raises a number of questions as to influence. He was in Parliament fifty-five years. He was for years a leader of the English bar, but his all-embracing interests—including mathematics, economics, languages—produced the contemporary quip that if he only knew some law he would have known a little of everything. As a young man he had written on economics for the *Edinburgh Review* and in a two-volume work, *An Inquiry into the Colonial Policy of the European Powers*, and to the end of his life he repeatedly brought economic concepts into his analysis of public issues. His very versatility—his distinction in fields other than economics—and his tireless campaigns on behalf of civil rights, parliamentary reform, suppression of the slave trade, and abolition of slavery sometimes have obscured the fact that Brougham was an able, albeit sometimes erratic economist. He supported repeal of the Corn Laws, opposed sinecures and other needless government expenditures, had much to say on tax reform and on the need for railroad regulation. Yet

11. John Morley, *The Life of Richard Cobden* (Boston: Robert Brothers, 1881), p. 213.

no member of Parliament, economist or not, was a more determined opponent of regulation of hours and conditions of labor, even for women in mines and for young children, and he was a vigorous defender of the Navigation Acts, appealing to political economy to support his position. Brougham was a great but paradoxical figure of his age, and his influence was felt in many fields.

An intriguing question, to which an answer, if it ever could be given, could come only after intensive research, is how much influence Perronet Thompson had in Parliament. He was a maverick politically, and a man of independent thought and high moral courage who was well ahead of his time in urging reforms on a broad front, even at the risk of losing political support. He was elected three times, serving a total of nine years, and was defeated eight times. Ridiculed by his Tory opponents, and never admitted to the councils of the Whigs, it is a temptation to write him off as a dreamer without political influence, but the record of the reforms for which he campaigned, both in and out of Parliament, and which were accepted only years later, is impressive.

Theoretical Framework of the Parliamentary Economists

It is impossible to speak of the economic theory of sixty-two economists, covering a period of nearly ninety years, as one could speak of the views of an individual economist at a particular time. When the parliamentary economists got into theoretical discussions, as David Ricardo, Thornton, Torrens, Alexander Baring, Parnell, Scrope, and Mill did a number of times, it was not to win a theoretical argument with a fellow economist but to bolster the case for particular legislative action. So an analysis of the economic theory, explicit or implicit, in the parliamentary speeches of a particular economist, rarely if ever would reveal his full theoretical system. Yet if faced with the direct question, What economist was most responsible for the thinking of the parliamentary economists covered in this study? the answer must be Adam Smith. He was referred to more often than any other economist, almost invariably in favorable terms. Even those who favored a particular measure of control—an example is Brougham's defense of the Navigation Acts—generally could find support for their view in the writings of Adam Smith. Such subtleties as the labor theory of value, or the wages fund, rarely figured in the parliamentary speech of economists; and there is little basis for tracing the changes, in the years here covered, of economists' views on finer points of theory. Insofar as the main lines of thinking of parliamentary economists did change over the period of some ninety years, it was still within the main framework of Smithian thinking, but with a widening sector of interferences with the free market to deal with particular situations as being reasonable or natural.

With the aspects of Ricardian theory that are likely to be emphasized today in a graduate class in economics—in particular the labor theory of value, the relation between profits and rent, or the effect of machinery—there was little concern. The Ricardian influence appears to have been more important in the monetary and banking field, notably support of a metallic standard, and a desire to restrict or eliminate entirely the note issues of private banks. Although there were few specific references to Ricardo's views, the thinking that lay back of Peel's Bank Act of 1844 was strongly in the Ricardian tradition.

Much of what the economists had to say about poor relief and emigration reflected Malthusian thinking. But it was Malthusianism of the second edition, which recognized that workers could rise above the minimum of subsistence, and not the fatalistic Malthusianism of the first edition. When Malthusian ideas, either expressly or by implication, were brought into economists' discussions of the poor laws, emigration, or even the problems of the Irish, it was rarely, if ever, for the purpose of showing that it was futile to try to put an end to poverty, but for the purpose of suggesting what was necessary to alleviate poverty. There was hardly a trace, in what any of the economists said, of the differences between Ricardo and Malthus over the importance of demand.

Shifting Nature of Parliamentary Economists' Role between 1780 and 1868

In an evaluation of the influence of economists in Parliament between 1780 and 1868 it is important to keep in mind that the nature of the economic problems that held the center of the parliamentary stage, and the general outlook of economists, shifted at least twice during the period of nearly ninety years. For most of the first two decades, close on the publication of *The Wealth of Nations*, few economic issues were debated in Parliament, and on the two most important economic measures discussed—the Irish trade proposals and the commercial treaty with France—the economists had little to say.

The suspension of cash payments in 1797, the concern about poverty and poor relief dramatized by Malthus's *Essay* of 1798, the increasing import of corn, the extension of cultivation to poorer land, and the advance of industrialization presented a series of problems that called for the type of analysis that a generation who had read Adam Smith were eager to apply. Repeatedly the questions were asked, What are the consequences of changes in economic forces, and what public policy is best suited to minimize the damage or maximize the benefits from these changes? Increasingly men in and out of Parliament were saying that the answers were to be found in the elimination of ancient controls and in the operations of the market. The economists were emerging as a separate group, saying proudly that they were economists and that as economists they were able to provide answers. And the answers, in the spirit of Adam Smith, usually were the loosening or abandonment of ancient controls and obstacles to change. A manifestation of this increasing pride and confidence was the organization in 1821 of the Political Economy Club.

During the years from 1780 to 1868 there was a shift in the nature of the problems that economists discussed, and also a shift in the relation of their political and social philosophy to dominant British opinion. Until the late 1790s the economists' contribution in Parliament was largely by way of incidental comment rather than organized presentation of a peculiarly economist position. Beginning with the monetary issue around 1800, then with restrictions on international trade a few years later and a whole series of issues involving the broad issue of freedom of choice versus authority as the determinant of economic and political action, the economists in Parliament came to approach a consensus in opposition to organization thinking. To the theory back of the cash resumption legislation of 1819 Boyd, Grenfell, Horner, Huskisson, Parnell, Thornton, Lord King, and in his preparliamentary writings David Ricardo made important contributions; even though the timing of the resumption legislation was strongly influenced by political considerations. On other issues, until Catholic Emancipation in 1829 and the passage of the Reform Act of 1832, the economists were generally on the losing side of both economic and political issues. They were overwhelmingly for change but still a minority voice on most issues. Increasingly with pride they defended their position as in accord with the principles of political economy and of liberty.

The decades of the thirties and forties were the years of the economists' greatest influence and greatest legislative victories. The Reform Act of 1832, the new Poor Law of 1834, repeal of the Corn Laws and of the Navigation Acts, some tax reforms, reform of municipal corporations, more self-government for colonies, and a whittling down of the special privileges of the Established Church in Ireland and England were accomplishments to which economists made major contributions. On regulation of working conditions the economists played a mixed role, but as suggested earlier their opposition was not as united as much popular thinking has assumed.

On a number of noneconomic reforms which the great majority of economists had supported, such as removal of Jewish disabilities, the secret ballot, further parliamentary reforms, disestablishment of the Church of Ireland, abolition of church rates, and abolition of religious tests at Cambridge and Oxford, the economists' goals had not yet been won by 1850. Yet on all these by the early 1850s the ultimate victory seemed assured. In several cases only the Lords had blocked legislative action, and even in situations where the Commons had not yet given approval, the handwriting on the wall seemed clear; it was simply a question of when, and not whether, the old citadels of privilege would fall.

The greatest number of economists was in the first Reform Parliament of 1833–35—twenty-three in the Commons and nine in the Lords. From then on the numbers slowly declined: in the Parliament of 1847–52 there were fourteen in the Commons and nine in the Lords; in the Parliament of 1865–68 there were eight in the Commons and four in the Lords, and one member of the Commons—Scrope—resigned, and two of the Lords—Brougham and Monteagle—died during that Parliament. It was not merely that there were fewer economists in Parliament, but the great economic controversies of the first half-century had either been settled for that generation, or continued only in a minor key. During much of the period from 1800 to 1850 the role of economists had been to argue why and how economic, political, and social changes should be made; in the 1850s and 1860s there was less of a crusading fire, less criticism of existing institutions and practices, more concern with details rather than with great issues. A generalization to which there are many individual exceptions is that most of the parliamentary economists up to around 1850 had strong antiestablishment leanings, in both the economic and political fields. In the next two decades economists came more to explain and interpret the arrangements of the new establishment than to press for reforms. It is true that Scrope, who had first gone to Parliament in 1833 and had repeatedly pressed for economic change, was a member until 1867. John Stuart Mill was in the Parliament of 1865–68. But Scrope did not play an active role in Parliament after 1852, and Mill never was the force in Parliament that he had been in the field of ideas. Parliamentary economists by the 1860s had become much more spokesmen for the prevailing establishment view than their predecessors of a few decades back, but it was these predecessors who had helped to change the nature of prevailing establishment thinking. After the 1860s the parliamentary economists might use their powers of economic analysis to suggest legislative improvements, but no longer were they pressing for far-reaching changes.

A small matter, but symbolic of the changing status of parliamentary economists, was the presence in the Parliament of 1865–68 of three directors of the bank of England—Goschen, Hankey, and Hubbard—whereas previous to Hankey's election to Parliament in 1853 the only parliamentary economist to serve on the bank's directorate was Alexander Baring, and he for only a brief period. Four of the seven economists in the Commons in 1868 were subsequently raised to the peerage—Goschen, Hubbard, Lowe, and Northcote. By the time John Stuart Mill left Parliament classical economics, since Adam Smith a powerful voice for change, was being displaced by neoclassical economics, the voice of the new establishment.

Appendix I

Economists in Parliament: 1780–1868

Date at left of name is year of entering Parliament.
Members of the Political Economy Club are identified by an asterisk preceding the name.

1819   Matthias Attwood (1779–1851)

Fowey	1819–
Callington	1820–30
Boroughbridge	1830–32
Whitehaven	1833–47

Unseated on petition in Fowey in 1819; did not stand in 1847.

Brother of Thomas Attwood and partner in London private bank. Author of *Observations Concerning the Distress of the Country* (London, 1817), and *A Letter to Lord Archibald Hamilton on Alterations in the Value of Money* (published anonymously in London in 1823, reprinted in 1847).

Tory

1833   Thomas Attwood (1783–1856)

Birmingham	1833–39

Resigned seat in 1839.

Partner in Birmingham private bank of Attwood and Spooner, and organizer of the Birmingham Political Union, which was influential in pressing for the Reform Act of 1832. Author of many brochures and books on money and banking. A list of his publications and a reprint of several of the more important is in *Selected Economic Writings of Thomas Attwood*, edited by Frank Whitson Fetter (London School of Economics and Political Science, London, 1964).

Whig and Radical

1806   Alexander Baring (1st Baron Ashburton, 1835) (1774–1848)

Taunton	1806–26
Callington	1826–31
Thetford	1831–32
North Essex	1833–35
House of Lords	1835–48

Defeated in Taunton, 1826.

Son of Sir Francis Baring. Member of the banking house of Baring Brothers and Co., and commissioner who negotiated the Webster-Ashburton Treaty of 1842 fixing the American-Canadian boundary. Author of *An Inquiry into the Causes of the*

Orders in Council (London, 1807), and *The Financial and Commercial Crises Considered* (London, 1847).

Whig in early life, but joined Tories in late 1820s over Parliamentary Reform.

1784   Sir Francis Baring (1740–1810)

Grampound	1784–90
Chipping Wycombe	1794–96, 1802–6
Calne	1796–1802

Did not stand in 1806.

London merchant, founder of Baring Brothers and Co. Author of *The Principle of the Commutation Act Established by Facts* (1786); *Observations on the Establishment of the Bank of England, and on the Paper Circulation of the Country* (1797); *Further Observations on the Establishment of the Bank of England, and on the Paper Circulation of the Country* (1797); *Observations on the Publication of Walter Boyd* (1801).

Whig

1796   Walter Boyd (c. 1754–1837)

Shaftesbury	1796–1802
Lymington	1823–30

Did not stand in 1802 or 1830.

Financier and partner in London banking house of Boyd, Benfield and Co., which went into bankruptcy in 1799. Author of *Letter to the Right Honourable William Pitt on the Influence of the stoppage of issues in specie at the Bank of England on the prices of provisions and other commodities* (1801); *Reflections on the financial system of Great Britain, and particularly on the sinking fund* (1815); *Observations on Lord Grenville's essay on the sinking fund* (1828).

Independent

1810   Henry Brougham (1st Baron Brougham & Vaux, 1830) (1778–1868)

Camelford	1810–12
Winchelsea	1815–30
Knaresborough	1830–
Yorkshire	1830–
House of Lords	1830–68

Defeated in Liverpool, 1812; in Sterling Burghs, 1812; in Westmorland, 1818, 1820, and 1826. When elected for both Knaresborough and Yorkshire in 1830, Brougham took his seat for Yorkshire.

Lawyer; attended Dugald Stewart's Edinburgh lectures on Political Economy; Lord Chancellor 1830–34. A prolific writer in many fields, but his principal economic writings were articles in the early issues of the *Edinburgh Review; An Inquiry into the Colonial Policy of the European Powers*, 2 vols. (1803); *An Inquiry into the State of the Nation, at the Commencement of the Present Administration* (1806); *A letter to Sir Samuel Romilly, M.P. from Henry Brougham . . . upon the Abuses of Charities* (1818); *Practical Observations upon the Education of the People, Addressed to the Working Classes and their Employers* (1818).

Whig, but in later years sided with Tories on a number of issues and at times sat on the Tory benches.

1852   Isaac Butt (1813–79)

Harwich   1852–
Youghal   1852–65
Limerick City   1871–79
Defeated in Mayo, 1850; in Youghal, 1865; in Monaghan, 1871. Died in office.
Irish lawyer, second professor of political economy at Trinity College (Dublin), and in the 1870s leader of the Irish Home Rule party in Parliament. He wrote on a variety of topics, but his principal publications on economics were *An Introductory Lecture Delivered before the University of Dublin* (1837); *The Poor Law for Ireland, Examined in a Letter to Lord Viscount Morpeth* (1837); *Protection to Home Industry* (1846); *A voice for Ireland—the Famine in the Land* (1847); *The Rate in Aid: a Letter to the Earl of Roden* (1849); *Land tenure in Ireland* (1866); *The Irish People and the Irish Land: a Letter to Lord Lifford* (1867); *The Irish Querist: Ireland's Social Condition* (1867).
Originally a Tory, but gradually shifted toward a Whig and Irish Nationalist position.

1833   Edward S. Cayley (1802–62)

Yorkshire (North Riding)   1833–62
Died in office.
Country gentleman, who wrote *On Commercial Economy in Six Essays* (1830), and a number of brochures on the Corn Laws and agriculture. A full list of his publications is in Barry Gordon, *Non-Ricardian Political Economy* (Harvard School of Business Administration, Cambridge, Mass., 1967), pp. 47–48.
Independent

1833   *Sir William Clay (1791–1869)

Tower Hamlets   1833–57
Defeated in Tower Hamlets, 1857.
Merchant and director of water companies. His principal publications on economics were: *Speech in Moving for a Committee to Inquire into the Operations of the act Permitting the Establishment of Joint Stock Banks* (1836); *Remarks on the expediency of Restricting the Issue of Promissory Notes to a Single Issuing Body* (1844); *Remarks on the Water Supply of London* (1849); *Statement of the Plan of Supplying London with Water* (1850).
Whig

1833   William Cobbett (1762–1835)

Oldham   1833–35
Defeated in Bristol, 1812; in Coventry, 1820; in Preston, 1826; in Manchester, 1832. Died in office.
Journalist and editor of *Cobbett's Political Register*. His writings cover a wide field, but the principal economic ones were: *Paper against gold* (1815); *Gold for Ever! Real Causes of the Fall of the Funds* (1825); and *Surplus Population and Poor-law bill, a comedy in three acts* (1835). A French doctoral thesis, Marie de Kergaradec, *William Cobbett. L'inflation et la déflation* (Paris, 1933), deals with Cobbett's monetary views.
Radical

1841   Richard Cobden (1804–65)

Stockport   1841–47

Yorkshire (West Riding)   1847–57
Rochdale   1859–65
Defeated in Stockport, 1837; in Huddersfield, 1857. Died in office.

Cotton manufacturer, prime mover in the Anti-Corn Law League, and negotiator of Cobden-Chevalier commercial treaty of 1860. Author of the anonymous *England, Ireland, and America. By a Manchester Manufacturer* (1835), and *Russia. By a Manchester Manufacturer* (1836); translated, with an Introduction, Michel Chevalier's *On the Probable Fall in the Value of Gold* (1859). His economic ideas, however, were expressed more in speeches than in writing, and two of the nonparliamentary speeches reprinted are *Speech of Richard Cobden . . . at Sheffield, November 23, 1842* (1842), and *Speech of Richard Cobden . . . on the Russian loan . . . January 18, 1850* (1850).
Whig

1827   Edward Copleston, Bishop of Llandaff (1776–1849)

House of Lords   1827–49
Clergyman and Bishop of Llandaff, 1827–49. Author of *A letter to the Right Hon. Robert Peel . . . on the Pernicious Effects of a Variable Standard of Value* (1819); *A Second Letter to the Right Hon. Robert Peel . . . on the Causes of the Increase in Pauperism and in the Poor Laws* (1819); and "State of the Currency" in *Quarterly Review*, art. xi, April 1822, reprinted in 1830 as an anonymous pamphlet, *An Examination of the Currency Question and of the Project for Altering the Standard of Value.*
No party affiliation, but favorable to Tory views.

1826   Edward D. Davenport (1778–1847)

Shaftesbury   1826–30
Defeated in Lincoln, 1820; in Stockport, 1832 and 1835; in Warrington, 1837.

Country gentleman. Author of *How to Improve the Condition of the Labouring Classes* (1845); reputed author of anonymous pamphlet, *The Corn Question, in a Letter Addressed to the Right Hon. W. Huskisson* (1825).
Independent

1865   *Henry Fawcett (1833–84)

Brighton   1865–74
Hackney   1874–84
Defeated in Cambridge, 1863; in Brighton, 1864. Died in office.

Professor of political economy at Cambridge University. Author of *Manual of Political Economy* (1863); *The Economic Position of the Labourer* (substance of a course of lectures given in 1864) (1865); "Strikes, their tendencies and remedies," in *Westminster Review*, July 1860; several articles on economic subjects in *Macmillan's Magazine*. A full list of his publications is in Leslie Stephen, *Life of Henry Fawcett* (1885), pp. 469–72.
Liberal

1833   John Fielden (1784–1849)

Oldham   1833–47
Defeated in Oldham, 1847.

Cotton manufacturer. Author of *The Mischief and Iniquities of Paper Money* (1832);

The Curse of the Factory System (1836); and *A Selection of the Facts and Arguments in Favour of the Ten Hours Bill* (1845).
  Independent

1812   Kirkman Finlay (1773–1842)

  Glasgow   1812–18
  Malmesbury   1818–20 (Resigned 1820)
Defeated in Glasgow, 1830; in Malmesbury, 1830; in Glasgow, 1831; in Malmesbury, 1831.
  Merchant, textile manufacturer, and Lord Provost of Glasgow. Author of *Letter to the Right Hon. Lord Ashley, on the cotton factory system, and the ten hours factory bill* ... (1833).
  Whig

1804   Davies Gilbert (Giddy until 1817) (1767–1839)

  Helston   1804–6
  Bodmin   1806–32
Did not stand in 1832.
  Scientist, and president of the Royal Society. Wrote on a wide variety of topics, but his economic publications were: *Cursory Observations on the act for ascertaining the Bounties and for the Exportation and Importation of Corn* (1804) and *A Plain Statement on the Bullion Question in a Letter to a Friend* (1810, in 1819 reprinted in the *Pamphleteer*, vol. 14, no. xxvi). *Beyond the Blaze: A Biography of Davies Gilbert*, by Arthur Cecil Todd (D. Bradford Barton, Truro, 1967), has a list of Gilbert's writings, pp. 810–12.
  Independent

1830   Thomas Gisborne (1794–1852)

  Stafford   1830–32
  North Derbyshire   1833–37
  Carlow Borough   1839–41
  Nottingham   1843–47
Defeated in Galway City, 1826; in Totnes, 1840; in South Leister, 1841; in Newport, 1841; in Ipswich, 1842; in Nottingham, 1847; in Kidderminster, 1849.
  Country gentleman and businessman. Published three articles on agriculture in *Quarterly Review*, which together with a heretofore unpublished manuscript on "High Farming," were reprinted in *Essays on Agriculture* (1854); *Letter to the Council of the Anti-Corn-Law League* (1842); *A second letter to the Council of the Anti-Corn-Law League* (1842).
  Whig

1863   *George Joachim Goschen (1st Viscount Goschen, 1900) (1831–1907)

  London   1863–80
  Ripon   1880–85
  East Edinburgh   1885–86
  St. George   1887–1900

House of Lords   1900–1907
Merchant, and director of the Bank of England at age twenty-seven. Author of *Theory of the Foreign Exchanges* (1861); and *Essays and Addresses on Economic Questions 1865–1893* (London, 1905). Thomas J. Skinner, *George Joachim Goschen. The Transformation of a Victorian Liberal* (University Press, Cambridge, 1973), p. 247, has a bibliography of Goschen's publications.
Liberal

1818   Sir James R. G. Graham (1792–1861)

Hull	1818–20
St. Ives	1820–21 (resigned 1821)
Carlisle	1826–29
Cumberland	1829–32
East Cumberland	1833–37
Pembroke	1838–41
Dorchester	1841–47
Ripon	1847–52
Carlisle	1852–61

Defeated in East Cumberland, 1837. Died in office.
Country gentleman, and several times cabinet minister. Author of *Corn and Currency* (1826), which went into four editions; supposed author of anonymous *A Compendium of the Laws, Passed from Time to Time, for Regulating and Restricting the Importation, Exportation, and Consumption of Foreign Corn, from the Year 1666* (London, 1826); *Free Trade in Corn* (London, 1826); and *Free Trade in Corn, the Real Interest of the Landlord, and the True Policy of the State* (1828).
Whig; went over to Tories in 1838; rejoined Liberals in 1852.

1802   Pascoe Grenfell (1761–1838)

Great Marlow	1802–20
Penryn	1820–26

Did not stand in 1826; defeated in Buckinghamshire in 1831.
Businessman and governor of Royal Exchange Insurance Company. Author of *The Speech of Pascoe Grenfell . . . on Certain Transactions Subsisting between the Public and the Bank of England. With an Appendix (1816); On the Application of the Sinking Fund* (A reprint, with an Introduction, of a speech given in the House of Commons on 28 April 1814) (1817); *The Government and the Bank* (1818). Probable author of anonymous *Letters Addressed to the Proprietors of Bank Stock* (1816).
Independent

1826   *Henry George Grey (Viscount Howick; 3d Earl Grey, 1845) (1802–94)

Winchelsea	1826–30
Higham Ferrers	1830–31
Northumberland	1831–32
North Northumberland	1832–41
Sunderland	1841–45
House of Lords	1845–94

Defeated in Northumberland, 1826 and 1841.

Country gentleman who attended McCulloch's London lectures on political economy. Author of *The Colonial Policy of Lord John Russell's Administration*, 2 vols. (1853); *Free Trade with France* (1881); *Ireland, The Causes of Its Present Position* (1882); *The Commercial Policy of British Colonies and the McKinley Tariff* (1892).
Whig

1833   *George Grote (1794–1871)

London   1833–41
Did not stand in 1841.
Banker, backer of University of London, historian of Greece, and friend of David Ricardo and John Stuart Mill.
In the Ricardo papers is Grote's unpublished manuscript on Foreign Trade (referred to in Ricardo, *Works*, 6, p. xxxiv), and in the British Museum (Add MS. 29, 530) is his unpublished manuscript of 231 pages on political economy. Professor William Thweatt of Vanderbilt University has in preparation the publication, with an Introduction, of the British Museum manuscript.
Whig

1853   *Thomson Hankey (1805–93)

Peterborough   1853–68, 1874–80
Defeated in Boston, 1852; in Peterborough, 1868 and 1880.
Merchant, long-time director of Bank of England, and governor (1851–53). Author of *The Principles of Banking* (1867); *Taxes and Expenditures* (1864); *On Bi-Metallism* (1879); and translator of Leon Faucher: *Remarks on the Production of the Precious Metals* (1852).
Liberal

1806   Francis Horner (1778–1817)

St. Ives   1806–7
Wendover   1807–12
St. Mawes   1813–17
In 1812 resigned Wendover seat to permit election of Lord Carrington. Died in office.
Lawyer; attended Dugald Stewart's Edinburgh lectures on political economy; cofounder of *Edinburgh Review*. Author of a number of economic articles in *Edinburgh Review* (reprinted in Frank Whitson Fetter, *The Economic Writings of Francis Horner in the Edinburgh Review* [London School of Economics and Political Science, 1957]); and of anonymous *A Short Account of a Late Short Administration* (1807).
Whig

1818   *Robert John Wilmot Horton (Wilmot until 1823; knighted in
        1831; succeeded to baronetcy, 1834) (1784–1841)

Newcastle-under-Lyme   1818–30
Defeated in Newcastle-under-Lyme, 1815; did not stand in 1830.
Country gentleman, colonial governor. Author of several pamphlets on the Catholic question, on emigration, and on the causes of poverty, including *A Letter* [to Sir Francis Burdett] *in Reply to his Speech Opposing a Parliamentary Grant of £20,000 for the Purposes of Emigration* (1826); *The Causes and Remedies of Pauperism in*

the United Kingdom Considered (1829); *An Inquiry into the Causes and Remedies of Pauperism* (1830); *Lectures Delivered at the London Mechanics Institute . . . on Statistics and Political Economy, as Affecting the . . . Labouring Classes* (1831); *Observations upon Taxation as Affecting the Operative and Labouring Classes* (1840).

Tory

1859   *John Gellibrand Hubbard (1st Baron Addington, 1887) (1805–89)

Buckingham	1859–68
London	1874–87
House of Lords	1887–89

Defeated in Buckingham, 1868.

Merchant, and director of the Bank of England. Author of *Vindication of a Fixed Duty on Corn* (1841); *The Currency and the Country* (1843); *A Letter to the Right Honourable Sir Charles Wood . . . Chancellor of the Exchequer, on the Monetary Pressure and Commercial Crisis of 1847 . . .* (1848); *How Should the Income Tax be Levied* (1852); *Reform or Reject the Income Tax* (1852).

Conservative

1812   Joseph Hume (1777–1855)

Weymouth and Melcombe Regis	1812–
Aberdeen Burghs	1818–30
Middlesex	1830–37
Kilkenny City	1837–41
Montrose	1842–55

Defeated in Middlesex, 1837; in Leeds, 1841. Died in office.

Surgeon, and official of the East India Company, who at the age of thirty retired with a fortune that enabled him to devote his life to travel, study, and politics. Author of *The Substance of a Speech of Joseph Hume . . . at an Adjourned General Court of the Proprietors of East India Stock* (1813); *An Account of the Provident Institution for Savings* (1816); reputed author of anonymous pamphlet, *Thoughts on the New Coinage, with Reflections on Money and Coins, and a New System of Weights and Measures, on a Simple and Uniform Principle* (1816).

Radical and Whig

1796   William Huskisson (1770–1830)

Morpeth	1796–1802
Liskeard	1804–7
Harwich	1807–12
Chichester	1812–23
Liverpool	1823–30

Defeated in Dover, 1802. Died in office.

Country gentleman and government pensioner. Author of *The Question concerning the Depreciation of the Currency Stated and Examined* (1810, eight editions in all); *A Letter on the Corn Laws* (1826); *Shipping Interest Speech . . . With an Appendix, containing the several accounts referred to* (1826).

Tory

1808   William Jacob (?1762–1851)

    Westbury   1806–7
    Rye   1808–12
Defeated in Great Yarmouth, 1807. Did not stand in 1812.

    Traveler, and statistician of the Board of Trade. Author of *Considerations on the Protection required by British Agriculture* . . . (1814); *An Inquiry into the Causes of Agricultural Distress* (1816); *A View of the Agriculture, Manufacture, Statistics, and State of Society of Germany and Parts of Holland and France* (1820); *A Report on the Trade in Foreign Corn, and of the Agriculture of the North of Europe* . . . (1820); *An Historical Inquiry into the Production and Consumption of the Precious Metals* (1831).

    Tory

1761   Charles Jenkinson (1st Baron Hawkesbury, 1786; 1st Earl of

        Liverpool, 1796) (1727–1808)

    Cockermouth   1761–66
    Appleby   1767–72
    Harwich   1772–74
    Hastings   1774–80
    Saltash   1780–86
    House of Lords   1786–1808

    Government official. Author of *Reflections on the Present State of the Resources of the Country* (1796); *State of the Country in the Autumn of 1798* (1798); *A Treatise on the Coins of the Realm* (1805).

    Tory

1797   Peter King (7th Baron King of Ockham) (1776–1833)

    House of Lords   1797–1833
    Country gentleman and biographer of John Locke. Author of *Thoughts on the Restriction of Payments in Specie at the Banks of Ireland and England* (1803), later published in an enlarged version as *Thoughts on the Effects of the Bank Restrictions* (1804); *On the Conduct of the British Government towards the Catholics in Ireland* (1807); *A Short History of the Job of Jobs* (written in 1825 but first published in 1846 as an anti-Corn Law pamphlet). *A Selection from the Speeches and Writings of the Late Lord King, with a Short Introductory Memoir by Earl Fortescue* (1844) reprints these writings and most of King's parliamentary speeches.

    Whig

1847   *Sir George Cornewall Lewis (1806–63)

    Herefordshire   1847–52
    New Radnor   1855–63
Defeated in Herefordshire, 1852; in Peterborough, 1852. Died in office.

    Author, editor of *Edinburgh Review*, Poor Law Commissioner, and chancellor of the exchequer. His principal writings on economics were, in addition to several articles in the *Edinburgh Review*, *Report on the State of the Irish Poor in Great Britain* (1836); *Remarks on the Third Report of the Irish Poor Inquiry Commissioner* (1837); *The Finances and Trade of the United Kingdom at the Beginning of the Year 1852* (1852).

    Whig

1852   *Robert Lowe (1st Viscount Sherbrooke, 1880) (1811–92)

Kidderminster	1852–59
Calne	1859–68
London University	1868–1880
House of Lords	1880–92

Lawyer, for seven years member of the Legislative Council of New South Wales, journalist.
Liberal

1819   *Samuel Jones Loyd (1st Baron Overstone, 1850) (1796–1883)

Hythe	1819–26
House of Lords	1850–83

Did not stand in 1826; defeated in Manchester, 1832.
    Banker, witness before several parliamentary committees. Author of brochures on monetary problems including *Reflections Suggested by a Perusal of Mr. J. Horsley Palmer's Pamphlet on the Causes and Consequences of the Pressure on the Money Market* (1837); *Further Reflections on the State of the Currency and the Action of the Bank of England* (1837); *Thoughts on the Separation of the Departments of the Bank of England* (1844). Dennis O'Brien, *Correspondence of Lord Overstone*, 3 vols. (Cambridge University Press, 1971), includes a bibliography of Overstone's writings in vol. 3.
    Whig

1780   James Maitland (8th Earl of Lauderdale [Scotland], 1789; 1st
         Baron Lauderdale, 1806) (1759–1839)

Newport (Cornwall)	1780–84
Malmesbury	1784–89
House of Lords (Scottish Representative Peer)	1790–96
House of Lords	1806–39

Country gentleman and lawyer; attended Dugald Stewart's Edinburgh lectures on political economy. Author of *Inquiry into the Nature and Origin of Public Wealth* (1804, enlarged edition in 1819, and translated into French and Italian), and of a number of brochures, including *Thoughts on Finance Suggested by the Measures of the Present Session* (1797); *A Letter on the Present Measures of Finance* (1798); *Thoughts on the Alarming State of the Circulation and of the means of Redressing the Pecuniary Grievances of Ireland* (1805); *The Depreciation of the Paper currency of Great Britain proved* (1812); *Letter on the Corn Laws* (1814); *Three Letters to the Duke of Wellington* (1829).
    Whig, but beginning in 1820 sided increasingly with the Tories.

1865   *John Stuart Mill (1806–73)

Westminster	1865–68

Defeated in Westminster, 1868.
    Philosopher, and official of the East India Company. Nineteen volumes of *Collected Works of John Stuart Mill* (University of Toronto Press, Toronto, 1965–77) have already appeared; subsequent volumes will include his parliamentary speeches.
    Liberal

1833   Sir William Molesworth (1810–55)

> East Cornwall   1833–37
> Leeds   1837–40
> Southwark   1845–55

Did not stand in 1841. Died in office.

Country gentleman. Founder of *London Review*, editor of Hobbes's *Works*, disciple of George Grote and James Mill, and colonial reformer. A number of his speeches, both in and out of Parliament, are reprinted in *Selected Speeches of Sir William Molesworth, edited with an Introduction by Hugh Edward Egerton* (J. Murray, London, 1903).

Whig

1830   *James Morrison (1790–1857)

> St. Ives   1830–31
> Ipswich   1831–34; 1835–37
> Inverness Burghs   1840–47

Defeated in Great Marlow, 1826; in Ipswich, 1835; did not stand in 1847.

Merchant. Author of *Observations Illustrative of the Defects of the English System of Railway Legislation* (1846); *The Influence of English Railway Legislation on Trade and Industry* (1848).

Whig

1840   George Frederick Muntz (1794–1857)

> Birmingham   1840–57

Died in office.

Birmingham manufacturer. Author of *The True Cause of the Late Sudden Change in the Affairs of the Country* (1837; 2d edition with additions, 1843); *Letters upon Coin and Currency* (1841).

Whig

1855   *Sir Stafford Henry Northcote (1st Earl of Iddesleigh, 1885) (1818–87)

> Dudley   1855–57
> Stamford   1858–66
> North Devon   1866–85
> House of Lords   1885–87

Defeated in North Devon, 1857

Country gentleman, lawyer, and public official; chairman of the Hudson's Bay Company. Author of the anonymous *A Short Review of the Navigation Laws from the Earliest Times* (1849); *Twenty Years of Financial Policy* (1862).

Conservative

1802   *Sir Henry Brooke Parnell (1st Baron Congleton, 1841) (1776–1842)

> Queen's County   1802–, 1806–32
> Portarlington   1802–

Dundee	1833–41
House of Lords	1841–42

Withdrew from Queen's County contest in 1832. Did not stand in 1841.

Irish country gentleman. Author of *Observations upon the State of the Currency of Ireland* (1804; 3d edition enlarged in 1804); *The Principles of Currency and Exchange* (1805); *Treatise on the Corn Trade and Agriculture* (1809); *Observations on Paper Money, Banking, and Over-Trading* (1827); *Financial Reform* (1830; 4th ed. enlarged, 1832); *A Plain Statement of the Power of the Bank of England* (1832); *A Treatise on Roads* (1833, 2d ed. enlarged, 1838).

Whig

1809   Sir Robert Peel (1788–1850)

Cashel	1809–12
Chippenham	1812–17
Oxford University	1817–29
Westbury	1829–30
Tamworth	1830–50

Defeated in Oxford University, 1829. Died in office.

Politician; prime minister. Chairman of Commons Committee of 1819 on Resumption of Cash Payments; sponsor of Bank Act of 1844, and of repeal of the Corn Laws in 1846.

Tory

1802   *Henry Petty-Fitzmaurice (Lord Henry Petty; 3rd Marquess of Lansdowne, 1809) (1780–1863)

Calne	1802–6
Cambridge University	1806–7
Camelford	1807–9
House of Lords	1809–63

Defeated in Cambridge University, 1807.

Country gentleman; attended Dugald Stewart's Edinburgh lectures on political economy; chancellor of the exchequer, 1805–7. Author of *Statement of a Plan of Finance* (1807).

Whig

1833   *George Pryme (1781–1868)

Cambridge	1833–41

Defeated in Cambridge, 1820 and 1826. Did not stand in 1841.

Lawyer and professor of political economy at Cambridge. Author of Syllabus of a *Course of Lectures on Political Economy* (1815, with several editions in subsequent years); *An Introductory Lecture* (1823).

Whig

1819   *David Ricardo (1772–1823)

Portarlington	1819–23

Died in office.

Stockbroker. Ricardo's writings, letters, speeches, and an account of his life are in

The Works and Correspondence of David Ricardo, vols. 1–11, edited by Piero Sraffa (Cambridge University Press, 1952–73). A complete list of his publications is in vol. 10, pp. 355–83; his parliamentary speeches and evidence before parliamentary committees are in vol. 5.

Independent

1841   *John Lewis Ricardo (1812–62)

Stoke-on-Trent   1841–62

Died in office.

Financier, railroad developer, and nephew of David Ricardo. Author of *The Anatomy of the Navigation Acts* (1847); *The War History of Commerce* (1857).

Whig

1852   *Samson Ricardo (1792–1862)

New Windsor   1855–57

Defeated in Kidderminster, 1841; in Totnes, 1847; in New Windsor, 1852 and 1857.

Brother of David Ricardo, member of London Stock Exchange, underwriting member of Lloyds. Author of *Observations on the Recent Pamphlet of J. Horsley Palmer . . .* (1837); and *A National Bank the Remedy for the Evils Attendant upon our Present Paper of Currency* (1838). The second pamphlet reprinted, as an Appendix, David Ricardo's *Plan for a National Bank.*

Liberal

1820   *Thomas Spring Rice (1st Baron Monteagle, 1839) (1790–1866)

Limerick City   1820–32
Cambridge   1833–39
House of Lords   1839–66

Defeated in Limerick City, 1818.

Irish country gentleman, contributor to *Edinburgh Review*, and chancellor of the exchequer. Author of several economic articles in *Edinburgh Review*; anonymous *Considerations on the Present State of Ireland* (1822); (joint author) *Report on the Burdens on Real Property, and the Impediments to Agricultural Transactions* (1846).

Whig

1784   George Rose (1744–1818)

Launceton   1784–88
Lymington   1788–90
Christchurch   1790–1818

Died in office.

Naval officer and government official. Author of *The Proposed System of Trade with Ireland* (1792); *A Brief Examination into the Increase of the Revenue, Commerce, and Manufactures of Great Britain from 1792 to 1799* (1799) (both of these volumes went into several editions, and the second was translated into French); *Considerations on the Debt of the Civil List* (1802); *Observations Respecting the Public Expenditure and the Influence of the Crown* (1810); *Observations on Banks for Savings* (1816).

1833   George Julius Poulett Scrope (1797–1876)

    Stroud   1833–67
Defeated in Stroud, 1832; resigned in 1867.

    Geologist, contributor to *Quarterly Review*, pamphleteer, and brother of Poulett Thomson. Author of *The Principles of Political Economy* (1833); twelve economic articles in the *Quarterly Review*, and a score or more of pamphlets. Redvers Opie, "A Neglected English Economist: George Poulett Scrope," *Quarterly Journal of Economics*, 44 (Nov. 1928): 101–37, has on pp. 134–37 an incomplete bibliography of Scrope's economic publications.
    Whig

1780   Sir John Sinclair (1754–1835)

Caithness	1780–84
Lostwithiel	1784–90
Caithness	1790–96
Petersfield	1797–1802
Caithness	1802–6, 1807–11

Defeated in Kirkwall, 1784; resigned in 1811.

    Country gentleman, agricultural innovator, and first president of the Board of Agriculture. His writings covered a variety of subjects, of which the more important ones on economics were *History of the Public Revenue of the British Empire*, 2 vols. (1784; 3d ed. expanded, in 1803–4); *General View of the Agriculture of the Northern Counties and Islands of Scotland* (1795); *Letters Written to the Governor and Directors of the Bank of England . . .* (1797); *Observations on the Report of the Bullion Committee* (1810); *On the Approaching Crisis* (1818); *An Answer to a Tract Recently Published by David Ricardo, on Protection to Agriculture* (1822); *The Late Prosperity* (1826); *Thoughts on Currency* (1829). *Memoirs of the Life and Work of the Late Right Honourable Sir John Sinclair, bart. by his son the Rev. John Sinclair*, 2 vols. (1837) has list, probably incomplete, of 367 publications.
    Whig

1804   *John Charles Spencer (Viscount Althorp; 3d Earl Spencer, 1834) (1782–1845)

Okehampton	1804–6
Northamptonshire	1806–32
South Northamptonshire	1833–34
House of Lords	1834–45

Defeated in Cambridge University, 1806.

    Country gentleman. Leader of Whigs in the Commons, 1830–34, chancellor of the exchequer, 1830–34.
    Whig

1835   *Thomas Perronet Thompson (1783–1869)

Hull	1835–37
Bradford	1847–52, 1857–59

Defeated in Preston, 1835; in Maidstone, 1837; in Marylebone, 1838; in Manchester, 1839; in Hull, 1841; in Cheltenham, 1841; in Sunderland, 1845; in Bradford, 1852. Did not stand in 1859.

Army officer, governor of Sierra Leone, Proprietor of *Westminster Review*. Extensive contributor of economic articles to *Westminster Review*, and author of influential *Catechism on the Corn Laws* (1827) that went through eighteen editions. In 1842 an edition of all his writings to that time was published in six volumes, *Exercises, Political and Others*; and in the same year Richard Cobden, for the Anti-Corn Law League, in support of repeal of the Corn Laws, published *Extracts from the Works of T. P. Thompson*.

Whig and Radical

1826   *Charles Edward Poulett Thomson (1st Baron Sydenham, 1840) (1799–1841)

Dover	1826–32
Manchester	1833–39
House of Lords	1840–41

Resigned Commons seat in 1839 to become governor general of Canada.

London merchant, vice-president of the Board of Trade.

Whig

1782   Henry Thornton (1760–1815)

Southwark	1782–1815

Died in office.

Banker, philanthropist, and leader of the Clapham Sect. Author of *Enquiry into the Nature and Effects of the Paper Credit of Great Britain* (1802), translated into French and German, and reprinted several times.

Independent

1826   *Robert Torrens (1780–1864)

Ipswich	1826–27
Ashburton	1831–32
Bolton	1833–35

Defeated in Rochester, 1818; unseated on petition in Ipswich, 1827; defeated in Pontrefact, 1830; in Bolton, 1835.

Colonel of Marines, newspaper proprietor, promoter of Australian colonization. Lord Robbins, *Robert Torrens and the Evolution of Classical Economics* (Macmillan, London, 1958), in a Bibliographical Appendix, pp. 259–349, lists and summarizes Torrens's many publications.

Whig

1796   Nicholas Vansittart (1st Baron Bexley, 1823) (1766–1851)

Hastings	1796–1802
Old Sarum	1802–12
East Grinstead	1812–
Harwich	1812–23
House of Lords	1823–51

Lawyer and chancellor of the exchequer (1812–23). Author of *Reflections on the*

Propriety of an Immediate Conclusion of Peace (1793); *Letters to Mr. Pitt on the Conduct of the Bank Directors* (1795); *An Inquiry into the State of the Finances of Great Britain* (1796); *Outlines of a Plan of Finance: Proposal to be Submitted to Parliament* (1813).
  Tory

1790   Charles Callis Western (1st Baron Western, 1833)(1767–1844)

>   Maldon   1790–1806), 1807–12
>   Essex   1812–32
>   House of Lords   1833–44

Defeated in Maldon, 1806; in Essex, 1832.
  Country gentleman, and prison reformer. Author of numerous pamphlets on prison reform, agriculture, and monetary policy, including: *Letter. . . . to his Constituents, on the Subject of the Foreign Corn Trade* (1822); *A Letter to the Earl of Liverpool on the Cause of our Present Embarrassment and Distress* (1826); *A Letter on the Present Distress of the Country. Addresses to his Constituents* (1829); *A Third Letter on the Present Distress of the Country* (1830); *The Maintenance of the Corn Laws Essential to the General Prosperity of the Empire* (1828); *A Letter from Lord Western to Lord John Russell, on his Proposed Alterations of the Corn Laws and on the Causes of Commercial Distress* (1841).
  Whig

1833   *Richard Whately, Archbishop of Dublin (1787–1869)

>   House of Lords   1833–69

Professor of political economy at Oxford (1828–31), and Archbishop of Dublin (1831–63). In addition to extensive writings on church matters, Whately published the anonymous *Introductory Lectures on Political Economy* (1831); *The Evidence of His Grace the Archbishop of Dublin, As Taken before the Select Committe of the House of Lords, Appointed to Inquire into the Collection and Payment of Titles in Ireland, and the State of the Laws Relating Thereto* (1832); *Easy Lessons on Money Matters* (1835), which came out in many editions, and in French, Gaelic, Japanese, and Maori translations.
  No party affiliation, but favorable to Whig views

1820   *William Wolryche Whitmore (1787–1858)

>   Bridgnorth   1820–32
>   Wolverhampton   1833–34

Did not stand in 1835.
  Country gentleman. Author of *A Letter on the Present State and Future Prospects of Agriculture* (1822); *A Letter to the Electors of Bridgenorth, upon the Corn Laws* (1826); *Letter on the Corn Laws to the Manchester Chamber of Commerce* (1839); *A Second Letter on the Corn Laws, to the Manchester Chamber of Commerce* (1839); *A Letter to the Agriculturalists of the County of Salop* (1841); *A Second Letter to the Agriculturalists of the County of Salop* (1847); *A Letter to Lord John Russell on Railways* (1847); *A Few Plain Thoughts on Free Trade as Affecting Agriculture* (1849).
  Whig

1847   James Wilson (1805–60)

>   Westbury   1847–57
>   Devonport   1857–59

Resigned 1859 to become financial member of the Council of India.

Businessman, founder and editor of *The Economist*. Author of *Influences of the Corn Laws* (1839); *Fluctuations of Currency, Commerce, and Manufactures* (1840); *The Revenue: or, What Should the Chancellor Do* (1841); *The Cause of the Present Commercial Distress* (1843); *Capital, Currency and Banking* (1847) (later came out in Italian and Portuguese translations).

Whig

Appendix II

Members of Political Economy Club in Parliament but Not Included in List of Economists

Date at left of name is year of entering Parliament.
An asterisk following name indicates inclusion in the DNB.

1826   William Bingham Baring* (2nd Baron Ashburton, 1848) (1799–
        1864)

Thetford	1826–30
Callingham	1830–31
Winchester	1832–37
North Staffordshire	1837–41
Thetford	1841–48
House of Lords	1848–64

1850   Frederick Temple Hamilton-Temple Blackwood* (1st Baron
        Clandeboye, 1850; 1st Earl of Dufferin and Ava, 1871; 1st
        Marquess of Dufferin and Ava, 1888) (1826–1902)

House of Lords	1850–1902

1837   William John Blake (1805–75)

Newport	1837–41

1844   Edward Pleydell Bouverie* (1818–89)

Kilmarnock	1844–74

1830   Charles Buller* (1806–48)

West Looe	1830–31
Liskeard	1832–48

1865   Lord Frederick Charles Cavendish* (1836–82)

York (West Riding, northern division) 1865–82

1832   William Ewart Gladstone* (1809–98)

Newark-on-Trent	1832–47
Oxford University	1847–65
Lancashire (southern division)	1865–68
Greenwich	1868–80
Midlothian	1880–95

1832   Sir Benjamin Hawes* (1797–1862)

Lambeth	1832–47
Kinsdale	1848–52

1857   Kirkman Daniel Hodgson (1814–79)

Bridgeport	1857–68
Bristol	1868–78

1846   Edward Frederick Leveson-Gower* (1819–1907)

Derby	1846–48
Stoke-on-Trent	1852–57
Bodmin	1859–85

1836   Granville George Leveson Gower* (Lord Leveson; 2nd Earl
       Granville, 1846) (1815–91)

Morpeth	1837–40
Lichfield	1841–46
House of Lords	1846–91

1833   George Lyall* (d. 1853)

London	1833–35
	1841–47

1819   Col. William Maberly* (1798–1885)

Westbury	1819–20
Northampton	1820–30
Shaftesbury	1831–32
Chatham	1832–34

1852   George Montagu Warren Peacocke (in 1868 changed name to
       Sandford) (1821–78)

Maldon	1854–57;
	1859–68;
	1874–78

1832   William Thomas Petty-Fitzmaurice (Earl of Kerry) (1811–36)

    Calne   1832–36

1832   Sir John Romilly* (1st Baron Romilly, 1865) (1802–74)

    Bridport   1832–35
                                      1846–47
    Devenport   1847–52
    House of Lords   1865–74

1830   John Abel Smith* (1802–71)

    Midhurst   1830–31
    Chichester   1831–59
                                      1863–68

1830   Edward Strutt* (1st Baron Belper, 1856) (1801–80)

    Derby   1830–48
    Arundel   1851–52
    Nottingham   1852–56
    House of Lords   1856–80

1835   Charles Pelham Villiers* (1802–98)

    Wolverhampton   1835–98

1838   George Villiers* (4th Earl of Clarendon, 1838) (1800–70)

    House of Lords   1838–70

1836   Thomas Hyde Villiers* (1801–32)

    Hedon   1826–30
    Wootton Bassett   1830–31
    Bletchingley   1831–32

1826   Henry Warburton* (c. 1784–1858)

    Bridport   1826–41
    Kendal   1843–47

1857   Sir Edward William Watkin* (1819–1901)

    Great Yarmouth   1857–58
    Stockport   1864–68
    Hythe   1874–95

1852   William Arthur Wilkinson (1793–1865)

    Lambeth   1852–57

1846   John Wodehouse* (3d Baron Wodehouse, 1846; 1st Earl of
        Kimberley, 1866) (1826–1902)

   House of Lords   1847–1902

Appendix III

Parliaments and Economists Who Were in Them: 1780–1868

For each of the parliaments covered below the names of the economists participating are given, in roman type, in a single column to the left. For a complete listing see Appendix I.

From 58 George III, a second column to the right gives, in italic type, the names of participants who are not included in the list of economists which comprises Appendix I, but who were members of the Political Economy Club. For a full listing of these, see Appendix II. It should be noted that this supplementary listing includes men who were members of the Political Economy Club up to 1868, even though they may not have been members of the club in their earlier years in Parliament.

1.   21 George III   31 Oct. 1780–25 Mar. 1784

Charles Jenkinson
James Maitland (Earl of Lauderdale)
John Sinclair
Henry Thornton (24 Sept. 1782)

2.   24 George III   18 May 1784–11 June 1790

Francis Baring
Charles Jenkinson (raised to peerage
   as Lord Hawkesbury, 21 Aug. 1786)
James Maitland (Earl of Lauderdale)
George Rose
John Sinclair (created baronet, 14 Feb.
   1786)
Henry Thornton
   LORDS
Lord Hawkesbury (21 Aug. 1786)

3.   30 George III   7 Aug. 1790–20 May 1796

Francis Baring (1 Feb. 1794; created
   baronet, 29 May 1793)
George Rose
Sir John Sinclair
Henry Thornton
Charles Callis Western

LORDS
Lord Hawkesbury
Earl of Lauderdale (Representative Peer for Scotland)

4. 36 George III 12 July 1796–29 June 1802

Sir Francis Baring
Walter Boyd
William Huskisson
Henry Parnell (5 Apr. 1802)
George Rose
Sir John Sinclair (7 Jan. 1797)
Henry Thornton
Nicholas Vansittart
Charles Callis Western
LORDS
Lord King (1797)
Earl of Liverpool

5. 42 George III 31 Aug. 1802–24 Oct. 1806

Sir Francis Baring
Davies Giddy (26 May 1804; resigned
   April 1806)
Pascoe Grenfell (14 Dec. 1802)
William Huskisson (9 Mar. 1804)
Henry Parnell (resigned Dec. 1802;
   reelected 17 Feb. 1806)
Henry Petty-Fitzmaurice (Lord Henry
   Petty)
George Rose
Sir John Sinclair
John Charles Spencer (Lord Althorp)
   (27 Apr. 1804)
Henry Thornton
Nicholas Vansittart
Charles Callis Western
LORDS
Lord King
Earl of Liverpool
Earl of Lauderdale (created Baron in
   peerage of United Kingdom, 22 Feb.
   1806)

6. 46 George III 3 Dec. 1806–29 Apr. 1807

Alexander Baring
Davies Giddy
Pascoe Grenfell
Francis Horner
William Huskisson
Henry Parnell

Henry Petty-Fitzmaurice (Lord Henry
   Petty)
George Rose
John Charles Spencer (Lord Althorp)
Henry Thornton
Nicholas Vansittart
Charles Callis Western
     LORDS
Lord King
Earl of Lauderdale
Earl of Liverpool

7.   47 George III   22 June 1807–29 Sept. 1812

Alexander Baring
Henry Brougham (5 Feb. 1810)
Davies Giddy
Pascoe Grenfell
Francis Horner (20 July 1807)
Joseph Hume (18 Jan. 1812)
William Huskisson
William Jacob (15 July 1808)
Henry Parnell (succeeded to baronetcy,
   30 July 1812)
Robert Peel (15 Apr. 1809)
Henry Petty-Fitzmaurice (Lord Henry
   Petty; succeeded to peerage as
   Marquess of Lansdowne, 15 Nov.
   1809)
George Rose
Sir John Sinclair (resigned 26 June
   1811)
John Charles Spencer (Lord Althorp)
Henry Thornton
Nicholas Vansittart
Charles Callis Western
     LORDS
Lord King
Marquess of Lansdowne (15 Nov.
   1809)
Earl of Lauderdale
Earl of Liverpool (died 17 Dec. 1808)

8.   53 George III   24 Nov. 1812–10 June 1818

Alexander Baring
Henry Brougham (21 June 1815)
Kirkman Finlay
Davies Giddy (changed name to
   Gilbert, 10 Dec. 1817)
Pascoe Grenfell

Francis Horner (17 Apr. 1813; died 8
  Feb. 1817)
William Huskisson
Sir Henry Parnell
Robert Peel
George Rose (died 13 Jan. 1818)
John Charles Spencer (Lord Althorp)
Henry Thornton (died 16 Jan. 1815)
Nicholas Vansittart
Charles Callis Western
    LORDS
Lord King
Marquess of Lansdowne
Earl of Lauderdale

9. 58 George III 4 Aug. 1818–29 Feb. 1820

Matthias Attwood (unseated 11 May   *Col. William Maberly (1 May 1819)*
  1819)
Alexander Baring
Henry Brougham
Kirkman Finlay
Davies Gilbert
James Graham
Pascoe Grenfell
Joseph Hume
William Huskisson
Samuel Jones Loyd (20 May 1819)
Sir Henry Parnell
Robert Peel
David Ricardo (26 Feb. 1819)
John Charles Spencer (Lord Althorp)
Nicholas Vansittart
Charles Callis Western
Robert Wilmot
    LORDS
Lord King
Marquess of Lansdowne
Earl of Lauderdale

10. 1 George IV 21 Apr. 1820–2 June 1826

Matthias Attwood   *Col. William Maberly*
Alexander Baring
Walter Boyd (3 Apr. 1823)
Henry Brougham
Kirkman Finlay (resigned 23 June
  1820)
Davies Gilbert
James Graham (resigned 20 May 1821)
Pascoe Grenfell

Joseph Hume
William Huskisson
Samuel Jones Loyd
Sir Henry Parnell
Robert Peel
David Ricardo (died 11 Sept. 1823)
Thomas Spring Rice
Nicholas Vansittart (raised to peerage
 as Lord Bexley, 1 Mar. 1823)
Charles Callis Western
William Wolryche Whitmore
Robert Wilmot (changed name to
 Horton, 8 May 1823)
  LORDS
Lord Bexley (1 Mar. 1823)
Lord King
Marquess of Lansdowne
Earl of Lauderdale

11. 7 George IV 25 July 1826–24 July 1830

Matthias Attwood
Alexander Baring
Walter Boyd
Henry Brougham
Edward Davenport
Davies Gilbert
Sir James Graham (succeeded to
 baronetcy 13 Apr. 1824)
Henry George Grey (Lord Howick)
Robert Wilmot Horton
Joseph Hume
William Huskisson
Sir Henry Parnell
Robert Peel (succeeded to baronetcy, 3
 May 1830)
Thomas Spring Rice
John Charles Spencer (Lord Althorp)
Charles Edward Poulett Thomson
Robert Torrens (unseated 23 Feb.
 1827)
Charles Callis Western
William Wolryche Whitmore
  LORDS
Lord Bexley
Lord King
Marquess of Lansdowne
Earl of Lauderdale
Bishop of Llandaff (Edward Copleston)
 (14 Feb. 1828)

William Bingham Baring
Charles Buller (Feb. 1830)
Col. William Maberly
Thomas Hyde Villiers
Henry Warburton

12.   1 William IV   14 Sept. 1830–23 Apr. 1831

Matthias Attwood
Alexander Baring
Henry Brougham (raised to peerage as
    Lord Brougham and Vaux, 22 Nov.
    1830)
Davies Gilbert
Thomas Gisborne
Sir James Graham
Henry George Grey (Lord Howick)
Joseph Hume
William Huskisson (died 15 Sept.
    1830)
James Morrison
Sir Henry Parnell
Sir Robert Peel
Thomas Spring Rice
John Charles Spencer (Lord Althorp)
Charles Edward Poulett Thomson
Charles Callis Western
William Wolryche Whitmore
    LORDS
Lord Bexley
Lord Brougham (22 Nov. 1830)
Lord King
Marquess of Lansdowne
Earl of Lauderdale
Bishop of Llandaff (Edward Copleston)

William Bingham Baring
Charles Buller
Col. William Maberly (12 Apr. 1831)
John Abel Smith
Edward Strutt
Thomas Hyde Villiers
Henry Warburton

13.   1 William IV   14 June 1831–3 Dec. 1832

Matthias Attwood
Alexander Baring
Davies Gilbert
Thomas Gisborne
Sir James Graham
Henry George Grey (Lord Howick)
Joseph Hume
James Morrison
Sir Henry Parnell
Sir Robert Peel
Thomas Spring Rice
John Charles Spencer (Lord Althorp)
Charles Edward Poulett Thomson
Robert Torrens
Charles Callis Western
William Wolryche Whitmore
    LORDS
Lord Bexley
Lord Brougham
Lord King

Col. William Maberly
John Abel Smith
Edward Strutt
Thomas Hyde Villiers (died 3 Dec. 1832)
Henry Warburton

Marquess of Lansdowne
Earl of Lauderdale
Bishop of Llandaff (Edward Copleston)

14.   3 William IV   29 Jan. 1833–29 Jan. 1835

Matthias Attwood
Thomas Attwood
Alexander Baring
Edward Cayley
William Clay
William Cobbett
John Fielden
Thomas Gisborne
Sir James Graham
Henry George Grey (Lord Howick)
George Grote
Joseph Hume
Sir William Molesworth
James Morrison
Sir Henry Parnell (17 Apr. 1833)
Sir Robert Peel
George Pryme
Thomas Spring Rice
George Julius Poulett Scrope (27 May
    1833)
John Charles Spencer (Lord Althorp)
    (succeeded to peerage as Earl
    Spencer, 10 Nov. 1834)
Charles Edward Poulett Thomson
Robert Torrens
William Wolryche Whitmore
    LORDS
Lord Bexley
Lord Brougham
Lord King (died 4 June 1833)
Marquess of Lansdowne
Earl of Lauderdale
Earl Spencer (10 Nov. 1834)
Lord Western
Bishop of Llandaff (Edward Copleston)
Archbishop of Dublin (Richard
    Whately) (1 Feb. 1833)

William Bingham Baring
Charles Buller
William Ewart Gladstone
Benjamin Hawes
George Lyall (27 Feb. 1833)
Col. William Maberly (resigned June 1835)
William Thomas Petty-Fitzmaurice (Earl of
    Kerry)
John Romilly
John Abel Smith
Edward Strutt
Henry Warburton

15.   5 William IV   19 Feb. 1835–17 July 1837

Matthias Attwood
Thomas Attwood
Alexander Baring (raised to peerage as
    Lord Ashburton, 10 Apr. 1835)
Edward Cayley
William Clay

William Bingham Baring
Charles Buller
William Ewart Gladstone
Benjamin Hawes
Granville George Leveson-Gower (Lord
    Leveson) (8 Feb. 1837)

William Cobbett (died 18 June 1835)
John Fielden
Thomas Gisborne
Sir James Graham
Henry George Grey (Lord Howick)
George Grote
Joseph Hume
Sir William Molesworth
James Morrison (10 June 1835)
Sir Henry Parnell
Sir Robert Peel
George Pryme
Thomas Spring Rice
George Julius Poulett Scrope
Thomas Perronet Thompson (28 June 1835)
Charles Edward Poulett Thomson
LORDS
Lord Ashburton (10 Apr. 1835)
Lord Bexley
Lord Brougham
Marquess of Lansdowne
Earl of Lauderdale
Earl Spencer
Lord Western
Bishop of Llandaff (Edward Copleston)
Archbishop of Dublin (Richard Whately)

William Thomas Petty-Fitzmaurice (Earl of Kerry) (died 31 Aug. 1836)
John Abel Smith
Edward Strutt
Charles Pelham Villiers
Henry Warburton

16. 1 Victoria 11 Sept. 1837–23 June 1841

Matthias Attwood
Thomas Attwood (resigned Dec. 1839)
Edward Cayley
William Clay
John Fielden
Thomas Gisborne (11 July 1839)
Sir James Graham (20 Feb. 1838)
Henry George Grey (Lord Howick)
George Grote
Joseph Hume
Sir William Molesworth
James Morrison (4 Mar. 1840)
George Frederick Muntz (25 Jan. 1840)
Sir Henry Parnell
Sir Robert Peel
George Pryme
Thomas Spring Rice (raised to peerage as Lord Monteagle, 5 Sept. 1839)
George Julius Poulett Scrope

William Bingham Baring
William John Blake
Charles Buller
William Ewart Gladstone
Benjamin Hawes
Granville George Leveson-Gower (Lord Leveson) (resigned 22 Feb. 1840)
John Abel Smith
Charles Pelham Villiers
Henry Warburton

Charles Edward Poulett Thomson
  (resigned August 1839 to
  become governor general
  of Canada)
    LORDS
Lord Ashburton
Lord Bexley
Lord Brougham
Marquess of Lansdowne
Earl of Lauderdale (died 13 Sept.
  1839)
Lord Monteagle (5 Sept. 1839)
Earl Spencer
Lord Sydenham (19 Aug. 1840)
Lord Western
Bishop of Llandaff (Edward Copleston)
Archbishop of Dublin (Richard
  Whately)

17. 5 Victoria   19 Aug. 1841–23 July 1847

Matthias Attwood
Edward Cayley
William Clay (created baronet, 21 Sept.
  1841)
Richard Cobden
John Fielden
Thomas Gisborne (5 Apr. 1843)
Sir James Graham
Henry George Grey (Lord Howick) (17
  Sept. 1841; succeeded to peerage as
  Earl Grey, 17 July 1845)
Joseph Hume (16 Apr. 1842)
Sir William Molesworth (12 Sept. 1845)
James Morrison
George Frederick Muntz
Sir Robert Peel
John Lewis Ricardo
George Julius Poulett Scrope
    LORDS
Lord Ashburton
Lord Bexley
Lord Brougham
Lord Congleton (raised to peerage, 23
  Aug. 1841; died 8 June 1842)
Earl Grey (17 July 1845)
Marquess of Lansdowne
Lord Monteagle
Earl Spencer (died 1 Oct. 1845)
Lord Sydenham (died 4 Sept. 1841)
Lord Western (died 4 Nov. 1844)
Bishop of Llandaff (Edward Copleston)

William Bingham Baring
Edward Pleydell Bouverie (20 May 1844)
Charles Buller
William Ewart Gladstone
Benjamin Hawes
Edward Frederick Leveson-Gower (16 June
  1847)
Granville George Leveson-Gower (Lord
  Leveson) (succeeded to peerage as Earl
  Granville, 8 Jan. 1846)
George Lyall
John Romilly (7 Mar. 1846)
John Abel Smith
Edward Strutt
Charles Pelham Villiers
Henry Warburton (resigned 15 Sept. 1841;
  reelected 9 Nov. 1843)
    LORDS
Earl of Clarendon
Earl Granville (8 Jan. 1846)
Lord Wodehouse (succeeded to peerage, 29
  May 1846)

Archbishop of Dublin (Richard
  Whately)

18.   11 Victoria   21 Sept. 1847–1 July 1852

Isaac Butt (8 May 1852)
Edward Cayley
Sir William Clay
Richard Cobden
Sir James Graham
Joseph Hume
George Cornewall Lewis
Sir William Molesworth
George Frederick Muntz
Sir Robert Peel (died 2 July 1850)
John Lewis Ricardo
George Julius Poulett Scrope
Thomas Perronet Thompson
James Wilson
  LORDS
Lord Ashburton (died 13 May 1848)
Lord Brougham
Lord Bexley (died 8 Feb. 1851)
Earl Grey
Marquess of Lansdowne
Lord Monteagle
Lord Overstone (raised to peerage, 5
  Mar. 1850)
Bishop of Llandaff (Edward Copleston)
  (died 14 Oct. 1849)
Archbishop of Dublin (Richard
  Whately)

William Bingham Baring (succeeded to
  peerage as Lord Ashburton, 13 May
  1848)
Edward Pleydell Bouverie
Charles Buller (died 29 Nov. 1848)
William Ewart Gladstone
Benjamin Hawes (11 Mar. 1848; resigned
  12 Feb. 1852)
Edward Frederick Leveson-Gower (resigned
  8 Sept. 1848)
John Romilly
John Abel Smith
Edward Strutt (resigned 9 Sept. 1848)
Charles Pelham Villiers
  LORDS
Lord Ashburton (13 May 1848)
Lord Clandeboye (raised to peerage 22 Jan.
  1850)
Earl of Clarendon
Earl Granville
Lord Wodehouse

19.   16 Victoria   20 Aug. 1852–21 Mar. 1857

Isaac Butt
Edward Cayley
Sir William Clay
Richard Cobden
Sir James Graham
Thomson Hankey (25 June 1853)
Joseph Hume (died 20 Feb. 1855)
Sir George Cornewall Lewis (8 Feb.
  1855; succeeded to baronetcy, 23
  Jan. 1855)
Robert Lowe
Sir William Molesworth (died 22 Oct.
  1855)
George Frederick Muntz
Sir Stafford Henry Northcote (4 Mar.
  1855)
John Lewis Ricardo
Samson Ricardo (14 Feb. 1855)

Edward Pleydell Bouverie
William Ewart Gladstone
Edward Frederick Leveson-Gower
George Montagu Warren Peacocke
  (resigned 21 June 1853; reelected 17
  Aug. 1854)
John Abel Smith
Edward Strutt (raised to peerage as Lord
  Belper, 29 Aug. 1856)
Charles Pelham Villiers
William Arthur Wilkinson
  LORDS
Lord Ashburton
Lord Belper (29 Aug. 1856)
Lord Clandeboye
Earl of Clarendon
Earl Granville
Lord Wodehouse

George Julius Poulett Scrope
James Wilson
   LORDS
Lord Brougham
Earl Grey
Marquess of Lansdowne
Lord Monteagle
Lord Overstone
Archbishop of Dublin (Richard
  Whately)

20.   20 Victoria   30 Apr. 1857–23 Apr. 1859

Isaac Butt
Edward Cayley
Sir James Graham
Thomson Hankey
Sir George Cornewall Lewis
Robert Lowe
George Frederick Muntz (died 30 July
  1857)
Sir Stafford Henry Northcote (17 July
  1858)
John Lewis Ricardo
George Julius Poulett Scrope
Thomas Perronet Thompson
James Wilson
   LORDS
Lord Brougham
Earl Grey
Marquess of Lansdowne
Lord Monteagle
Lord Overstone
Archbishop of Dublin (Richard
  Whately)

Edward Pleydell Bouverie
William Ewart Gladstone
Kirkman Daniel Hodgson
John Abel Smith
Charles Pelham Villiers
Edward William Watkin (resigned Aug.
  1858)
   LORDS
Lord Ashburton
Lord Belper
Lord Clandeboye
Earl of Clarendon
Earl Granville
Lord Wodehouse

21.   22 Victoria   31 May 1859–6 July 1865

Isaac Butt
Edward Cayley (died March 1862)
Richard Cobden (died 2 Apr. 1865)
George Joachim Goschen (2 June
  1863)
Sir James Graham (died 25 Oct. 1861)
Thomson Hankey
John Gellibrand Hubbard
Sir George Cornewall Lewis (died 13
  Apr. 1863)
Robert Lowe
Sir Stafford Henry Northcote
John Lewis Ricardo (died 20 Aug.
  1862)

Edward Pleydell Bouverie
William Ewart Gladstone
Kirkman Daniel Hodgson
Edward Frederick Leveson-Gower
George Montagu Warren Peacocke
John Abel Smith (21 Feb. 1863)
Charles Pelham Villiers
Edward William Watkin (9 May 1864)
   LORDS
Lord Ashburton (died 23 Mar. 1864)
Lord Belper
Lord Clandeboye
Earl of Clarendon
Earl Granville

George Julius Poulett Scrope
James Wilson (resigned Aug. 1859)
    LORDS
Lord Brougham
Earl Grey
Marquess of Lansdowne (died 31 Jan.
  1863)
Lord Monteagle
Lord Overstone
Archbishop of Dublin (Richard
  Whately) (died 1 Oct. 1863)

Lord Wodehouse

22.   28 Victoria 15 Aug. 1865–11 Nov. 1868

Henry Fawcett
George Joachim Goschen
Thomson Hankey
John Gellibrand Hubbard
Robert Lowe
John Stuart Mill
Sir Stafford Henry Northcote
George Julius Poulett Scrope (resigned
  Aug. 1867)
    LORDS
Lord Brougham (died 7 May 1868)
Earl Grey
Lord Monteagle (died 7 Feb. 1866)
Lord Overstone

Edward Pleydell Bouverie
Frederick Charles Cavendish (Lord
  Cavendish)
William Ewart Gladstone
Kirkman Daniel Hodgson
Edward Frederick Leveson-Gower
George Montagu Warren Peacocke
John Abel Smith
Charles Pelham Villiers
Edward William Watkin
    LORDS
Lord Belper
Lord Clandeboye
Earl Granville
Lord Romilly (raised to peerage, 19 Dec.
  1865)
Lord Wodehouse (created Earl of
  Kimberley, 1 June 1866)

Appendix IV

Participation of Economists in Parliamentary Activities

The record of speeches, as given in the indexes to *Hansard*, includes a number of cases where all the man did was to ask a short question, or express dissent in a word or two. There are also some mistakes in the *Hansard* index, in particular where men with similar names were confused. The committee memberships—which do not include standing committees—are based on the information given in the Commons and Lords Journals when members were first appointed, but in some cases members originally appointed did not serve, and in other cases new members were later appointed. I caught a number of such changes, but undoubtedly missed some. Such mistakes as may have arisen from these situations do not alter, however, the broad picture of the activity of each economist in parliamentary business.

Names of economists	Speeches	Committee memberships	Witness before parliamentary committees
Matthias Attwood	169	20	1
Thomas Attwood	150	7	3
Alexander Baring (Lord Ashburton)	1008	113	6
Francis Baring	18	6	1
Walter Boyd	2	0	2
Henry Brougham (Lord Brougham & Vaux)	4960	181	8
Isaac Butt	463	7	2
Edward S. Cayley	197	22	5
Sir William Clay	272	64	0
William Cobbett	262	1	0
Richard Cobden	482	24	2
Edward Copleston (Bishop of Llandaff)	41	11	0
Edward D. Davenport	50	4	0
Henry Fawcett	118	5	1
John Fielden	139	9	2
Kirkman Finlay	71	49	6
Davies Gilbert	178	209	3
Thomas Gisborne	218	217	0
George J. Goschen (Lord Goschen)	132	17	0
Sir James Graham	2492	183	9
Pascoe Grenfell	260	23	1
Henry George Grey (Viscount Howick, Earl Grey)	1780	103	5
George Grote	176	27	1

Thomson Hankey	274	23	2
Francis Horner	227	28	0
Robert Wilmot Horton	160	36	0
John Gellibrand Hubbard (Lord Addington)	204	10	1
Joseph Hume	7311	266	6
William Huskisson	575	132	1
William Jacob	14	2	3
Charles Jenkinson (Earl of Liverpool)	74	7	1
Peter King (Lord King)	336	41	0
Sir George Cornewall Lewis	1933	35	11
Robert Lowe (Lord Sherbrooke)	527	53	4
Samuel Jones Loyd (Lord Overstone)	90	44	6
James Maitland (Earl of Lauderdale)	459	54	1
John Stuart Mill	150	54	1
Sir William Molesworth	259	29	0
James Morrison	35	16	1
George Frederick Muntz	329	13	5
Sir Stafford Northcote (Earl of Iddesleigh)	700	32	0
Sir Henry Parnell (Lord Congleton)	361	175	11
Sir Robert Peel	4850	307	3
Henry Petty-Fitzmaurice (Lord Henry Petty, Marquess of Lansdowne)	2139	254	0
George Pryme	152	9	1
David Ricardo	124	8	5
John Lewis Ricardo	171	13	3
Samson Ricardo	0	0	0
Thomas Spring Rice (Lord Monteagle)	2115	263	10
George Rose	507	212	6
George Poulett Scrope	289	22	3
Sir John Sinclair	29	47	1
John Charles Spencer (Lord Althorp, Earl Spencer)	2314	124	0
Thomas Perronet Thompson	245	4	0
Charles Edward Poulett Thomson (Lord Sydenham)	419	58	3
Henry Thornton	84	103	2
Robert Torrens	104	7	4
Nicholas Vansittart (Lord Bexley)	949	232	1
Charles C. Western (Lord Western)	194	53	2
Richard Whately (Archbishop of Dublin)	44	2	2
William Wolryche Whitmore	116	34	3
James Wilson	849	45	2

Appendix V

Economists in Government: 1783–1868

This appendix is based on the information in Sir Llewellyn Woodward, *The Age of Reform* (Clarendon Press, Oxford, 1938), pp. 575–583, 658–667.

Members of the Political Economy Club are identified by an asterisk preceding the name.

First Administration of William Pitt (1783–1801)

Lord Hawkesbury (created 1st Earl of Liverpool in 1796)—President of the Board of Trade, 1791–1801 (also Chancellor of the Duchy of Lancaster, 1794–1801)

Addington Administration (1801–4)

Lord Liverpool—President of the Board of Trade, 1801–4 (also Chancellor of the Duchy of Lancaster, 1801–4)

Second Pitt Administration (1804–6)

No economists.

"Ministry of All the Talents" (1806–7)

*Lord Henry Petty (later 3d Marquess of Lansdowne)—Chancellor of the Exchequer, 1806–7

Portland Administration (1807–9)

No economists.

Perceval Administration (1809–12)

No economists.

Lord Liverpool's Cabinet (1812–27)

Nicholas Vansittart (created 1st Baron Bexley in 1823)—Chancellor of the Exchequer, 1812–23
Lord Bexley—Chancellor of the Duchy of Lancaster, 1823–27
Robert Peel—Home Secretary, 1822–27
William Huskisson—President of the Board of Trade and Treasurer of the Navy, 1823–27

Canning's Cabinet (1827)

William Huskisson—President of the Board of Trade and Treasurer of the Navy, 1827

Lord Bexley—Chancellor of the Duchy of Lancaster, 1827
*Marquess of Lansdowne—Minister without Portfolio; later Home Secretary, 1827

Goderich's Cabinet (1827–28)

*Marquess of Lansdowne—Home Secretary, 1827–28
William Huskisson—Secretary for War and Colonies, 1827–28
Lord Bexley—Chancellor of the Duchy of Lancaster, 1827–28

Wellington's Cabinet (1828–30)

Robert Peel—Home Secretary, 1828–30
William Huskisson—Secretary for War and Colonies, 1828

Grey's Cabinet (1830–34)

Lord Brougham—Lord Chancellor, 1830–34
*Lord Althorp (later 3d Earl Spencer)—Chancellor of the Exchequer, 1830–34
*Marquess of Lansdowne—Lord President of the Council, 1830–34
Sir James Graham—First Lord of the Admiralty, 1830–34
*T. Spring Rice—Secretary for War and Colonies, 1834
*Sir Henry Parnell was Secretary of War, 1831–32, but was not in the cabinet.
*C. E. Poulett Thomson was Vice-President of the Board of Trade and Treasurer
 of the Navy, 1830–34, but was not in the cabinet.

Melbourne's First Cabinet (1834)

Lord Brougham—Lord Chancellor, 1834
*Marquess of Lansdowne—Lord President of the Council, 1834
*Lord Althorp—Chancellor of the Exchequer, 1834
*T. Spring Rice—Secretary for War and Colonies, 1834
*C. E. Poulett Thomson—President of the Board of Trade and Treasurer of the
 Navy, 1834

Peel's First Cabinet (1834–35)

Sir Robert Peel—Prime Minister and First Lord of the Treasury; Chancellor of the
 Exchequer, 1834–35
Alexander Baring—President of the Board of Trade; Master of the Mint, 1834–
 35

Melbourne's Second Cabinet (1835–41)

*Marquess of Lansdowne—Lord President of the Council, 1835–41
*T. Spring Rice—Chancellor of the Exchequer, 1835–39
*C. E. Poulett Thomson—President of the Board of Trade, 1835–39
*Lord Howick (later 3d Earl Grey)—Secretary of War, 1835–39

Peel's Second Cabinet (1841–46)

Sir Robert Peel—Prime Minister and First Lord of the Treasury, 1841–46
Sir James Graham—Home Secretary, 1841–46

Russell's First Cabinet (1846–52)

*Marquess of Lansdowne—Lord President of the Council, 1846–52

*Earl Grey—Secretary for War and Colonies, 1846–52
*James Wilson was Joint Secretary of the Board of Control, 1848–52, but was not
   in the cabinet.

Derby's First Cabinet (1852)

No economists.

Aberdeen's Cabinet (1852–55)

Sir James Graham—First Lord of the Admiralty, 1852–55
Sir William Molesworth—First Commissioner of Works, 1852–55
*Marquess of Lansdowne—Cabinet Minister without office, 1852–55
*James Wilson was Joint Secretary of the Board of Control (1853–55), but was not
   in the cabinet.
*Robert Lowe was Joint Secretary of the Board of Control (1852–55), but was not
   in the cabinet.

Palmerston's First Cabinet (1855–58)

Sir James Graham—First Lord of the Admiralty, 1855
Sir William Molesworth—First Commissioner of Works, 1855
Sir William Molesworth—Secretary for the Colonies, 1855
*Sir G. Cornewall Lewis—Chancellor of the Exchequer, 1855–58
*Marquess of Lansdowne—Cabinet Minister without office, 1855–58
*James Wilson was Joint Secretary of the Board of Control, 1855–58, but was not
   in the cabinet.
*Robert Lowe was Joint Secretary of the Board of Control, 1855, and Vice-Presi-
   dent of the Board of Trade and Paymaster-General, 1855–1858, but was not in
   the cabinet.

Derby's Second Cabinet (1858–59)

No economists.

Palmerston's Second Cabinet (1859–65)

*Sir G. Cornewall Lewis—Home Secretary, 1859–61
*Sir G. Cornewall Lewis—Secretary of War, 1861–63
*James Wilson was Vice-President of the Board of Control, and Paymaster-General
   (1859), but was not in the cabinet.

Russell's Second Cabinet (1865–66)

*J. G. Goschen (later 1st Viscount Goschen)—Chancellor of the Duchy of Cornwall,
   1866

Derby's Third Cabinet (1866–68)

*Sir Stafford Northcote (later 1st Earl of Iddesleigh)—President of the Board of
   Trade, 1866–67
*Sir Stafford Northcote—Secretary for India, 1867–68

Disraeli's First Cabinet (1868)

*Sir Stafford Northcote—Secretary for India, 1868

Appendix VI

Economists Unsuccessful in Their Parliamentary Aspirations

In addition to the economists covered in this study, several others before 1868 either considered standing for Parliament or stood and were defeated. All of these men, except Wheatley, are in the DNB.

Walter Bagehot (1826–74)

Editor of *The Economist*, 1860–74, author of *Lombard Street*, and member of the Political Economy Club. In 1860 considered standing for London University; in 1865 candidate for Manchester but withdrew before the voting; in 1866 stood for Bridgwater in a by-election and was defeated by seven votes; in 1868 sought Liberal nomination for London University, but was beaten by Robert Lowe. In 1869 refused invitations to stand for Freeman and Chichester Fortesque, and in 1873 to stand for Liverpool.

A recent biography is by Alastair Buchan: *The Spare Chancellor. The Life of Walter Bagehot* (Chatto and Wurdus, London, 1959).

Samuel Bailey (1791–1870)

Unsuccessful candidate for Sheffield in 1832 and in 1834.

Businessman and later philosophical writer. His principal economic writings were: *Questions in Political Economy* (1823); *A Critical Dissertation on the Nature, Measure, and Causes of Value* (1825); *A Letter to a Political Economist* (1826); *Money and Its Vicissitudes in Value* (1837); *A Defense of Joint-stock Banks and Country Issues* (1840).

Sir John Lubbock (Baron Avery) (1834–1913)

Banker and Merchant, member of Political Economy Club, and sponsor of Bank Holiday Act of 1871. Refused nomination to stand for London in 1863, and was defeated as Liberal candidate for West Kent in 1865 and 1868. Represented Maidstone 1870–80, University of London 1880–1900, raised to peerage in 1900. Wrote on a wide range of subjects, scientific, political, and economic. A partial bibliography of his publications is in Horace G. Hutchinson, *Life of Sir John Lubbock*, 2 vols. (Macmillan, London, 1914), 2:321–22.

John Horsley Palmer (1779–1858)

Director of Bank of England for fifty-six years and governor, 1830–32.

Author of *Reasons against the Proposed Indian Joint-Stock Bank* (1836); *The Causes and Consequences of the Pressure upon the Money Market* (1837); *Reply to the Reflections . . . of Mr. Samuel Jones Loyd in the Pamphlet Entitled Causes and Consequences* (1837).

In 1837 was defeated as candidate for London, polling six votes fewer than George Grote; in 1835 and 1843 defeated as candidate for Ashburton.

John Wheatley (1770–1830)

Wheatley never was formally a candidate, but it is evident from his letter of 18 November 1812 to Sir William Watkins Wynn (in the National Library of Wales, Aberystwyth) that he had been urged to be a candidate that year and had seriously considered doing so. "I was applied to to stand both for Dover and Sandwich. I made a show at Sandwich, but ran away upon Sir Joseph Yorke coming down. Dover might have been carried by any man for £500, but £500 was not at my command." Joseph Yorke was elected for Sandwich in 1812, but I can find no reference in either Dover or Sandwich newspapers to suggest that Wheatley might be a candidate.

An account of Wheatley's life and of his writings is in Frank Whitson Fetter, "The Life and Writings of John Wheatley," *Journal of Political Economy* 50 (June 1942): 357–76.

Principal Sources

Parliamentary Records

Cobbett, William. *Parliamentary History of England from the Earliest Times to the Year 1803*. London, 1806–12.

Hansard, T. C., *Parliamentary Debates*, 1803–68. The first series of Hansard covers 1803–20; a New Series, 1820–30; and a Third Series from 1830 on.

Journals of the House of Commons, 1780–1868.

Journals of the House of Lords, 1780–1868.

Reports of Parliamentary Committees. All committees through 1834 are listed in Hansard's *Catalogue and Breviate of Parliamentary Papers 1696–1834*. (Ordered, by the House of Commons, to be Printed 15 August 1834. Reprinted in facsimile, with an Introduction by P. Ford and G. Ford. Basil Blackwell, Oxford, 1953.) The principal committee reports for succeeding years are given in *Select List of British Parliamentary Papers 1833–1899*, compiled by P. Ford and G. Ford. Basil Blackwell, Oxford, 1953.

Manuscripts

Henry Brougham Papers. University College, London.

Isaac Butt, material relating principally to. Public Record Office of Northern Ireland.

Earl of Clarendon Papers. Bodleian Library, Oxford.

E. D. Davenport Papers. John Rylands Library, Manchester.

Election Records. Institute of Historical Research, London.

Sir James Graham Papers. Microfilm at Cambridge University, of originals in possession of Sir Fergus Graham.

Lord Howick (3d Earl Grey) Papers. Department of Palaeography and Diplomatics, University of Durham.

Francis Horner Papers. London School of Economics.

Sir Robert Wilmot Horton Papers. Public Library of Derby.

William Huskisson Papers. British Museum.

Sir George Cornewall Lewis Papers. National Library of Wales, Aberystwyth.

Miscellaneous material relating to several elections. University of Nottingham Library.

Miscellaneous papers. National Library of Scotland.

Miscellaneous papers, in large part relating to military career of Robert Torrens. Scottish Record Office.

Papers relating to C. C. Western campaigns, and to Robert Torrens's military career. Ipswich and East Suffolk Record Office.

Sir Henry Parnell (1st Lord Congleton) Papers. In possession of Lord Congleton, Ebbisbourne Wake (Wilts).

Sir Robert Peel Papers. British Museum.

Francis Place Papers. British Museum.
Thomas Spring Rice (Lord Monteagle) Papers. National Library of Ireland.
T. Perronet Thompson Papers. University of Hull.
Henry Thornton Papers. Cambridge University; Church Missionary Society (London).
Robert Torrens, material relating principally to candidacy of. Public Libraries of Bolton.
Nicholas Vansittart (Lord Bexley) Papers. British Museum.

Newspapers

The Times (London)	1780–1868
Aberdeen Journal	
Hume; J. L. Ricardo	11 August 1847
Berrow's Worcester Gazette	
Graham; Lewis; Northcote	3 March 1855
Clay; Cobden; Lowe; Northcote	4 April 1857
Birmingham Chronicle	
Cobbett	23 November 1830
Bolton Chronicle	
Torrens	15 December 1832
Torrens	3 January 1835
Torrens; Perronet Thompson	10 January 1836
Bradford Observer	
Cobden; Perronet Thompson	8 July 1852
Cobden; Perronet Thompson	15 July 1852
Cobden; Perronet Thompson	22 July 1852
Brighton Examiner	
Fawcett	11 July 1865
Fawcett	18 July 1865
Brighton Gazette	
Fawcett	13 July 1865
Brighton Observer	
Fawcett	11 July 1865
Bucks Chronicle and Bucks Gazette	
Hubbard	4 May 1859
Hubbard	15 July 1865
Bury and Norwich Post	
Alexander Baring	4 May 1831
Caledonian Mercury (Edinburgh)	
Brougham	5 November 1812
Hume	16 July 1818
Hume	3 April 1820

Matthias Attwood · 25 April 1833
Morrison · 5 March 1840
Hume · 18 April 1842
Hume · 9 August 1847

Cambrian (Swansea)
Graham · 2 February 1838

Cambridge Chronicle and Huntingtonshire Gazette
Pryme · 10 March 1820
Pryme · 16 June 1826
Pryme and Rice · 14 December 1832
Rice · 20 June 1834
Pryme and Rice · 6 January 1835
Pryme and Rice · 29 July 1837

Carlisle Examiner and Northern Advertiser
Graham · 30 August 1859

Carlisle Journal
Graham · 14 May 1831
Graham · 22 May 1832
Graham · 22 July 1837
Graham · 12 August 1837
Graham · 9 July 1852
Graham · 1 January 1853
Graham · 3 April 1857

Carlisle Patriot
Grenfell · 14 May 1831
Grote; Matthias Attwood · 15 December 1832
Graham · 8 July 1837
Graham · 11 July 1837
Graham · 14 July 1837
Graham · 15 July 1837
Graham · 8 January 1843
Graham and Perronet Thompson · 10 July 1852
Graham · 4 August 1857

Carlow Sentinel
Gisborne · 9 February 1839
Gisborne · 16 February 1839
Gisborne · 2 March 1839
Gisborne · 13 July 1839
Gisborne · 22 May 1841
Gisborne · 12 June 1841

Cheltenham Chronicle
Scrope · 29 July 1837

Chester Chronicle
Davenport · 18 May 1832

Colchester Gazette
   Western   7 May 1831

Cumberland Pacquet
   Graham   3 May 1859

Daily Telegraph
   Goschen; Mill   12 July 1865

Devizes and Wiltshire Gazette
   Scrope   5 May 1841
   Wilson   15 July 1847
   Wilson   5 August 1847

Devon Weekly News
   Northcote   11 May 1866

Dublin Evening Post
   Brougham; Rice   9 July 1818
   Parnell; Rice   1 March 1820
   Rice   27 June 1826
   Parnell   9 December 1832
   Parnell   29 June 1836
   Hume   10 August 1837
   Gisborne   28 February 1839
   Gisborne   11 July 1839
   Butt   15 July 1852

Durham Chronicle
   Howick   17 September 1841

Edinburgh Advertiser
   Finlay   14 July 1818

Essex Independent
   Western   28 December 1832

Exchange Herald (Manchester)
   Brougham   20 October 1812

Exeter Journal
   Northcote   4 April 1857

Glamorgan, Monmouth, and Brecan Gazette and Methyr Guardian
   Graham   February 1838

Gloucestershire Chronicle
   Scrope   3 July 1841

Hereford Journal
   Lewis   21 July 1852

Hereford Times
   Lewis   24 July 1852

Hull Advertiser
Graham	27 June 1818
Graham	4 July 1818
Brougham; Graham	11 July 1818
Graham	18 July 1818
Perronet Thompson	19 June 1835
Perronet Thompson	26 June 1835
Hume; Muntz; Peel; Perronet Thompson	2 July 1841

Hull Observer
Perronet Thompson	16 June 1835
Perronet Thompson	23 June 1835

Hull Packet
Perronet Thompson	19 June 1835
Hume; Perronet Thompson	26 June 1835
Cayley; Perronet Thompson	25 June 1841
Perronet Thompson	2 July 1841

Ipswich Journal
Torrens	17 June 1826
Torrens	24 June 1826
Torrens	26 February 1827

Kent Herald
Poulett Thomson	22 June 1826

Kentish Chronicle
Torrens	19 June 1818
Cobbett	22 January 1826
Poulett Thomson	10 August 1832

Kentish Gazette
Poulett Thomson	29 April 1831

Kilkenny Journal
Hume	12 August 1837

Kilkenny Moderator
Hume	9 August 1837

Lancaster Gazette
Brougham; Graham	11 July 1818
Brougham	25 March 1820
Brougham; Cobbett; Howick	1 July 1826

Leeds Intelligencer
Molesworth	15 July 1837
Molesworth	22 July 1837
Molesworth	29 July 1837
Cobden	7 August 1847
Cobden	14 August 1847

Leeds Mercury
Graham	15 July 1837

Cayley; Molesworth	22 July 1837
Molesworth	29 July 1837
Cobden; Fielden; Graham; Wilson	7 August 1847
Cobden	14 August 1847
Cobden	17 July 1852
Cobden	24 July 1852

Limerick Herald
Rice	9 May 1831

Lincoln, Rutledge and Stanford Mercury
Cobbett; Davenport	17 March 1820

Liverpool Advertiser
Huskisson	18 February 1823
Huskisson	17 June 1826

Liverpool Mercury
Brougham	21 July 1815

Liverpool Times
Cobbett; Fielden; Loyd; Poulett Thomson; Torrens	10 December 1832

Manchester Guardian
Cobbett; Fielden; Grote, Torrens	10 January 1835
Cobden; Fielden	4 August 1847

Newcastle Chronicle
Howick	22 December 1832

Northampton Herald
Lewis	11 December 1852

Northern Warder
Hume	12 August 1847

North Staffordshire Mercury
J. L. Ricardo	3 July 1841

Nottingham Journal
Gisborne	7 April 1843
Gisborne	29 July 1847

Nottingham Review
Gisborne	7 April 1843

Salisbury and Winchester Journal, and General Advertiser
Lowe	23 April 1859

Salisbury and Windsor Journal, and General Advertiser of Wilts, Hants, Dorset, and Somerset
Peel	9 March 1829
Wilson	30 July 1847

Shrewsbury Chronicle and North Wales Advertiser
Whitmore	6 August 1830

Staffordshire Advertiser
Peel; J. L. Ricardo   31 July 1847

Staffordshire Examiner
J. L. Ricardo   26 June 1841

Staffordshire Mercury
Whitmore   22 December 1832

Staffordshire Sentinel
J. L. Ricardo   4 April 1857

Stockport Advertiser
Davenport   14 December 1832
Cobbett; Davenport; Fielden   15 January 1835
Davenport; Torrens   16 January 1835
Cobden   28 July 1837
Cobden   2 July 1841
Cobden   6 August 1847

Suffolk Chronicle
Torrens   24 June 1826
Torrens   26 February 1827
Morrison   10 January 1837
Gisborne; Morrison   20 June 1835

Sunderland and Durham Country Herald
Howick   17 September 1841

Taunton Courier
Alexander Baring   8 October 1812
Alexander Baring   15 October 1812

Treman's Exeter Flying Post
Torrens   12 May 1831

Tyne Mercury
Howick   27 June 1826
Howick   13 July 1841

Western Times (Ashburton)
Molesworth; Torrens   14 May 1831

Western Times (Exeter)
Northcote   11 May 1866

Westmoreland Gazette and Kendall Advertiser
Brougham   14 July 1818

Whitehaven Herald
Matthias Attwood   15 December 1832

Wiltshire County Mirror
Lowe   4 May 1859

Wiltshire Independent
Wilson   5 August 1847

Wilson	8 July 1852
Wilson	15 July 1852

Windsor and Eton Express

Samson Ricardo	10 July 1852
Samson Ricardo	17 February 1855
Samson Ricardo	28 March 1857

Worcestershire Chronicle and Provincial Railway Gazette

Lowe	7 July 1852

Worcestershire Chronicle

Cobden; Graham; Lowe; Northcote; Perronet Thompson	25 March 1857

York Chronicle

Cayley	27 December 1832
Cayley	15 January 1835
Cayley	22 January 1835

York Courant

Cayley	24 December 1832
Cayley; Hume	22 January 1835

York Herald

Brougham; Hume	26 June 1830
Brougham; Huskisson	9 August 1830
Cayley	29 December 1832
Cayley; Cobden	4 April 1857
Cayley	11 April 1857

Yorkshire Gazette

Cayley; Hume	17 January 1835
Cayley	2 July 1841
Cayley; Clay; Cobden	4 April 1857
Cayley; Clay; Cobden; Wilson	6 April 1857
Cayley	14 August 1857

The Yorkshiremen

Cayley	17 January 1835
Cayley; Hume	5 August 1837

Periodicals

The Economist	1843–68
Punch	1841–68

Books About Elections

Bean, William Mardell. *The Parliamentary Representation of the Six Northern Counties of England.* Hull, 1890.

Crosby, George. *Crosby's Parliamentary Record,* 2 vols. Leeds, 1849.

Dod, Charles R. *Electoral Facts from 1832 to 1852*. London, 1852.
Dod, R. P. *The Parliamentary Pocket Companion* (annual). London, 1833–68.
Judd, Gerrit P. *Members of Parliament 1734–1832*. New Haven, Conn.: Yale University Press, 1955.
Jupp, Peter. *British and Irish Elections*. Newton Abbot: David and Charles, 1973.
Oldfield, T. H. B. *The Representative History of Great Britain and Ireland*, 6 vols. London, 1816.
Philbin, H. Holliday. *Parliamentary Representation, 1832: England and Wales*. New Haven, Conn.: Yale University Press, 1965.
Porritt, Edward. *The Unreformed House of Commons*. 2 vols. Cambridge, Eng.: Cambridge University Press, 1903.
Vincent, J., and M. Stenton, eds. *McCalmont's Parliamentary Poll Book*, 8th ed. Essex: Harvester Press, 1971.

.

Books and Articles Relating to Individual Economists

All of the economists listed in Appendix I are included in the *Dictionary of National Biography*, except Matthias Attwood, Edward S. Cayley, Edward D. Davenport, Samson Ricardo, and William Wolryche Whitmore. There are many biographies of William Cobbett, John Stuart Mill, and Sir Robert Peel; the ones listed here present the best discussions of the parliamentary careers of Cobbett and Mill and are the most recent for Peel.

Thomas Attwood

Fetter, Frank Whitson, ed. *Selected Economic Writings of Thomas Attwood*. London: London School of Economics and Political Science, 1964.
Wakefield, C. M. *The Life of Thomas Attwood*. London, 1885.

Henry Brougham

Aspinall, Arthur. *Lord Brougham and the Whig Party*. Manchester, 1927.
Garratt, G. T. *Lord Brougham*. London: Macmillan, 1935.
Hawes, Francis Richard. *Henry Brougham*. New York: St. Martin's Press, 1958.
New, Chester William. *The Life of Henry Brougham to 1830*. Oxford: Clarendon Press, 1961.

Isaac Butt

Thornley, David. *Isaac Butt and Home Rule*. London: MacGibbon and Lee, 1964.

Edward S. Cayley

Gordon, Barry. *Non-Ricardian Political Economy*. Boston: Graduate School of Business Administration, 1967. Chap. 2, "Edward Stillingsfleet Cayley: Principles and Practice," pp. 13–19, 47–48.

William Cobbett

Cole, G. D. H. *The Life of William Cobbett*. New York: Harcourt Brace, 1924.

Richard Cobden

Morley, John. *The Life of Richard Cobden*. Boston: Roberts Brothers, 1881.
Read, Donald. *Cobden and Bright, A Victorian Political Partnership*. New York: St. Martin's Press, 1968.

Edward Copleston, Bishop of Llandaff

Copleston, William J. *Memoir of Edward Copleston, D.D., Bishop of Llandaff, With Selections from his Diary and Correspondence.* London: J. W. Parker, 1851.

Henry Fawcett

Stephen, Leslie. *Life of Henry Fawcett.* London: Smith Elder and Co., 1885.

Kirkman Finlay

Anonymous. *James Finlay and Company, Limited.* Glasgow: Jackson Son, 1951. Chaps. 2, 3, and 4.
———. "Kirkman Finlay: Merchant, Manufacturer and Mentor," *Three Banks Review* (March 1957).

Davies Gilbert

Todd, Arthur Cecil. *Beyond the Blaze: A Biography of Davies Gilbert.* Truro: D. Bradford Barton, 1967.

George Joachim Goschen (1st Viscount Goschen)

Eliot, Arthur Ralph Douglas. *The Life of George Joachim Goschen.* London: Longmans, 1911.

James R. G. Graham

Erickson, Arvel B. *The Public Career of Sir James Graham.* Oxford: Blackwell, 1952.
Parker, Charles Stuart. *Life and Letters of Sir James Graham,* 2 vols. London: James Murray, 1907.
Ward, John Trevor. *Sir James Graham.* London: Macmillan, 1967.

George Grote

Bain, Alexander. *The Minor Works of George Grote.* London: John Murray, 1873.
Clark, M. L. *George Grote: A Biography.* London: Athlone Press, 1962.
Grote, Harriet (Mrs. George). *The Personal Life of George Grote.* London: John Murray, 1873.
———. *Posthumous Papers of the Late George Grote.* London: Clowes, 1874.

Francis Horner

Fetter, Frank Whitson, ed. *The Economic Writings of Francis Horner.* London: The London School of Economics and Political Science, 1964.
Horner, Leonard, ed. *Memoirs and Correspondence of Francis Horner, M.P.,* 2 vols. London: John Murray, 1843.

Sir Robert Wilmot Horton

Ghosh, R. N. "The Colonization Controversy: R. J. Wilmot-Horton and the Classical Economists." *Economica* r.s., 31 (Nov. 1964): 385–400.

William Huskisson

[Benjamin, Lewis Saul]. *The Huskisson Papers.* Edited by Lewis Melville [pseud.]. London: Constable, 1931.
Brady, Alexander. *William Huskisson and Liberal Reform.* London: Oxford University Press, 1928.

Lord King

A Selection from the Speeches and Writings of the Late Lord King. With a Short Introductory Memoir by Earl Fortesque. London: Longmans, 1844.

Sir George Cornewall Lewis

Lewis, Rev. Sir Gilbert Frankland, Bart., ed. *Letters of the Right Hon. Sir George Cornewall Lewis, Bart., to Various Friends.* London: Green and Co., 1870.

Robert Lowe (1st Viscount Sherbrooke)

Knight, Ruth. *Illiberal Liberal: Robert Lowe in New South Wales, 1842–1850.* Melbourne: Melbourne University Press, 1966.

Martin, Arthur Patchett. *Life and Letters of the Right Honourable Robert Lowe, Viscount Sherbrooke,* 2 vols. Longmans: London, 1893.

Sylvester, D. W. *Robert Lowe and Education.* London: Cambridge University Press, 1974.

Samuel Jones Loyd (1st Baron Overstone)

O'Brien, D. P., ed. *The Correspondence of Lord Overstone,* 3 vols. Cambridge: Cambridge University Press, 1971.

John Stuart Mill

Collected Works of John Stuart Mill. Toronto: Toronto University Press, 1977–. 19 vols. to date.

Packe, Michael St. John. *The Life of John Stuart Mill.* London: Secker and Warburg, 1954.

Sir William Molesworth

Fawcett, Millicent. *Right Hon. Sir William Molesworth,* Bart. London: Macmillan, 1901.

Grote, Harriet. *The Philosophical Radicals of 1832, comprising the Life of Sir William Molesworth and some Incidents connected with the Reform Movement from 1832 to 1842.* London, 1866. Reprint. New York: Burt Franklin, 1970.

Sir Stafford Henry Northcote (1st Earl of Iddesleigh)

Lang, Andrew. *Life, Letters, and Diaries of Sir Stafford Northcote, First Earl of Iddesleigh.* 2 vols. Edinburgh and London: William Blackwood and Sons, 1890.

Sir Robert Peel

Gash, Norman. *The Life of Sir Robert Peel to 1830.* Cambridge, Mass.: Harvard University Press, 1961.

———. *The Life of Sir Robert Peel after 1830.* Totowa, N.J.: Roman and Littlefield, 1972.

George Pryme

Autobiographical Recollections of George Pryme. Edited by his daughter. Cambridge, 1870.

David Ricardo

Cannan, Edwin. "Ricardo in Parliament." *Economic Journal* 6 (Jan. and Sept. 1894): 249–61, 409–28.

Shoup, Carl. *Ricardo on Taxation.* New York: Columbia University Press, 1960.

Sraffa, Piero, ed., with the collaboration of M. H. Dobb. *The Works and Correspondence of David Ricardo,* 11 vols. Cambridge: Cambridge University Press, 1951–73.

Weatherall, David. *David Ricardo: A Biography.* The Hague: Martinus Nyhoff, 1976.

George Rose

Vernon-Harcourt, Leveson, ed. *Diaries and Correspondence of the Right Hon. George Rose,* 2 vols. London, 1860.

George Julius Poulett Scrope

Opie, Redvers. "A Neglected British Economist, George Poulett Scrope." *Quarterly Journal of Economics* 44 (Nov. 1928): 101–37.

Sir John Sinclair

Mitchison, Rosalind. *Agricultural Sir John: The Life of Sir John Sinclair of Ulbster, 1754–1835.* London: Geoffrey Bles, 1962.

John Charles Spencer (Viscount Althorp; 3d Earl Spencer)

Le Marchant, Sir H. D., ed. *Memoir of John Charles Spencer, third Earl Spencer.* London, 1876.

Meyers, Ernest James. *Lord Althorp.* London: R. Bentley and Son, 1890.

Thomas Perronet Thompson

Johnson, L. G. *General T. Perronet Thompson.* London: George Allen and Unwin, 1957.

Moyse-Bartlett, H. *The Pirates of Trucial Oman.* London: MacDonal, 1966.

Charles Edward Poulett Thomson (1st Baron Sydenham)

Scrope, George Poulett. *Memoir of the Right Honble. Charles, Lord Sydenham.* London, 1843.

Henry Thornton

Hayek, F. A. Introduction to reprint of Thornton's *An Enquiry into the Nature and Effects of the Paper Credit of Great Britain.* London: George Allen and Unwin, 1939. Pp. 11–63.

Meacham, Standish. *Henry Thornton of Clapham.* Cambridge, Mass.: Harvard University Press, 1964.

Robert Torrens

Fetter, Frank Whitson. "Robert Torrens, Colonel of Marines and Political Economist." *Economica,* n.s., 29 (May 1962): 152–65.

Robbins, Lionel. *Robert Torrens and the Evolution of Classical Economics.* London: Macmillan, 1958.

Richard Whately (Archbishop of Dublin)

Whately, Elizabeth Jane. *Life and Correspondence of Richard Whately.* London: Longmans, 1875.

Other Books

Adams, William Forbes. *Ireland and Irish Emigration to the New World.* New Haven, Conn.: Yale University Press, 1932.

Anonymous. *The Black Book of England.* London, 1847.

Arbuthnot, Harriet. *The Journal of Mrs. Arbuthnot.* Edited by Francis Bamford and the Duke of Wellington. 2 vols. London: Macmillan, 1950.

Aspinall, Arthur. *Three Nineteenth Century Diaries.* London: Williams & Norgate, 1952.

———, ed. *The Diary of Henry Hobhouse.* London: Horne & Van Thal, 1947.

Barnes, Donald Grove. *A History of the English Corn Laws from 1660–1846.* New York: F. S. Croft & Co., 1930.

Best, G. F. A. *Shaftesbury.* New York: Arco Publishing Company, 1964.

Black, R. D. C. *Economic Thought and the Irish Question, 1817–1870.* Cambridge: Cambridge University Press, 1960.

Bloomfield, Paul. *Edward Gibbon Wakefield.* London: Longmans, 1961.

Briggs, Asa. *The Age of Improvement.* London: Longmans, 1959.

———, ed. *Chartist Studies.* London: Macmillan, 1959.

———. *Victorian People: A Reassessment of Persons and Themes, 1851–1867,* rev. ed. Chicago: University of Chicago Press, 1970.

Brown, Ford K. *Fathers of the Victorians.* Cambridge: Cambridge University Press, 1961.

Brown, Lucy M. *The Board of Trade and the Free Trade Movement.* Oxford: Clarendon Press, 1958.

Brose, Olive J. *Church and Parliament: The Reshaping of the Church of England, 1828–1860.* Stanford, Calif.: Stanford University Press, 1959.

Broughton, Lord. *Recollections of a Long Life.* Edited by his daughter, Lady Dorchester. 5 vols. London: James Murray, 1909–11.

Butler, J. R. M. *The Passing of the Great Reform Bill.* London: Longmans, 1914.

Bythell, Duncan. *The Handloom Weavers.* Cambridge: Cambridge University Press, 1969.

Checkland, S. G. *The Gladstones: A Family Biography 1764–1851.* Cambridge: Cambridge University Press, 1971.

Clapham, Sir John. *Economic History of Modern Britain.* Vols. 1 and 2. Cambridge: Cambridge University Press, 1926.

Conacher, J. B. *The Peelites and the Party System: 1846–1852.* Hamden, Conn.: Archon Books, 1972.

Cookson, J. E. *Lord Liverpool's Administration: The Crucial Years.* Edinburgh and London: Scottish Academic Press, 1975.

Cowan, Helen I. *British Emigration to British North America,* rev. and enlg. ed. Toronto: University of Toronto Press, 1961; orig. ed. 1928.

Cowherd, R. G. *The Humanitarians and the Ten Hour Movement in England.* Boston: Harvard Graduate School of Business Administration, 1956.

———. *Politics of English Dissent.* New York: New York University Press, 1956.

———. *Political Economists and the English Poor Laws.* Athens, Ohio: Ohio University Press, 1977.

Crowther, M. A. *Church Embattled: Religious Controversy in Mid-Victorian England.* Newton Abbot: David and Charles [Devon], 1970.

Darvall, Frank Ongley. *Popular Disturbances and Public Order in Regency England.* London: Oxford University Press, 1934.

Denison, John (Viscount Ossington). *Notes from My Journal When Speaker of the House of Commons.* London: John Murray, 1890.

Derry, John W. *Reaction and Reform: England in the Early Nineteenth Century.* London: Blandford Press, 1963.

Edsall, Nicholas C. *The Anti-Poor Law Movement, 1834–44.* Manchester: Manchester University Press, 1971.

Egerton, H. E. *Selected Speeches of Sir William Molesworth on Questions Relating to Colonial Policy.* London, 1903.

Fetter, Frank Whitson. *Development of British Monetary Orthodoxy 1797–1875.* Cambridge, Mass.: Harvard University Press, 1965.

———. *The Irish Pound 1797–1826. A Reprint of the Report of the Committee of 1804 of the British House of Commons on the Condition of the Irish Currency.* London: George Allen and Unwin, 1955.

Fraser, Derek, ed. *The New Poor Law in the Nineteenth Century.* New York: St. Martin's Press, 1976.

Gash, Norman. *Politics in the Age of Peel: A Study in the Technique of Parliamentary Representation.* New York: Longmans Green and Co., 1953.

George, M. D. *Catalogue of Political and Personal Satire,* vols. 5–11. London: British Museum, 1935–54.

Ghosh, R. N. *Classical Economics and the Case for Colonies.* Calcutta: New Age Publishers, 1967.

Gillespie, Frances Elma. *Labor and Politics in England: 1850–1867.* Durham, N.C.: Duke University Press, 1927.

Gordon, Barry. *Political Economy in Parliament, 1819–1823.* New York: Barnes and Noble, 1976.

Grammp, William Dyer. *The Manchester School of Economics.* Stanford, Calif.: Stanford University Press, 1960.

Halévy, Elie. *A History of the English People in the Nineteenth Century.* Translated from the French by E. I. Watkin and D. A. Barker. London: Ernest Benn, 1949–52.

Hamburger, Joseph. *Intellectuals in Politics: John Stuart Mill and the Philosophic Radicals.* New Haven and London: Yale University Press, 1965.

Hammond, J. L., and Barbara Hammond. *The Age of the Chartists: 1832–1854. A Study of Discontent.* London: Longmans Green, 1930.

———. *Lord Shaftesbury.* London: Constable, 1923.

———. *The Skilled Labourer: 1760–1832.* London: Longmans Green, 1920.

———. *The Town Labourer: 1760–1832.* London: Longmans Green, 1918.

———. *The Village Labourer: 1760–1832.* London: Longmans Green, 1912.

Harrison, Brian. *Drink and the Victorians.* Pittsburgh: University of Pittsburgh Press, 1971.

Hayek, F. A., ed. *Capitalism and the Historians.* Chicago: University of Chicago Press, 1953.

Henriques, Ursula. *Religious Liberation in England, 1787–1833.* London: Routledge and Kegan Paul, 1961.

Hobhouse, John Cab (Lord Brighton). *Recollections of a Long Life,* 6 vols. London: John Murray, 1909.

Hope-Jones, Arthur. *Income Tax in the Napoleonic Wars.* Cambridge: Cambridge University Press, 1938.

Ilbert, Sir Courtenay. *Parliament: Its History, Constitution and Practice.* New York: Henry Holt and Co., 1911.

Ilchester, Earl of, ed. *The Journal of the Hon. Henry Edward Fox (4th Earl Holland), 1818–1830.* London: T. Butterworth, 1923.

Jeans, William. *Parliamentary Reminiscences.* London: Chapman and Hall, 1912.

Johnston, H. J. M. *British Emigration Policy 1815–1830: "Shovelling Out Paupers."* Oxford: Clarendon Press, 1972.

Knorr, Klaus. *British Colonial Theories, 1570–1850.* Toronto: University of Toronto Press, 1944.

Lubenow, William C. *The Politics of Government Growth.* Hamden, Conn.: Archon Books, 1971.

McCord, Norman. *The Anti-Corn Law League, 1830–1846.* London: Allen and Unwin, 1968.

Machin, G. I. T. *The Catholic Question in English Politics.* Oxford: Clarendon Press, 1964.

Mackay, Thomas. *A History of the English Poor Law . . . A Supplementary Volume to "A*

History of the English Poor Law, by Sir John Nicholls." Reissue. London: P. S. King and Son, 1904.

Macoby, S. *English Radicalism 1786–1832 from Paine to Cobbett.* 3 vols. London: George Allen and Unwin, 1955.

Marshall, John Duncan. *The Old Poor Law, 1795–1834.* London: Macmillan, 1968.

Maxwell, the Right Hon. Sir Herbert. *The Creevey Papers.* London: John Murray, 1923.

Nicholls, Sir George. *A History of the English Poor Law.* New ed., 2 vols. London: P. S. King and Son, 1904.

——. *A History of the Irish Poor Law* [1856]. Repr. New York: Augustus M. Kelley, 1967.

O'Brien, D. P. *J. R. McCulloch. A Study in Classical Economics.* London: George Allen and Unwin, 1970.

Owen, David. *English Philanthropy: 1660–1960.* Part 2. Cambridge, Mass.: Harvard University Press, 1963.

Parris, Henry. *Government and the Railways in Nineteenth-Century Britain.* London: Routledge and Kegan Paul, 1965.

Polanyi, Karl. *The Great Transformation.* New York: Rinehart, 1944.

Political Economy Club, 1821–1920, Minutes of Proceedings, 1899–1920, Roll of Members and Questions Discussed, 1821–1920, vol. 6. London: Macmillan, 1921.

Poynter, J. R. *Society and Pauperism: English Ideas on Poor Relief, 1795–1834.* London: Routledge and Kegan Paul, 1969.

Reynolds, James A. *The Catholic Emancipation Crisis in Ireland, 1823–1829.* New Haven, Conn.: Yale University Press, 1954.

Robbins, Lionel. *The Theory of Economic Policy in English Classical Political Economy.* London: Macmillan, 1952.

Roberts, David. *Victorian Origins of the British Welfare State.* New Haven, Conn.: Yale University Press, 1960.

Robson, Robert, ed. *Ideas and Institutions of Victorian England.* New York: Barnes and Noble, 1967.

Rose, Michael E., ed. *The English Poor Law 1780–1930.* Newton Abbot: David and Charles, 1971.

Russell, Rollo, ed. *The Early Correspondence of Lord John Russell.* London: J. F. Unwin, 1913.

Semmel, Bernard. *The Rise of Free Trade Imperialism: Classical Political Economy, The Empire of Free Trade and Imperialism.* Cambridge: Cambridge University Press, 1970.

Shaw, A. G. L., ed. *Great Britain and the Colonies: 1815–1865.* London: Methuen, 1970.

Sherab, F. *Progressive Taxation.* Oxford: Clarendon Press, 1953.

Smart, William. *Economic Annals of the Nineteenth Century,* 2 vols. New York: Sentry Press, 1964.

Smith, F. D. *The Making of the Second Reform Bill.* Cambridge: The University Press, 1966.

Soloway, R. A. *Prelates and People: Ecclesiastical Thought in England, 1783–1852.* London: Routledge and Kegan Paul, 1969.

Southgate, Donald. *The Passing of the Whigs.* London: Macmillan, 1962.

Strachey, Lytton, and Roger Fulford, eds. *The Greville Memoirs,* 8 vols. London: Macmillan, 1938.

Thompson, E. P. *The Making of the English Working Class.* New York: Pantheon Books, 1964.

Turberville, A. B. *The House of Lords in the Age of Reform.* London: Faber and Faber, 1958.

Wade, John. *The Extraordinary Black Book.* London, 1831.

Wakefield, Edward Gibbon. *A Letter from Sydney.* London, 1829.

———. *A View of the Art of Colonization.* London, 1849.

Webb, Sidney, and Beatrice Webb. *The History of Liquor Licensing in England,* vol. 2 of *English Local Government.* London, 1903. Repr. Hamden, Conn.: Archon Books, 1963.

———. *English Poor Law History.* 3 vols. London: Longmans, 1927–29.

———. *English Poor Law Policy.* New York: Longmans, 1910.

West, E. G. *Education and the State.* London: Institute of Economic Affairs, 1965.

White, William. *The Inner Life of the House of Commons: Edited with a Preface by Justin McCarthy,* 2 vols. London: T. Fisher Unwin, 1898.

Winch, Donald. *Classical Political Economy and the Colonies.* Cambridge, Mass.: Harvard University Press, 1965.

Woodward, Sir Llewellyn. *The Age of Reform.* Oxford: Clarendon Press, 1938.

Other Articles

Aydelotte, W. O. "The Conservative and Radical Interpretations of Early Victorian Social Legislation." *Victorian Studies* 11 (Dec. 1967):225–36.

———. "Parties and Issues in Early Victorian England." *Journal of British Studies* 5 (May 1966):95–101.

———. "Voting Patterns in the British House of Commons in the 1840s." *Comparative Studies in Society and History* 5 (Jan. 1963):123–63.

Best, G. F. A. "The Religious Difficulties of National Education in England." *Cambridge Historical Journal* 12, no. 2 (1956):155–73.

Blaug, Mark. "The Classical Economists and the Factory Acts." *Quarterly Journal of Economics* 72 (May 1958):211–26.

———. "The Myth of the Old Poor Law and the Making of the New." *Journal of Economic History* 23 (June 1963):151–84.

———. "The Poor Law Report Reexamined." *Journal of Economic History* 24 (June 1964):229–45.

Brebner, J. Bartlett. "Laissez Faire and State Intervention in Nineteenth-Century Britain." *Journal of Economic History,* Supplement 8 (1948):59–73.

Fetter, Frank Whitson. "The Bullion Report Reëxamined." *Quarterly Journal of Economics* 56 (Aug. 1942):655–65.

———. "The Politics of the Bullion Report." *Economica,* n.s., 26 (May 1959):99–120.

Grammp, William D. "Politics of the Classical Economists." *Quarterly Journal of Economics* 62 (Nov. 1948):714–47.

Hollander, Samuel. "The Role of the State in Vocational Training: The Classical Economists' View." *Southern Economic Journal* 34 (Apr. 1968):513–25.

Kitson Clark G. "The Repeal of the Corn Laws and the Politics of the Forties." *Economic History Review,* second series, 4 no. 1 (1951):1–13.

Kittrell, Edward R. "The Classical Debate on Colonization: Reply." *Southern Economic Journal* 32 (Jan. 1966):346–49.

————. "The Development of the Theory of Colonization in English Classical Political Economy." *Southern Economic Journal* 31 (Jan. 1965):189–206.

Miller, William L. "The Economics of Education in English Classical Economics." *Southern Economic Journal* 32 (Jan. 1966):294–309.

Porter, J. "The British Timber Duties: 1815–60." *Economica*, n.s., 32 (May 1955):122–36.

Roberts, David. "How Cruel Was the Victorian Poor Law?" *Historical Journal* 6, no. 1 (1963):97–107.

Semmel, Bernard. "The Philosophic Radicals and Colonialism." *Journal of Economic History* 11 (Dec. 1961):513–25.

Sorenson, Lloyd R. "Some Classical Economists, Laissez Faire, and the Factory Acts." *Journal of Economic History* 12, no. 3 (1952):247–62.

Stewart, Robert. "The Ten Hours and Sugar Crises of 1844: Government and the House of Commons in the Age of Reform." *Historical Journal* 12 (1969):35–57.

Wagner, Donald A. "British Economists and the Empire." *Political Science Quarterly* 46 (March 1931):248–76; 47 (March 1932):57–74.

Walker, K. O. "The Classical Economists and the Factory Acts." *Journal of Economic History* 1 (Nov. 1941):168–77.

West, E. G. "Private versus Public Education: A Classical Economic Dispute." *Journal of Political Economy* 72 (Oct. 1964):465–75.

Winch, Donald N. "The Classical Debate on Colonization: Comment." *Southern Economic Journal* 32 (Jan. 1966):341–45.

————. "Classical Economics and the Case for Colonization." *Economica*, n.s., 30 (Nov. 1965):387–400.

Unpublished British and Irish Theses

Brewer, Robert Charles. "An Investigation into the Effects of the 1832 Act on the General Elections of 1832, 1835, and 1837 in Ireland." M.S. thesis, London, 1965.

Carrich, Anne E. "Three Northumberland Constituencies in the General Elections of 1852: North and South Northumberland and Tynemouth." M.A. Thesis, Durham, 1965.

Checkland, Sydney C. "The Political Economists and the Politicians from Waterloo to the Reform Bill." M. Com. Thesis, Birmingham, 1946.

————. "Studies in Economic Thought and Behaviour." Ph.D. Thesis, Liverpool, 1953.

Close, D. M. "The General Elections of 1835 and 1837 in England and Wales." Ph.D. Thesis, Oxford, 1967.

Cookson, J. E. "Lord Liverpool's Administration 1815–1822." Ph.D. Thesis, St. Andrews, 1969.

Doran, Patrick F. "The Irish Parliamentary Representation: 1832–1867." M.A. Thesis, University College, Cork, 1954.

Fenn, Robert Anthony. "The Politics of David Ricardo." M.Sc. Thesis, London School of Economics, 1959.

Hanrahan, Anthony K. "Irish Electioneering, 1850–1872." M.A. Thesis, University College, Dublin, 1965.

Hinton, Michael. "The General Elections of 1806 and 1807." Ph.D. Thesis, Reading, 1959.

Job, R. "The Political Career of Henry Third Earl Grey (1826–1852)." M.Litt. Thesis, Durham, 1959.

Jones, E. G. "Sir Robert John Wilmot Horton." M.A. Thesis, Bristol, 1936.

Jupp, Peter. "Irish Parliamentary Representation, 1801–1820." Ph.D. Thesis, Reading, 1966.

Kent, Gordon B. "Party Politics in the County of Staffordshire during the Years 1830 to 1847." M.A. Thesis, Birmingham, 1959.

McGrath, Brigid M. "Introduction of the Poor Law in Ireland, 1831–1838." M.A. Thesis, University College, Dublin, 1965.

Macintyre, A. D. "Daniel O'Connell and the Irish Parliamentary Party 1830–1847." Ph.D. Thesis, Oxford, 1963.

Meenai, S. A. "The Economics of Lord Lauderdale." Ph.D. Thesis, London, 1950.

Moses, John Henry. "Elections and Electioneering in the Constituencies of Nottinghamshire, 1762–1832." Ph.D. Thesis, Nottingham, 1965.

Rees, R. D. "Parliamentary Representation in South Wales, 1790 to 1830." Ph.D. Thesis, Reading, 1962.

Index of Persons

Index of Subjects